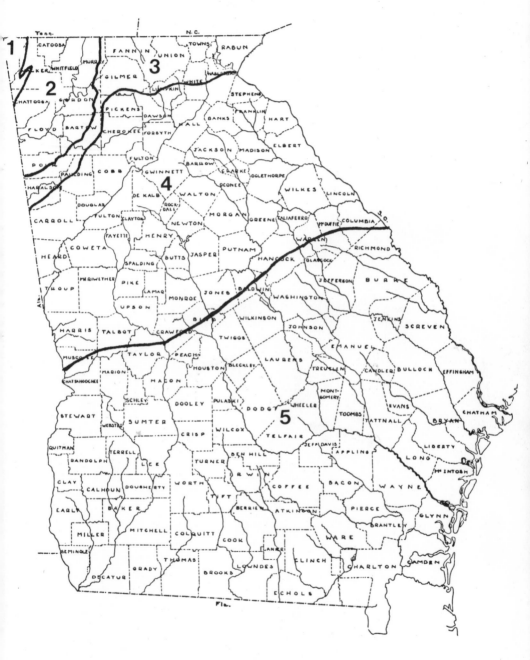

Physical Provinces of Georgia: Cumberland Plateau (1), Ridge and Valley (2), Blue Ridge Mountains (3), Piedmont (4), and Coastal Plain (5).

Trees of Georgia
and
Adjacent States

To: Anna Dorothy Warnell.

A Georgian whose heritage embodies a deep and abiding love for the good earth and the trees thereon. She inspires others to responsible stewardship of Georgia's greatest natural resource.

Trees of Georgia and Adjacent States

CLAUD L. BROWN

L. KATHERINE KIRKMAN

TIMBER PRESS
Portland, Oregon

ISBN 0-88192-148-3

LC #90-183964

Printed in Hong Kong

TIMBER PRESS, INC.
The Haseltine Building
133 S.W. Second Avenue, Suite 450
Portland, Oregon 97204, U.S.A.

Contents

Preface

Georgia, the largest state east of the Mississippi River, possesses one of the more diverse floras in the United States due mainly to its five distinct physiographic provinces, differing in topography, soils and climate. The seasonal climate on mountain summits in northern Georgia is comparable to that of some northeastern States, while that of the Coastal Islands resembles subtropical regions.

Although a complete taxonomic treatment with adequate keys to the flora of Georgia does not presently exist, the magnitude of plant diversity within the State is evident by the checklist of vascular plants compiled by Duncan and Kartesz (1981). These authors list a total of 3,686 taxa occurring in Georgia, whereas Radford *et al.* (1968) treat 3,442 taxa for the combined states of North and South Carolina.

The diversity of native tree species within the State is even more striking. Of approximately 680 tree species native to the United States and Canada, almost one third of these occur in Georgia, exclusive of many introduced and naturalized species. Approximately 235 native trees occur in the Southeast and 90 percent of these are native to Georgia.

This manual, *Trees of Georgia and Adjacent States*, was written because a current guide to native Georgia trees is not available. Two earlier sources of information, *Guide to Georgia Trees* by Duncan (1941) and *Native Trees of Georgia* by Bishop (1943), although useful in identifying numerous species, have become outdated because of many taxonomic revisions since the time of publication, nearly a half century ago.

This treatment includes 205 tree species or varieties which are native to Georgia. Our decision of which species to include as small trees or to exclude as large shrubs was somewhat arbitrary and may differ from the opinions of other authors. The size and form of individual trees vary regionally with genetic diversity and environmental conditions and the distinction between trees and shrubs based solely on size is not absolute. In general, we included those woody plants that reach 15 or more feet in height, which commonly possess a single trunk or stem 3 inches or more in diameter, and which terminate in an upright crown of branches. Introduced and naturalized trees have been excluded from the keys and descriptions, although a list of some commonly encountered species which have been introduced and naturalized in the State is presented in Appendix C.

The purpose of this guide is to provide students, laypersons and professionals interested in tree identification with a concise manual for field identification of 205 native taxa. This objective is met with the following features: 1) a standardized format describing important features of identification, 2) summer and winter keys with a minimum of technical terms, 3) 432 color photographs of leaves, flowers, fruit and bark accompanying the species description, 4) 95 black and white photographs of winter twigs, 5) discussion of specific recognition difficulties between taxa in the field, 6) natural habitat information, and 7) useful information of economic importance, ornamental considerations, value for birds and wildlife and frequently a glimpse of natural history.

The tree taxa presented have been studied in their native habitats during each season of the year, in addition to examination of voucher specimens in the University of Georgia Herbarium. Photographs were made in the field, both in Georgia and adjacent states.

Claud L. Brown

L. Katherine Kirkman

Acknowledgments

We are indebted to many persons who have helped with the publication of this book. Several persons have accompanied us on field trips to locate and observe uncommon species in their native habitats including: Lindsay Boring, Steve Bowling, Patrick Brewer, Bernard Ebel, Gary Green, Lawrence Nix, Merve Reines and Francis Thorne. Sincere appreciation is expressed to Angus Gholson for considerable time in the field and for sharing much valuable information on trees of the region.

Special recognition is due William Lott for his enthusiastic assistance on numerous field trips and for helping with the photography of most specimens. We extend thanks to Robert McReynolds for the use of his photograph of *Sapindus marginatus* flowers and to Rebecca Sharitz for the habitat photograph of *Taxodium distichum*.

We gratefully acknowledge the valuable editorial assistance and suggestions of Nancy Coile in reviewing the entire manuscript. Sue Sherman-Broyles reviewed and made helpful suggestions of the Ulmaceae and Greg Krakow provided detailed information concerning *Ilex*. Sue Lawrence prepared all of the line drawing illustrations.

The species distribution maps were reproduced from the *Atlas of United States Trees*, Volumes 1 and 4, prepared by Elbert Little, USDA-Forest Service, with the exception of those presented for *Quercus geminata*, *Q. austrina*, *Q. margaretta*, *Nyssa sylvatica* var. *biflora*, and *Tilia americana*. Modifications of the maps of *Taxodium distichum* and *Quercus falcata* were made to separate the varieties or taxa which were indicated by Little by broken lines. The ranges of *Acer nigrum*, *A. pensylvanicum*, *A. spicatum*, *A. saccharum*, *Aesculus glabra*, *Clethra acuminata*, *Cotinus obovatus* and *Illicium floridanum* were modified to indicate occurrence or extension into Georgia by more recent documented collections in the University of Georgia Herbarium.

We are pleased to acknowledge the support of the School of Forest Resources, University of Georgia, and the University of Georgia Foundation, Warnell Fund, for monetary assistance in making this publication possible.

Introduction

Identification of trees requires observation and study. Whether one learns to recognize trees by a self-taught approach through the use of field manuals and appropriate keys, or by formal training in taxonomy or dendrology, adeptness is achieved by repeated observation and experience in the field. A certain intuitiveness of plant recognition, encompassing the variability within a species, is attained only with repeated exposure to trees in natural habitats.

The use of field guides and keys require a basic understanding of the terminology describing features such as leaves, twigs, bark and reproductive structures. We have attempted to present this information with a minimum use of technical terms so that the book can be used by student or layperson without previous training in botany or other plant sciences. However, a certain amount of scientific terminology is essential to convey meaning that would otherwise require repetitive lengthy explanation. For effective use of this guide, the reader should become familiar with the material and illustrations presented in this section. A glossary is also provided defining terms used in the text.

CATEGORIES OF PLANT CLASSIFICATION

Plants are grouped by taxonomists into categories which attempt to reflect their evolutionary relationships. These are ranked such that higher categories are more inclusive than lower ones. The major categories include the following relative positions.

Kingdom
Division
Order
Family
Genus
Species
Variety

For purposes of identification, the species unit is usually the most important. In this manual, tree species are grouped by families in phylogenetic order (a classification scheme based on evolutionary history) according to the Engler System as presented by Dalla Torre and Harmes (1900–1907). Within each family, we have listed the genera and species in alphabetical order. Two major groups of families are recognized, the Gymnosperms (Conifers) and Angiosperms (Flowering Plants).

NOMENCLATURE

Both scientific and common names are used in this manual. Because common names vary from region to region and some are applicable to more than one species, it is necessary to have a standardized system of scientific names that is universal in acceptance. Scientific names of plants are governed by The International Code of Botanical Nomenclature, a detailed set of rules adopted by systematic botanists. All scientific names of plants consist of two Latin words, first the genus name, followed by the species name, or specific epithet. The scientific name is then followed by the authority, i.e., the name of the person or persons who originally described and named the species, sometimes abbreviated. For example, all maples belong to the genus *Acer*. Red Maple is known as *Acer rubrum* L. A variety is indicated by adding the word var., and a third Latinized word, following the scientific name of the species followed again by the authority, such as *Nyssa sylvatica* var. *biflora* (Walter) Sarg. In this manual, a second scientific name in parentheses indicates a synonym, or previously accepted name for the species.

HOW TO USE THE KEYS

A key is a useful tool to aid in the identification of an unknown plant. It is simply an outline with contrasting pairs of features. By a sequence of choices, taxa are eliminated until the possibilities are reduced to one. This manual contains keys to native tree genera and species in summer and in winter condition. The characters used in the keys are ones that can be observed in the field with the naked eye or with the use of a hand lens. Where possible, two or more characteristics are included in each paired choice so that the decision can be made on more than one trait.

Tree identification requires observation. It is important to be aware of the amount of variation in plant characteristics between trees of the same species and even on the same tree. For instance, one should examine more than a single leaf to determine, size, shape, hairiness, and other characteristics. Often there is significant variation in leaf size and shape on the same tree depending on whether the leaf has developed in sun or shade or whether it possesses a juvenile form often common on sprouts along the lower trunk. Trees also vary in height and shape based on the environment in which they are growing. Flowers may vary in color. In addition, many species of trees hybridize. When hybridization occurs, traits are often intermediate between the parents, and trees of hybrid origin can be difficult to identify using a key based on traits of the individual parents.

Before using a key in the field, obtain samples of leaves, twigs, fruits and flowers, if available. Often, fruits can be found on the ground beneath the tree after fruiting season, especially if resistant to decay. Also, note the size and shape of the tree and examine the bark for distinctive characteristics such as color and texture.

The next step is to determine to what major grouping in the key the tree belongs, based on leaf and twig features. Is the specimen evergreen or deciduous, does it have simple or compound leaves, are the leaves opposite or alternately arranged on the twig? Each of these determinations will help place the specimen into a smaller group of possible taxa. One proceeds in a step-wise fashion, selecting the appropriate choice based on examination of the specimen until the genus is reached. By using the *Summer Key to Genera* to determine the genus, one then turns to the genus specified in the descriptions and uses the key to species for that genus. In the *Winter Key to Genera*, the tree is automatically identified to species if the genus is monotypic, i.e., containing only one species. If not monotypic, then locate the *Key to Species* for each genus (listed alphabetically).

After keying the specimen to species, verify the result by comparing the specimen with the color photographs and the narrative descriptions of leaves, twigs, bark, flowers, and fruit of that particular species. If the specimen does not fit these descriptions, then begin again with the key and determine where the wrong choice was made. In some genera in winter condition, it is almost impossible to distinguish with absolute certainty closely related species on the basis of dormant twig features alone. In such cases, persistent fruit or leaves on the tree or on the ground must be relied upon to identify the species.

IDENTIFICATION FEATURES OF TREES

Basic morphological traits, particularly of leaves and twigs, are utilized in the keys and species descriptions. These features are briefly discussed and illustrated by the line drawings in this section.

Leaves

Leaves are the photosynthetic organs of trees. A leaf usually consists of an expanded portion, the blade, and a stalk, the petiole. Associated with every leaf is a lateral bud which can give rise to secondary branches. Leaf characteristics of an individual species are often diagnostic for identification. Leaves of our native species range in size from a minute fraction of an inch in some conifers to several feet long in palms. The arrangement, shape, margins, apices and bases and venation patterns are traits which are useful in separating species.

Types. Leaves are either simple or compound. A simple leaf is a leaf with a single blade and a compound leaf is one composed of two or more separate leaflets. The arrangement of the leaflets in a compound leaf can be pinnate, palmate, or trifoliate. Plate 1.

Arrangement. Leaves are arranged in a definite pattern on the twig. The positioning of a single leaf at successive points of attachment (node) along the twig is referred to as alternate arrangement, whereas two leaves which oppose each other at the node are considered oppositely arranged. In trees where three or more leaves are attached at the node, the leaf arrangement is whorled. Plate 2.

Shapes. The shapes of leaves are highly variable, often even on the same tree. In general, leaf shape is a common diagnostic feature for many species. The more common shapes are illustrated in Plate 3.

Margins. Although leaf margins and patterns of lobing may vary considerably within a given species, they are under rigid genetic control in others. Consequently, leaf margins may be useful in identification. Plate 4 illustrates several types of leaf margins.

Apices and Bases. The apex of a leaf is the tip or distal portion, while the part of the blade nearest the petiole, or in the absence of a petiole nearest the point of attachment to the twig, is the base. The shapes of leaf apices and bases are often diagnostic and are diagrammed in Plate 5.

Venation. Several branching patterns of primary and secondary veins can be recognized in leaves which frequently aid in identification. These are shown in Plate 6.

LEAF TYPES

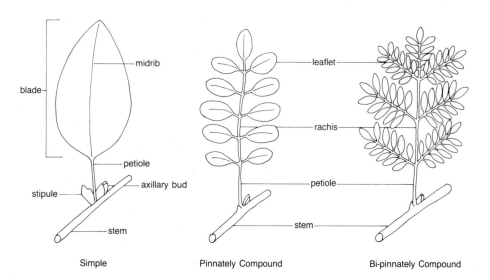

Simple   Pinnately Compound   Bi-pinnately Compound

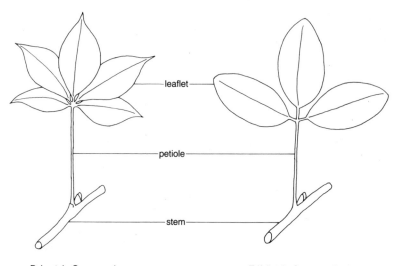

Palmately Compound   Trifoliately Compound

Plate 1

LEAF ARRANGEMENT

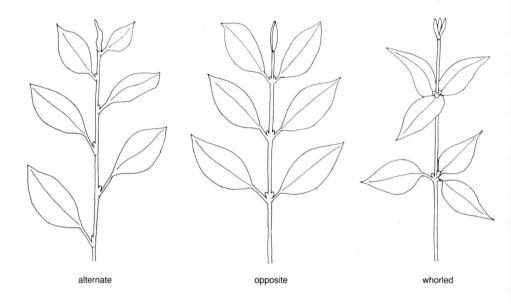

alternate   opposite   whorled

Plate 2

LEAF SHAPES

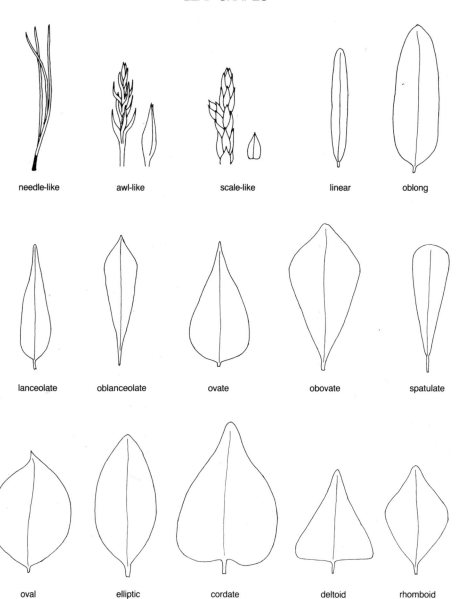

needle-like   awl-like   scale-like   linear   oblong

lanceolate   oblanceolate   ovate   obovate   spatulate

oval   elliptic   cordate   deltoid   rhomboid

Plate 3

LEAF MARGINS

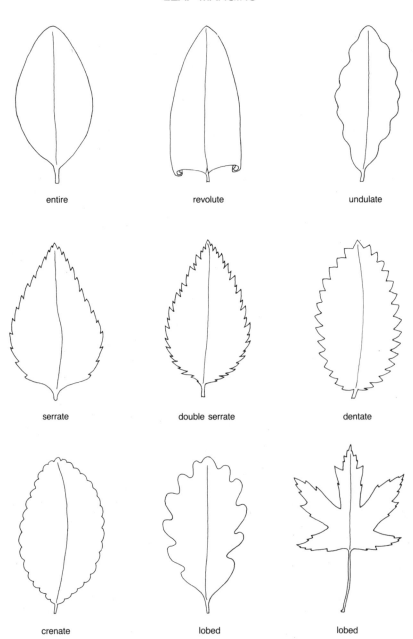

entire   revolute   undulate

serrate   double serrate dentate

crenate   lobed   lobed

Plate 4

LEAF APICES

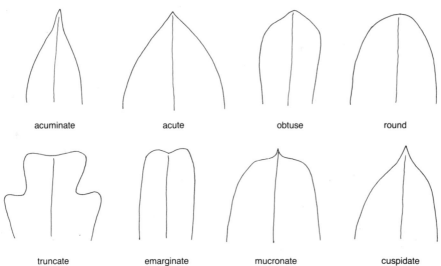

| acuminate | acute | obtuse | round |

| truncate | emarginate | mucronate | cuspidate |

LEAF BASES

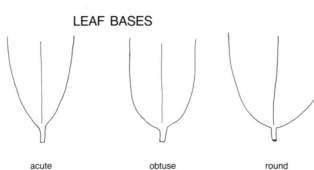

| cuneate | acute | obtuse | round |

| truncate | cordate | auriculate | inequilateral |

Plate 5

LEAF VENATION

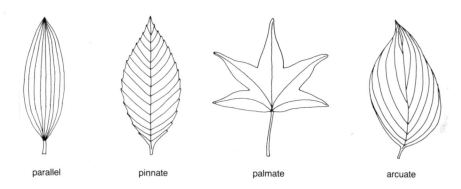

parallel   pinnate   palmate   arcuate

Plate 6

Twigs

A twig is the extended portion of the current year's shoot growth. Dormant twigs are useful for identifying trees in the winter in the absence of leaves and often provide diagnostic characteristics year round in some species. The following features are represented in Plates 7 and 8.

Buds and Bud Scales. Buds enclose embryonic shoot tissues and are either terminal or positioned in the axils of leaves. Superposed buds are accessory buds which are positioned directly above an axillary bud. A pseudoterminal bud is a lateral bud which occupies a terminal position due to the abscission of the shoot tip. In winter during the dormant season, buds are usually protected by a series of modified leaves, called bud scales. A bud lacking such scales is called naked.

Leaf Scars and Bundle Scars. The leaf scar is a mark at the node which is left by a fallen leaf. The size and shape of these scars are useful identification traits. Within the leaf scar are bundle scars which appear as small dots, indicating the connections of former vascular strands of the leaf with the twig. The number of these bundle scars vary among species and is often useful in identification. Plate 8.

Stipule Scars. Stipule scars are found on twigs that had leaf stipules. Most are inconspicuous slits along the upper edge of the leaf scar, but some completely encircle the twig.

Lenticels. Lenticels are small slitlike or corky protuberances occurring on the twig which function in aeration. Occasionally, they provide identification clues because of size, color or configuration.

TWIG FEATURES

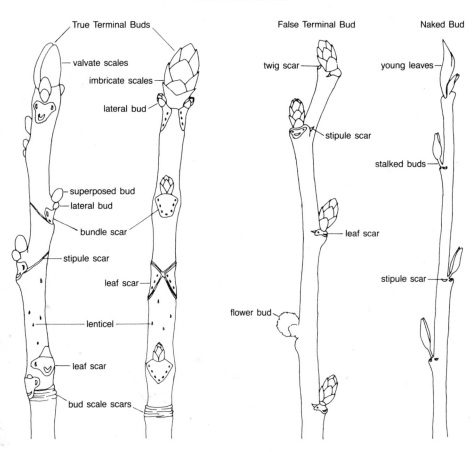

True Terminal Buds

valvate scales

imbricate scales

lateral bud

superposed bud

lateral bud

bundle scar

stipule scar

leaf scar

lenticel

leaf scar

bud scale scars

False Terminal Bud

twig scar

stipule scar

leaf scar

flower bud

Naked Bud

young leaves

stalked buds

stipule scar

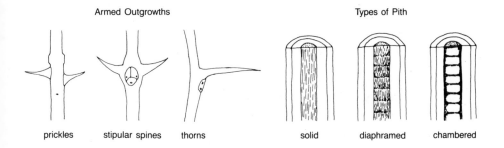

Armed Outgrowths

prickles

stipular spines

thorns

Types of Pith

solid

diaphramed

chambered

Plate 7

LEAF SCAR SHAPES

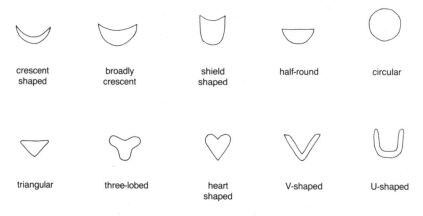

crescent shaped	broadly crescent	shield shaped	half-round	circular

triangular	three-lobed	heart shaped	V-shaped	U-shaped

Plate 8

Spines, Thorns, and Prickles. Although all of these outgrowths are usually very sharp to the touch, they have distinctly different anatomical origins. Spines are modified stipules which commonly occur in pairs at the node; thorns are woody outgrowths derived from axillary buds, and are therefore modified branches which may be straight, curved or branched; prickles are simply outgrowths derived from the epidermis of twigs, leaves, petioles or other organs in a random manner, not associated with nodes or axillary buds.

Pith. Pith is the central portion of tissue in a twig. The structural composition of the pith may be solid, hollow, or partitioned (diaphragmed or chambered) as illustrated in Plate 7.

Bark

Bark forms the outer covering of the trunk, branches and twigs. The color, thickness, roughness and patterns of furrowing are valuable identification traits, but take some experience to recognize. Bark features are difficult to describe because many of the traits are qualitative or relative characteristics. Also, the age of the tree is an important consideration since young trees may have thin, smooth bark, but develop thick, furrowed, rough or scaly bark with age. With considerable experience in the field, one may easily identify numerous trees simply by recognition of bark features alone.

Reproductive Structures

A basic difference in conifers and angiosperms (flowering plants) is in the type of reproductive structures. Conifers produce reproductive organs enclosed in a cone, or strobilus. These cones consist of scales, or bracts, with either pollen sacs (male organs) or ovules (female organs). Most conifers have both male and female cones on the same tree. Seeds develop within the female cone and are usually released when mature. The cones may be woody or fleshy and are very useful in identification.

Angiosperms produce flowers which bear stamens (pollen producing male structures) and pistils (female structures). Pistils are composed of an ovary (which contain the ovule), an extended neck of the ovary (style), and the receptive surface for the pollen (stigma). Angiosperms may have both male and female reproductive structures (bisexual) in the same flower, or may have only flowers of one kind or the other (unisexual). Some species produce unisexual flowers on different plants (dioecious) and others produce both male and female flowers on the same tree (monoecious). Some trees are polygamous, having bisexual and unisexual flowers on the same tree. The parts of a complete, bisexual flower are shown in Plate 9. It should be noted that some flowers lack either or both petals and sepals.

Types of Inflorescences. An inflorescence is a cluster of flowers. The type of arrangement of the flowers is used as an identification character and several commonly encountered types are illustrated in Plate 10.

Types of Fruit. A fruit is a ripened ovary, occurring only in angiosperms. There are numerous types of simple fruits which are useful for identification. Aggregate fruits are a cluster of simple fruits derived from numerous pistils of a single flower. A multiple fruit is a cluster of simple fruits produced by the pistils of numerous separate flowers. The many kinds of fruits produced by trees are illustrated in Plates 11 and 12, and definitions of each are included in the Glossary.

FLOWER STRUCTURE

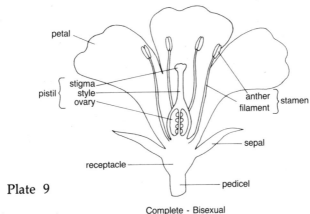

Plate 9

Complete - Bisexual

INFLORESCENCE TYPES

catkin

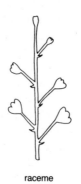

spike

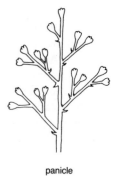

raceme

panicle

cyme

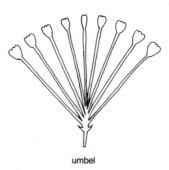

umbel

head

Plate 10

TYPES OF FRUITS - SIMPLE

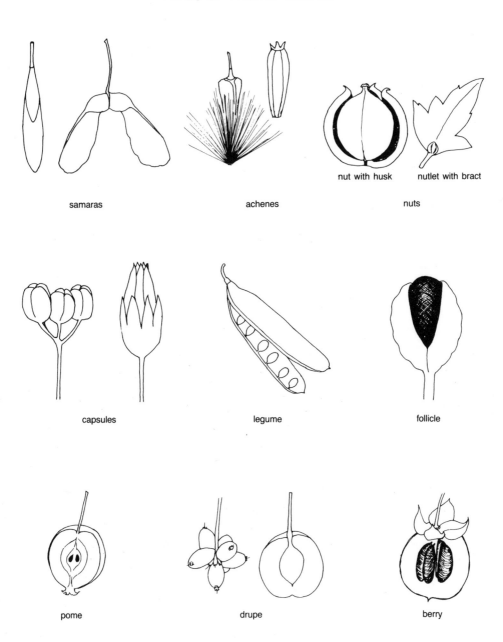

samaras   achenes   nuts

nut with husk   nutlet with bract

capsules   legume   follicle

pome   drupe   berry

Plate 11

TYPES OF FRUITS - COMPOUND

cone-like cluster
of nutlets

samaras

follicles

Aggregrate Fruits

capsules

achenes

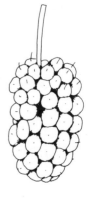

drupes

Multiple Fruits

Plate 12

Habit or Form of Trees

The size and shape of a tree can be useful in identification but requires experience and observation due to the amount of variation. Trees that are grown in the open usually have a different crown and bole form than the same species grown under a forest canopy and subjected to shade, competition for nutrients, water, and restricted crown development. Therefore, we have given little emphasis to form in this manual.

Habitat

Many species are highly adapted to specific sites and may be restricted to certain environmental conditions, either due to the inability to compete with other species in another habitat or due to certain physiological limitations. Knowledge of these habitat restrictions is useful in predicting the probability of a species occurrence in a given environment.

Distribution Maps

Because most of the native tree species in Georgia extend into many of the Southeastern States, we have included range maps for 200 of the 205 taxa covered in the manual. This information will be useful for users within Georgia as well as adjacent States. The maps are from Little (1971, 1977), as indicated in the acknowledgments. The distribution of each taxon in Georgia is briefly discussed in the manual.

Summer Key to the Genera

1. Leaves needle-like, scale-like, or awl-shaped .... (Conifers)
   Group A
1. Leaves not needle-like, scale-like or awl-shaped; seed enclosed in an ovary............................. (Flowering Plants) 2
   2. Leaves very large, up to 4–7' long, fan-like, stem un-branched .... (Monocotyledons) *Sabal* (p. 61)
   2. Leaves less than 4' long, stems branched..... (Dicotyledons) 3
      3. Leaves simple.................................... 4
         4. Leaves opposite or whorled .... **Group B**
         4. Leaves alternate........................ **Group C**
      3. Leaves compound .... **Group D**

KEY TO GROUP A (Conifers)

1. Leaves needle-like, borne in clusters of 2–5 with sheath at the base ...
   .... *Pinus* (p. 41)
1. Leaves linear, scale-like or awl-shaped, lacking sheath at the base ... 2
   2. Leaves closely appressed to twig, scale-like or awl-shaped ... 3
      3. Twigs decidedly flattened, branches flattened, spray-like ...
         .... *Chamaecyparis* (p. 58)
      3. Twigs rounded to 4-sided; branches not spray-like 4
         4. Cone fleshy, blue; base of trunk not buttressed; knees not formed............................ *Juniperus* (p. 59)
         4. Cone woody, base of trunk buttressed; knees formed ...
            .... *Taxodium* (p. 55)
   2. Leaves positioned or twisted to appear borne in a single plane ... 5
      5. Leaves less than 1" long, lacking pungent odor; cone woody .. 6
         6. Leaves with two white bands of stomates beneath; lacking knees; trunk not buttressed.............. *Tsuga* (p. 53)
         6. Leaves lacking white bands of stomates; forming knees; trunks buttressed..................... *Taxodium* (p. 55)
      5. Leaves 1" long or longer, pungent, disagreeable odor; seed sur-rounded by fleshy or leathery structure ..... *Torreya* (p. 39)

29

KEY TO GROUP B (leaves simple, opposite)

1. Leaves 3–5 lobed, palmately veined; fruit a samara . . . . . *Acer* (in part)
   (p. 185)
1. Leaves not lobed, not palmately veined; fruit not a samara. 2
   2. Leaves heart-shaped; fruit 12" long or longer. . . . . *Catalpa* (p. 245)
   2. Leaves not heart-shaped; fruit less than 1" long 3
      3. Leaves leathery, evergreen 4
         4. Leaves 4–5" (up to 9") long. . . . . *Osmanthus* (p. 243)
         4. Leaves ½–2½" long. . . . . *Viburnum* (in part) (p. 250)
      3. Leaves not leathery, deciduous. 5
         5. Stipules or stipular scars connecting opposite petioles. . . . 6
            6. Leaves pubescent on both surfaces; flowers and fruits in
               terminal clusters; sepals of some flowers petal-like, large,
               pink. . . . . *Pinckneya* (p. 247)
            6. Leaves usually glabrous above and sometimes below;
               flowers and fruits in globose heads; sepals not
               enlarged . . . . *Cephalanthus* (p. 246)
         5. Stipules or stipular scars not connecting opposite
            petioles 7
            7. Leaves finely serrate or remotely toothed. 8
               8. Leaf margins finely toothed; fruit not elliptical. 9
                  9. Twigs purplish-green, often with 4 ridges; fruit a
                     reddish 4-lobed capsule. . . . . *Euonymus* (p. 182)
                  9. Twigs brown to gray, lacking 4 ridges; fruit a blue-
                     black drupe . . . . *Viburnum* (in part) (p. 250)
               8. Leaf margins toothed from middle upwards; fruit an
                  elliptical drupe . . . . *Forestiera* (p. 238)
            7. Leaves entire. 10
               10. Leaf scars with single bundle scar; leaves 4–6" long;
                   bud scales keeled, sharp pointed . . . . *Chionanthus*
                   (p. 237)
               10. Leaf scars with more than 1 bundle scar; leaves less
                   than 4" long; bud scales not keeled, not sharply
                   pointed 11
                   11. Young twigs green, red or maroon; flower parts
                       in 4s; lateral veins arching toward tips of leaves
                       and reaching margins . . . . *Cornus* (in part)
                       (p. 214)
                   11. Young twigs gray to brown; flower parts in 5s;
                       lateral veins arching toward tips of leaves but
                       forming marginal loops . . . *Viburnum* (in part)
                       (p. 250)

KEY TO GROUP C (Leaves simple, alternate)

1. Leaves thick, evergreen.................................... 2
   2. Leaves spicy aromatic................................... 3
      3. Leaves nearly fleshy; lateral veins indistinct ... *Illicium* (p. 137)
      3. Leaves leathery, but not fleshy; lateral veins distinct...... 5
         5. Leaves irregularly serrate, glandular dotted ... *Myrica* (in part) (p. 66)
         5. Leaves entire, not glandular dotted....... *Persea* (p. 140)
   2. Leaves not spicy aromatic............................. 6
      6. Leaves glandular dotted .... *Myrica* (in part) (p. 66)
      6. Leaves not glandular dotted (or inconspicuously so) 7
         7. Twigs encircled at nodes with stipular scars, stout; buds hairy..................... *Magnolia* (in part) (p. 130)
         7. Twigs not encircled at nodes with stipular scars, not stout; buds not hairy 8
            8. Twigs usually thorny, spur shoots present, milky sap when cut .... *Bumelia* (in part) (p. 227)
            8. Twigs lacking thorns and spur shoots, without milky sap.. 9
               9. Uppermost lateral buds clustered toward tips of twigs 10
                  10. Bundle scars numerous; fruit an acorn ... . *Quercus* (in part) (p. 91)
                  10. Bundle scar one (sometimes broken into several); fruit not an acorn 11
                     11. Leaves 3½–12" long; flowers greater than 1" in diameter..... *Rhododendron* (p. 223)
                     11. Leaves 1–4" long; flowers 1" in diameter or less.................... 12
                        12. Leaves glabrous beneath; flowers saucer-shaped, with pouches, about 1" in diameter .... *Kalmia* (p. 220)
                        12. Leaves rusty scaly; flowers urn-shaped, without pouches, about ⅓" long .... *Lyonia* (p. 221)
               9. Uppermost lateral buds not clustered at end of twig..................................... 13
                  13. Leaf scar with 3-many bundle scars..... 14
                     14. Buds silky hairy; flowers about 3" in diameter; fruit a capsule...... *Gordonia* (p. 205)
                     14. Buds not silky hairy; flowers about ¼" or less in diameter; fruit a drupe .... *Prunus* (in part) (p. 149)
                  13. Leaf scar with one bundle scar........ 15
                     15. Pith chambered; leaves sweet to taste ... . *Symplocos* (p. 235)

15. Pith not chambered; leaves not sweet to taste. 16
    16. Leaf margins toothed . . . *Ilex* (p. 174)
    16. Leaf margins entire (sometimes remotely toothed) 17
        17. Flowers and fruits in racemes 18
            18. Leaves 2–4" long; fruits not winged; racemes just below previous season growth. . . . . *Cyrilla* (p. 172)
            18. Leaves 1–2" long; fruits 2–4 winged; racemes terminal . . . . *Cliftonia* (p. 171)
        17. Flowers and fruits in cymes or fascicles or solitary. . . . . *Ilex* (in part) (p. 174)
1. Leaves deciduous. 19
  19. Uppermost lateral buds clustered at ends of twigs; fruit an acorn . . . . *Quercus* (in part) (p. 91)
  19. Uppermost lateral buds not clustered at ends of twigs; fruit not an acorn. 20
    20. Twigs armed with thorns or sharp pointed spur shoots 21
      21. Twigs with milky sap. . . . . *Bumelia* (in part) (p. 227)
      21. Twigs lacking milky sap 22
        22. One or two conspicuous glands on the petiole near the blade or on the leaf base. . . . . *Prunus* (in part) (p. 149)
        22. Glands lacking on the petiole and blade 23
          23. Sharp pointed spur shoots formed from lateral buds, bearing leaves or distinct leaf scars. . . . . *Malus* (p. 147)
          23. Thorns formed from lateral buds, not bearing leaves or distinct leaf scars . . . . *Crataegus* (p. 147)
    20. Twigs not armed 24
      24. Leaves lobed, or with lobed and non-lobed leaves on same tree 25
        25. Leaves truncate or v-notched at apex; flower yellow-green, tulip-shaped; fruit a samara in cone-like aggregation . . . . *Liriodendron* (p. 129)
        25. Leaves not truncate nor V-notched at apex; flowers and fruit not as above. 26
          26. Leaves uniformly 5-lobed; fruit a prickly, globose head of capsules; twigs often winged. . . . . *Liquidambar* (p. 143)
          26. Leaves not uniformly 5-lobed; fruit not as above; twigs not winged. 27
            27. Bark exfoliating in plates, exposing white to greenish layers beneath; leaves irregularly toothed and lobed; stipules leaf-like; petiole base encircling the bud; fruit a globose head of achenes . . . *Platanus* (p. 144)

27. Bark not exfoliating in plates; leaves not toothed, or if toothed, teeth are regularly spaced; stipules not leaf-like, petiole base does not encircle bud; fruit a drupe or an aggregate of drupes resembling a berry.................................... 28

   28. Twigs aromatic, green, without milky sap; leaf base acute, margins entire; flower and fruit stalks bright red; fruit a simple drupe...... *Sassafras* (p. 144)

   28. Twigs not aromatic, gray to brown, milky sap; leaf base not acute, margins serrate; flower and fruit stalks not bright red; fruit an aggregate of drupes .... *Morus* (p. 127)

24. Leaves not lobed 29

   29. Petioles swollen at both ends......... *Cercis* (p. 157)

   29. Petioles not swollen at both ends 30

      30. Flowers and fruits attached to elongated bract; buds oblique at base .... *Tilia* (p. 202)

      30. Flowers and fruit not attached to elongated bract; buds not oblique at base......................... 31

         31. Leaves broadly deltoid-ovate or cordate-ovate; twigs roughened by 3-lobed leaf scars; pith 5-angled; buds resinous........... *Populus* (p. 62)

         31. Leaves not broadly deltoid-ovate or cordate-ovate; twigs not markedly roughened by leaf scars; pith not 5-angled 32

            32. Stipular scars forming a line around (or almost around) the stem of twig................. 33

               33. Lateral veins of leaves parallel from midrib to margin; leaves 2-ranked; fruit a triangular nut within a spiny bur........... *Fagus* (p. 90)

               33. Lateral veins of leaves not parallel from midrib to margin; leaves not 2-ranked; fruit an aggregate of follicles in a cone-like structure............ *Magnolia* (in part) (p. 130)

            32. Stipular scars not forming a line around the twig 34

               34. Foliage fetid-aromatic, buds reddish brown, hairy.................... *Asimina* (p. 138)

               34. Foliage not fetid-aromatic; buds not reddish brown and hairy..................... 35

                  35. Buds stalked...................... 36

                     36. Plants blooming in autumn; fruit a capsule; leaves 2-ranked ...... *Hamamelis* (p. 142)

                     36. Plants blooming in spring-summer; fruits in a woody cone; leaves more than 2-ranked............... *Alnus* (p. 81)

                  35. Buds not stalked; plants not blooming in autumn 37

      37. Pith chambered or diaphragmed... 38
38. Pith chambered only at nodes; bark with warty outgrowths ...
              Celtis (p. 118)
38. Pith chambered or diaphragmed entire length of twig; bark
  lacking warty outgrowths............................. 39
  39. Lateral buds superposed, the uppermost bud triangular; lower
    leaf surface with stellate hairs at least on midrib; fruit
    winged .... *Halesia* (p. 231)
  39. Lateral buds not superposed, or if superposed the uppermost
    bud not triangular; lower leaf surface glabrous; fruit not
    winged... 40
    40. Leaves commonly blemished with dark spots; leaf scar with
      single bundle scar; bark dark gray-black, broken into blocky
      rectangular plates .... *Diospyros* (p. 230)
    40. Leaves not blemished with dark spots; leaf scars with 3
      bundle scars; bark gray, fissured into narrow ridges... *Nyssa*
                  (p. 209)
 37. Pith not partitioned, solid............................... 41
 41. Leaves entire to slightly wavy, but not toothed........... 42
  42. Leaves leathery, leaf venation conspicuous.... *Leitneria* (p. 69)
  42. Leaves not leathery, leaf venation not markedly
    conspicuous 43
  43. Leaf apex blunt; fruits in feathery sprays.... *Cotinus* (p. 166)
  43. Leaf apex acute; fruits not in a feathery spray 44
    44. Leaves blemished with dark spots; fruit a berry, 1½" in
      diameter........................ *Diospyrus* (p. 230)
    44. Leaves not blemished with dark spots; fruit a drupe or
      capsule....................................... 45
      45. Lateral veins arching toward tips of leaves and reach-
        ing margins; leaf tip acuminate; flowers in a cyme; fruit
        a drupe, blue............. *Cornus* (in part) (p. 214)
      45. Lateral veins arching toward tips of leaves but forming
        marginal loops; leaf tip with short bristle; flowers in a
        long raceme; fruit a capsule, brown ... *Elliottia* (p. 219)
 41. Leaves toothed, sometimes irregularly or minutely so...... 46
  46. Twigs red or green; flowers and fruit in one-sided racemes;
    bark thick, deeply furrowed .... *Oxydendrum* (p. 222)
  46. Twigs brown or gray; flowers and fruit not in one-sided
    racemes; bark not thick and not deeply furrowed (exception:
    Salix nigra bark is sometimes deeply furrowed) 47
  47. Bundle scar 1..................................... 48
    48. Buds naked; leaves stellate pubescent beneath, at least
      along the veins or petiole (use hand lens)...... *Styrax*
                  (p. 233)
    48. Buds with scales; leaves lacking stellate pubescence
      beneath 49
      49. Leaf apex long acuminate; outer bark red-brown;
        flowers and fruits in dense racemes ... *Clethra* (p. 218)
      49. Leaf apex not long acuminate; bark gray; flowers and
        fruits not in dense racemes.................... 50

50. Leaves with ciliate margins; flowers 3½–4″ in diameter; fruit a capsule; bark shreddy...... *Stewartia* (p. 206)

50. Leaves without ciliate margins; flowers about ¼″ in diameter; fruit a berry-like drupe; bark smooth .... *Ilex* (in part) (p. 174)

47. Bundle scars 3 or more 51

51. Leaves 2-ranked 52

52. Marginal teeth of leaves bristle-tipped ..... *Castanea* (p. 88)

52. Marginal teeth of leaves not bristle-tipped. 53

53. Bark with scaly plates or peeling in papery layers; spur twigs on older branches; lenticels on young twigs conspicuous.............................. *Betula* (p. 82)

53. Bark not as above; lacking spur twigs; lenticels not conspicuous...................................... 54

54. Buds long tapered, ½–¾″ long; flowers showy; fruit a pome........................ *Amelanchier* (p. 146)

54. Buds pointed or rounded, but not long tapered, less than ½″ long; flower not showy; fruit not a pome 55

55. Bark blue-gray, smooth, trunk fluted; fruit subtended by foliaceous bract .... *Carpinus* (p. 85)

55. Bark not blue-gray or smooth, trunk not fluted; fruit not subtended by foliaceous bract. 56

56. Leaves distinctly asymmetrical, or if not asymmetrical, leaves very scabrous, or twigs with corky wings .... *Ulmus* (p. 122)

56. Leaves slightly or not at all asymmetrical; twigs without corky wings 57

57. Fruit with fleshy outgrowths, in leaf axils, not enclosed in a membranous sac, bark exfoliating in large scales exposing reddish areas of bark; leaves triangular ovate to rhombic ovate ....*Planera* (p. 121)

57. Fruit without fleshy outgrowths, enclosed in a membranous inflated sac; bark exfoliating in shreds; leaves ovate-oblong or elliptical .... *Ostrya* (p. 86)

51. Leaves not 2-ranked 58

58. Lateral veins of lower leaf surface raised, parallel from midrib to margin................................ *Rhamnus* (p. 201)

58. Lateral veins of lower leaf surface not raised, not parallel from midrib to margin.................................. 59

59. Twigs with bitter almond smell and taste; leaf scars half round or oval................ *Prunus* (in part) (p. 149)

59. Twigs lacking bitter almond smell and taste; leaf scars narrow, broadly V-shaped .... *Salix* (p. 64)

KEY TO GROUP D (leaves compound)

1. Leaves opposite. 2
  2. Leaves palmately or trifoliately compound 3
    3. Leaves with 5–7 leaflets; upper leaflet not stalked; petals longer than sepals; capsule leathery or prickly. . . . *Aesculus* (p. 195)
    3. Leaves with 3 leaflets; upper leaflet stalked; petals barely longer than sepals; capsule inflated. . . . . *Staphylea* (p. 183)
  2. Leaves pinnately compound. 4
    4. Leaf scar encirling stem; leaflets 3–5. . . . . *Acer* (in part) (p. 185)
    4. Leaf scar not encircling stem; leaflets 5–11 5
      5. Often shrubby; twigs stout, pith large; margins of leaflets conspicuously serrate; fruit a berry-like drupe, in dense panicles. . . . . *Sambucus* (p. 249)
      5. Tree; twigs moderate, pith small; margins of leaflets entire or shallowly serrate; fruit a samara, in racemes . . . . *Fraxinus* (p. 239)
1. Leaves alternate 6
  6. Twigs armed. 7
    7. Leaves with a pair of terminal leaflets; twigs stout; thorns often branched . . . . *Gleditsia* (p. 159)
    7. Leaves with a solitary terminal leaflet; spines or prickles slender, not branched. 8
      8. Leaves 2-several times compound. . . . . *Aralia* (p. 208)
      8. Leaves once pinnately compound 9
        9. Leaflet tip acute or acuminate. . . *Zanthoxylum* (p. 163)
        9. Leaflet tip blunt or notched . . . . *Robinia* (p. 161)
  6. Twigs not armed. 10
    10. Leaflets entire or wavy, not toothed. 11
      11. Leaflets asymmetrical; twigs fluted, greenish-yellow. . . . . *Sapindus* (p. 200)
      11. Leaflets symmetrical; twigs not fluted, gray to brown . . 12
        12. Leaves trifoliately compound; fruit a winged samara. . . . . *Ptelea* (p. 162)
        12. Leaves with 5 or more leaflets, pinnately compound; fruit not a winged samara. 13
          13. Lateral buds enclosed within hollow base of petiole; flowers in a raceme; fruit a legume . . . . *Cladrastis* (p. 158)
          13. Lateral buds not enclosed within base of petiole; flowers and fruits in terminal panicle; fruit a drupe 14
            14. Twigs stout; sap milky or watery, not turning black following injury to stem; flowers and fruits in dense terminal panicle; fruit red . . . . *Rhus* (in part) (p. 167)
            14. Twigs moderate; sap turning black following injury to stem; flowers and fruits in open

axillary panicles; fruit whitish . . . .
. . . . *Toxicodendron* (p. 170)
10. Leaflets toothed 15
  15. Pith chambered . . . . *Juglans* (p. 78)
  15. Pith not partitioned, solid. 16
    16. Fruit a nut with dehiscent husks; leaf scars heart-
    shaped to 3-lobed . . . . *Carya* (p. 70)
    16. Fruit a pome or drupe; bundle scars horseshoe-
    shaped to crescent-shaped. 17
      17. Lateral buds ¼" long or greater, pointed; flowers
      and fruits in flat-topped clusters; fruit a pome,
      more than ¼" long. . . . . *Sorbus* (p. 155)
      17. Lateral buds minute, rounded, often partly
      concealed; flowers and fruits in elongated panicle;
      fruit a drupe less than ¼" long . . . . . *Rhus* (in part)
                          (p. 167)

Family and Species Descriptions

Conifers

TAXACEAE–YEW FAMILY

The Taxaceae is a small family, with only two genera which occur in North America, *Taxus* and *Torreya*. Of these two genera, only two species of small trees occur in the southeastern United States, *Taxus floridana* Nutt. ex. Chapman and *Torreya taxifolia* Arn. Only *T. taxifolia* occurs in Georgia, and is an endangered species.

Members of this family are characterized by evergreen, alternate, spirally arranged, flattened, linear leaves. Trees are either dioecious or monoecious. Pollen cones are composed of overlapping scales containing four to eight pollen sacs and are borne in small clusters. The ovule is surrounded at the base by a fleshy bract. When the seed matures it is surrounded by a fleshy cup (aril).

Torreya–Torreya

Torreya taxifolia Arn.

Florida Torreya, Stinking Cedar

DESCRIPTION: Florida Torreya is a rare, small tree, seldom over 30' tall and 8–10" in diameter. Its distribution is limited to Decatur County, Georgia and to a few counties in northwest Florida along the Appalachicola River. A fungal root rot disease has killed most large specimens and only scattered young trees or individuals which have root sprouted exist today.

Needles – evergreen, persistent for several years; 1–1½" long, ⅛" wide; spirally arranged, but twisted to appear in one plane, flattened, linear-lanceolate, sharp-pointed; dark shiny green above, undersurface pale with two distinct longitudinal rows of light gray stomates; unpleasant fetid odor when crushed. Figure 1.

Twigs – slender, yellowish green becoming gray, stiff, mostly paired or opposite; buds angular, about ¼" long, covered with several brown overlapping scales.

Bark – brown, thin, irregularly fissured to form scaly ridges.

Young Cones – dioecious; pollen cones small, solitary, globular-ovate with several scales, each bearing 4 pollen sacs; ovulate cones consisting of a single ovule subtended by a fleshy sac; appearing March–April.

Mature Cones – ovoid, 1–1¼" long, dark green with purplish stripes, whitish bloom, solitary, fleshy; mature seed light brown; maturing at end of 2 seasons, June–July. Figure 1.

RECOGNITION DIFFICULTIES WITH OTHER TAXA: *Torreya taxifolia* resembles *Taxus floridana*; however, the latter is less aromatic, with more flexible leaves which are not nearly as sharp to the touch. The red, fleshy cup surrounding the seed of *Taxus floridana* is distinctive.

HABITAT: Florida Torreya occurs along steepheads (mesic limestone derived ravines) in Decatur County, Georgia and three counties in Florida. This species is very rare and is possibly near extinction in its native habitat. Clearcutting of adjacent hardwoods and conversion to pine monocultures in the region have likely altered local light, temperature and moisture regimes, adversely affecting these trees which are already in decline due to the fungal disease.

ECONOMIC, ORNAMENTAL AND OTHER USES: The species has been planted as an ornamental specimen in gardens and landscapes in several locations in the Southeast where it so far has escaped the fungal disease and continues to produce viable seed. The seeds require a long period (4–5 months) of moist, warm after-ripening followed by a similar period of mild, cold stratification to germinate. We have found seed germination and viability to be poor.

PINACEAE–PINE FAMILY

The Pinaceae include some of the most economically valuable trees in the world. The wood is commercially important as lumber, for paper, and for resins which are the source of rosin, turpentine, and numerous other derivatives. The family is composed of nine genera and about 210 species, primarily distributed in North America, Asia and Europe. In North America, this family includes the larches

(*Larix*), Douglas fir (*Pseudotsuga*), firs (*Abies*), spruces (*Picea*), pines (*Pinus*), and hemlocks (*Tsuga*). In Georgia, two genera are native, *Pinus* and *Tsuga*, with 10 and 2 species, respectively. Species of these two genera are characterized by evergreen, needle-like or linear leaves, reproductive structures in cones, and resinous wood. The plants are monoecious, the bracts and axis of the female cones becoming woody, enclosing the winged seeds which are released upon maturity.

Pinus–Pines

KEY TO SPECIES OF *PINUS*

1. Needles 5 per fascicle, bluish green due to vertical white stripes; cone narrow and elongated, cone scales lacking prickles. . . . . . *P. strobus*
1. Needles less than 5 per fascicle, cone not narrow and elongated, cone scales armed with prickles 2
　2. Needles 2 per fascicle 3
　　3. Needles stiff; cone scales thickened, prickles conspicuously stout . . . . *P. pungens*
　　3. Needles flexible; cone scales not thickened, prickles reduced, or if present not conspicuously stout 4
　　　4. Needles twisted 5
　　　4. Needles not twisted. . . . . *P. echinata*
　　　　5. Needles usually 2–4″ long; bark dark brown, ridged and furrowed; prickles minute, deciduous . . . . *P. glabra*
　　　　5. Needles usually less than 2½″ long; bark light gray-brown or orangish, scaly on older trunks; prickles sharp, slender, persistent. . . . . *P. virginiana*
　2. Needles 3 per fascicle, or in combination of 3s and 4s, or 2s and 3s per fascicle 6
　　6. Needles in fascicles of 3. 7
　　　7. Needles more than 10″ long; terminal buds silvery white; cones mostly over 6″ long. . . . . *P. palustris*
　　　7. Needles less than 10″ long; terminal buds brownish; cones usually less than 6″ long 8
　　　　8. Cones longer than broad, open when mature; needles mostly 7–9″ (rarely 6″) long. . . . . *P. taeda*
　　　　8. Cones as broad as long, often unopened when mature; needles mostly less than 7″ long 9
　　　　　9. Needles stiff, 3–5″ long, twisted; cones scales with stiff prickle. . . . . *P. rigida*
　　　　　9. Needles flexible, 5–7″ (rarely 8″) long, not twisted; cone scales with a small weak prickle that is usually absent (deciduous) . . . . *P. serotina*
　6. Needles in a combination of numbers per fascicle 10
　　10. Needles in 3s and 4s per fascicle; cones as broad as long, usually remaining closed on tree for several years . . . .
　　　. . . . . *P. serotina*

10. Needles in 2s and 3s; cones elongated to ovoid, opening and shedding seed at maturity 11
  11. Needles 7–12" long; cones 3–7" long, lustrous tan . . . . .
  . . . . *P. elliottii*
  11. Needles 2½–5" long; cones up to 2½" long, dull gray. . . . . .
  . . . . *P. echinata*

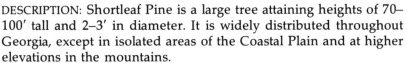

Pinus echinata Miller

Shortleaf Pine

DESCRIPTION: Shortleaf Pine is a large tree attaining heights of 70–100' tall and 2–3' in diameter. It is widely distributed throughout Georgia, except in isolated areas of the Coastal Plain and at higher elevations in the mountains.

Needles – evergreen, persistent for 3–4 seasons; 2½–5" long; 2 (occasionally 3) per fascicle, fascicle sheaths ⅛–¼" long; slender, flexible, not twisted. Figure 2.

Twigs – slender, pale green, often with purplish bloom, becoming reddish brown, scaly on older branchlets; buds ¼–½" long, scales red-brown.

Bark – dark brown, slightly scaly on young trees, becoming reddish brown, breaking into flat, irregular plates, often with numerous small conspicuous resin pockets. Figure 3.

Young Cones – pollen cones greenish yellow, ¼–½" long, in compact clusters at base of terminal bud; ovulate cones pinkish, usually 2–3 per cluster, occurring at end of elongating twigs; appearing March–April.

Mature Cones – ovoid, 1½–2½" long, scales transversely keeled, dull gray, prickle often deciduous, short, slightly recurved; almost stalkless; opening at maturity, but remaining on tree for 2 or more years. Figure 2.

RECOGNITION DIFFICULTIES WITH OTHER TAXA: In the upper Piedmont or mountains, Shortleaf and Virginia Pine may overlap in distribution. Shortleaf Pine has an open full crown and its needles are not twisted, whereas Virginia Pine is a scraggly tree with an irregular crown and twisted needles. In the mountains, Pitch Pine and Table Mountain Pine may be confused with Shortleaf Pine. The needles of these two species are twisted, and are coarser and less flexible than Shortleaf Pine. The cones of Table Mountain Pine are armed with broad, stout, recurved prickles, whereas those of Shortleaf Pine have short, slender prickles. In the Coastal Plain, Spruce Pine has somewhat similar needles and cones but the bark of Shortleaf Pine has broad, reddish brown plates with resin pockets rather than dark brown to gray bark with narrow scaly ridges of Spruce Pine.

HABITAT: Shortleaf Pine occurs on a wide variety of sites throughout the State from rocky ridges at lower elevations in the mountains to heavy clays in the Piedmont and on more sandy loams of the Coastal Plain. It invades abandoned fields and is moderately shade tolerant.

ECONOMIC, ORNAMENTAL AND OTHER USES: Shortleaf Pine is one of the most important lumber and pulp producing conifers in Georgia and the Southeast. Where natural stands are harvested, they are most often replanted with Loblolly or Slash Pine which grow more rapidly in managed plantations for short rotation pulpwood production.

Pinus elliottii Engelm.

Slash Pine

DESCRIPTION: Slash Pine is a medium to large-sized tree reaching 60–100' tall and 1½–2½' in diameter. In Georgia, it is restricted to the Coastal Plain.

   Needles – evergreen, persistent for 2 seasons; 7–12" long; 2 and 3 per fascicle, fascicle sheaths ½–¾" long; stout, stiff, not twisted, dark shiny green. Figure 4.

   Twigs – stout, light orange-brown, rough, ridged by compact arrangement of needles and scales; terminal buds ½–¾" long, scales rusty brown.

   Bark – dark reddish brown, furrowed and rough on young trees, becoming orange-brown and broken into broad, flat scaly plates on older trunks. Figure 5.

   Young Cones – pollen cones purplish brown, ½–2" long, in dense clusters at base of terminal buds; ovulate cones pink-purple, solitary or paired, at tip of elongating twigs; appearing February–early March. Figure 6, ovulate cones.

   Mature cones – ovoid to elongated, cylindrical, 3–7" long, scales lustrous tan with varnished appearance on face, scale prickle small, recurved, only slightly prickly to touch; open at maturity, usually falling from tree same season; maturing September–October. Figure 4.

RECOGNITION DIFFICULTIES WITH OTHER TAXA: Slash Pine and Loblolly Pine are most likely confused where the two species occur together. Slash Pine has two and three needles in fascicles while Loblolly Pine has three. The cones of the former are usually 6" in length with scales which are lustrous tan and weakly armed, while the cones of the latter are smaller, 4–5" long, dull brown and are armed with very sharp prickles. Longleaf Pine and Slash Pine often occur together. Longleaf Pine differs from Slash Pine by its needles in fascicles of 3, cones 5–10" long and its silvery terminal buds.

HABITAT: Slash Pine occurs in moist, wet, poorly drained sandy soils bordering shallow ponds and swamps of the flatwoods and on sandy loams of the upper Coastal Plain. It is maintained in pure stands throughout the region by periodic wildfires or prescribed burning.

ECONOMIC, ORNAMENTAL AND OTHER USES: Slash Pine is one of the most important pines in Georgia and the Southeast for lumber, pulpwood and plywood. Formerly it was tapped for crude gum or oleoresin for distillation into turpentine, rosin, pitch and tar. These products were used chiefly in tarring the decks and keels of wooden ships, hence, the usage of the term "naval stores." This industry has declined due to the cost of production and increased use of synthetics. Slash Pine is planted extensively in the Coastal Plain in short rotation plantations. It is also frequently used as an ornamental because of its rapid early growth and dense lustrous green foliage, although its heavy needle crops and brittle branches render it highly susceptible to ice damage and it is not widely planted outside the Coastal Plain.

Pinus glabra Walter
Spruce Pine

DESCRIPTION: Spruce Pine is an attractive medium-sized to large tree, 80–90' tall and 2–2½' in diameter. It occurs in Georgia along river systems in the lower Coastal Plain.

Needles – evergreen, persistent for 2 seasons; 2–4" long; 2 per fascicle, fascicle sheaths about ¼" long; slender, slightly flattened, twisted, dark green. Figure 7.

Twigs – slender, gray-green, smooth, becoming light brown and remaining smooth on older branches for several years.

Bark – grayish brown, smooth, thin on young trees, becoming dark gray-brown to almost black and furrowed into narrow scaly ridges with age, resembling spruces. Figure 8.

Young Cones – pollen cones greenish yellow, less than ½" long, clustered at the base of terminal buds; ovulate cones pale green with pinkish tinge, 1–3 on tips of fertile twigs; appearing February–March.

Mature Cones – conical-elliptical, small, 2–3½" long, scales slightly keeled on end with small, deciduous prickles; nearly stalkless; opening at maturity, but remaining on tree for 3–4 years. Figure 7.

RECOGNITION DIFFICULTIES WITH OTHER TAXA: Spruce Pine overlaps with Shortleaf Pine in the Coastal Plain. The smooth grayish green bark on the young branches and upper bole and the dark gray-brown, narrow furrowed bark on older trunks of Spruce Pine should distinguish it from Shortleaf Pine. See *P. echinata* for discussion of needle differences. Sand Pine (*P. clausa*) natively occurs in Florida in sandy soils in association with scrub oaks. It is planted in Georgia and has occasionally become naturalized. Sand Pine has ovulate cones with stout sharp prickles in contrast to the weak, usually deciduous prickles of Spruce Pine. Sand Pine cones remain on the tree longer than those of Spruce Pine and often the bases become nearly embedded in the twig.

HABITAT: *Pinus glabra* frequently occurs as a scattered tree, or occasionally in clumps on moist, alluvial flood plains, stream banks or hammocks with mixed hardwoods in the lower Coastal Plain.

ECONOMIC, ORNAMENTAL AND OTHER USES: Spruce Pine is utilized primarily for pulp. The wood is soft, light, and brittle and warps easily when sawed into lumber. The species is occasionally used as an ornamental shade and lawn tree because of its rapid growth on moist, sandy loams, its dark green foliage, and interesting bark features.

Pinus palustris Miller
Longleaf Pine

DESCRIPTION: Longleaf Pine is the most distinctive of southern conifers. It is a large tree reaching 80–100' in height and 2–2 ½' in diameter. The species occurs primarily in the Coastal Plain, but extends northward into the Ridge and Valley Province to Floyd, Bartow, and Chattooga counties.

Needles – evergreen, persistent for 2 seasons; 10–18" long; 3 per fascicle, fascicle sheaths ½–1" long; coarse, flexible, densely crowded, drooping, dark green. Figure 9.

Twigs – very stout, ½" or more in diameter, orange-brown, branches brown with rough flaky bark; buds large and conspicuous, scales silvery-white, fringed. Figure 10.

Bark – gray-brown, thin and scaly when young, becoming thick and broken into flat, scaly, reddish brown plates.

Young Cones – pollen cones dark purple-blue, 1–1½" long, in large clusters at base of terminal buds; ovulate cones rose-purple, usually in pairs or clusters of 3–4; appearing March. Figure 11, pollen cones.

Mature Cones – narrowly conical-cylindrical, 6–10" long, some scales raised, keeled on ends with small reflexed prickle; opening at maturity, falling from tree same season or by second year. Figure 9.

RECOGNITION DIFFICULTIES WITH OTHER TAXA: The large twigs and branches, long needles, large cones and conspicuous silvery-white buds make Longleaf Pine quite distinctive. A natural hybrid between Longleaf Pine and Loblolly Pine (*P.* × *sondereggii*) is a rapidly growing, but often poorly formed tree with wood quality that is inferior to either parent. It is generally intermediate in morphological traits, but, unlike Longleaf Pine, it does not possess the "grass stage" seedling habit, and initiates seedling height growth the first season.

HABITAT: Longleaf Pine occurs on well-drained, sandy soils throughout the flatwoods, in the deep sands of the scrub-oak sand hills, and on drier rocky ridges in the lower Piedmont and Ridge and Valley Province. During early seedling development, the bud is protected from fire by the compact arrangement of needles, hence the species is adapted to an environment frequently burned by wildfires. The seedling habit, referred to as the "grass stage" condition, resembles a clump of grass for 3–5 or longer years before height growth is initiated.

ECONOMIC, ORNAMENTAL AND OTHER USES: The wood of Longleaf Pine is strong, heavy, and durable. Longleaf Pine was a major source of lumber, construction timbers, and naval stores before the turn of the century. Today, much of the area formerly occupied by Longleaf Pine has been replaced by plantations of Slash and Loblolly Pines because its delayed period of seedling height growth is not compatible with maximizing yields in pulpwood rotations.

Pinus pungens Lamb.
Table Mountain Pine

DESCRIPTION: Table Mountain Pine is a small to medium-sized tree, 35–50' in height and 1–1½' in diameter. It occurs in a few counties of the upper Piedmont and in the Blue Ridge mountains of northeast Georgia.

Needles – evergreen, persistent for 2–3 years; 1½–3" long; 2 (rarely 3) per fascicle, fascicle sheaths less than ¼" long; stout, stiff, sharp pointed, twisted, dark green. Figure 12.

Twigs – stout, flexible, tough, difficult to break, orange-brown, becoming dark brown and rough, resinous; buds about ½" long, scales brown.

Bark – thin, dark reddish brown, scaly on young trees, becoming furrowed into scaly plates on older trunks.

Young Cones – pollen cones greenish yellow, ½–¾" long, in compact clusters; ovulate cones, pale green, clusters of 3–8, long-stalked; appearing April.

Mature Cones – broadly conical-ovoid, 2–3½" long, lopsided, scale tips prominently thickened, keeled, prickles stout, recurved; few opening at maturity, others remaining closed for 2–3 years; opened cones persistent for several years. Figure 12.

RECOGNITION DIFFICULTIES WITH OTHER TAXA: Table Mountain Pine may occur with Shortleaf Pine, Virginia Pine and Pitch Pine. It is readily distinguished from other southern pines by its unique, heavily armed persistent cones. The stout, sharp pointed twisted needles of Table Mountain Pine differ from those of Shortleaf which occur in 2s and 3s and are not twisted. Virginia Pine needles are flexible. Pitch Pine also has stiff, twisted needles but they occur in bundles of 3, rather than 2.

HABITAT: *Pinus pungens* occurs on drier, rocky slopes and ridges, frequently as a scattered tree in association with upland oaks and hickories. Following fires, it occasionally forms pure stands of limited extent on dry exposures.

ECONOMIC, ORNAMENTAL AND OTHER USES: Because of its smaller size and scattered occurrence, Table Mountain Pine is of minor economic importance. It is the only southern pine restricted exclusively to the Appalachian Mountains.

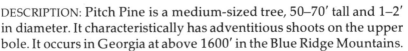

Pinus rigida Miller
Pitch Pine

DESCRIPTION: Pitch Pine is a medium-sized tree, 50–70' tall and 1–2' in diameter. It characteristically has adventitious shoots on the upper bole. It occurs in Georgia at above 1600' in the Blue Ridge Mountains.

Needles – evergreen, persistent for 2 years; 3–5" long; 3 per fascicle, fascicle sheaths less than ¼" long; stout, stiff, twisted, yellow-green. Figure 13.

Twigs – moderately stout, light grayish green at first, becoming orange-brown, branches brown, rough, flaky, highly resinous; buds about ¾" long, scales reddish brown.

Bark – dark brown, scaly on young trees, becoming fissured into irregular yellow-brown plates on older trunks.

Young Cones – pollen cones yellow-green with purple tinge, ½–¾" long, clustered at base of terminal buds; ovulate cones yellow-green, clusters of 3–8, short stalked; appearing April–May.

Mature Cones – elliptical-ovoid, broad as long, 1½–3" long, scales raised on end, keeled, prickle stiff, slender, sharp; cones often remaining closed after maturity for several years, opening and releasing seeds after a fire. Figure 13.

RECOGNITION DIFFICULTIES WITH OTHER TAXA: Pitch Pine superficially resembles Shortleaf Pine in needle and cone size, but the needles are stiff and twisted and in fascicles of 3, whereas those of the latter are not twisted and occur in fascicles of 2 (sometimes also 3). The buds of Pitch Pine are resinous and the bark scales lack the distinctive pitch pockets often found in Shortleaf Pine. In Georgia, the ranges of the two species seldom overlap, because Pitch Pine occurs only at higher elevations in the Blue Ridge Mountains where Shortleaf Pine infrequently occurs.

HABITAT: In Georgia, Pitch Pine occurs on rocky slopes and ridges in the Blue Ridge Mountains occasionally in pure stands, but more often in association with slow-growing oaks and other upland hardwoods. Since it sprouts from the lower trunk or stump after fire or mechanical injury, the species is adapted to fire environments.

ECONOMIC, ORNAMENTAL AND OTHER USES: Pitch Pine is occasionally harvested for lumber and pulpwood, but because of its size and distribution, it is of minor economic importance. In Colonial times, the wood was used for turpentine and charcoal, and pine knots attached to a pole were used as torches because they were naturally soaked with pitch.

Pinus serotina Michaux

Pond Pine

DESCRIPTION: Pond Pine is a medium-sized tree, 40–70' tall and 1–2' in diameter. Its branches tend to be gnarled and twisted, thus forming an irregularly shaped crown. Epicormic branching characteristically occurs on the main trunk. It occurs frequently throughout the Coastal Plain on wet sites.

Needles – evergreen, persistent for 3–4 years; 5–8" long; 3–4 per fascicle, fascicle sheaths ¼–½" long; slender, moderately stiff, yellow–green. Figure 14.

Twigs – moderately slender, greenish yellow at first, becoming light brown and scaly; buds ¾–1" long, scales brown.

Bark – dark gray to reddish brown, furrowed into small, scaly plates.

Young Cones – pollen cones yellow-orange, ½–1" long, clustered; ovulate cones greenish yellow, in pairs or clusters of 3–4; appearing March–April.

Mature Cones – subglobose to conic-ovoid, broad as long, 2–2½" long, yellow-brown, cone scales slightly raised, keeled, with weak deciduous prickles; usually remaining closed at maturity up to 10 years, frequently opening following hot fires. Figure 14.

RECOGNITION DIFFICULTIES WITH OTHER TAXA: Pond Pine is closely related to Pitch Pine and they often hybridize in regions where they overlap. In Georgia, the two species do not overlap in range. Some authorities consider Pond Pine to be a variety of Pitch Pine, *P. rigida* var. *serotina* (Michaux) R. T. Clausen. The needles of Pond Pine somewhat resemble those of Loblolly Pine although the needles of Pond Pine are 3 and 4 per fascicle and those of Loblolly are 3 per fascicle (only rarely 4). The globose, unopened cones and numerous tufted needles along the bole of Pond Pine help to separate the two rather easily.

HABITAT: Pond Pine occurs on wet, poorly drained sites of the Coastal Plain, often in shallow ponds and bays where the water table fluctuates widely. In addition to the serotinous cones, Pond Pine is adapted to a fire environment by readily sprouting from stumps, roots or trunks if injured by fire.

ECONOMIC, ORNAMENTAL AND OTHER USES: Because of its smaller size and inferior lumber quality on wet sites, Pond Pine is harvested largely for pulp, although on better drained soils some timber trees are produced.

Pinus strobus L.

Eastern White Pine

DESCRIPTION: Eastern White Pine, with its distinctive whorled branches, is the largest pine in the eastern United States. Trees over 100' in height and 3' in diameter still occur. Historical records indicate that trees, 150–175' tall, were common in the virgin forests of colonial days. In Georgia, it occurs throughout the mountains and into the foothills of the upper Piedmont.

Needles – evergreen, persistent for 2 seasons; 3–5" long; 5 per fascicle, fascicle sheaths about ⅛" long, early deciduous; soft, flexible, bluish green with whitish longitudinal rows of stomates. Figure 15.

Twigs – slender, smooth, green-gray, becoming darker with age; buds ¾–1½" long, scales reddish brown.

Bark – dark green-gray on young stems, thin, smooth, becoming thick and divided into long, narrow rectangular blocks by deep fissures. Figure 16.

Young Cones – pollen cones yellow-green, ⅓–½" long, in elongated clusters; ovulate cones, green, tinged with pink, narrowly cylindrical, stalked, 1–1½" long; appearing April–May.

Mature Cones – narrowly cylindrical and elongated, 5–8" long, cone scales thin, ends rounded, flat, without prickles, resinous, long-stalked; opening at maturity, falling from tree after 1–2 seasons. Figure 15.

RECOGNITION DIFFICULTIES WITH OTHER TAXA: Even when viewed at a distance, Eastern White Pine is quite distinctive because of its numerous tiers of whorled and slightly ascending lateral branches. It is easily separated from other native pines by its bluish green foliage with needles in fascicles of 5, its narrowly elongate, pendant cones and its smooth green-gray bark on upper stems and branches.

HABITAT: Eastern White Pine occurs on moist, well-drained slopes, along streams and moist coves in small pure stands or in association with hardwoods in the mountains and foothills of the upper Piedmont.

ECONOMIC, ORNAMENTAL AND OTHER USES: Eastern White Pine is a valuable timber tree. The wood is light, soft and easily worked. It is chiefly used for interior trim, paneling, cabinets, toys, and furniture stock. This species is widely used as a handsome shade and ornamental tree for lawns, parks and golf courses, although it is intolerant of drought and excessive heat.

Pinus taeda L.

Loblolly Pine

DESCRIPTION: Loblolly Pine is one of the largest southern pines. It frequently obtains heights of 90–100' and diameters of 2–3'. The species occurs throughout the State, but is most prevalent in the Piedmont.

Needles – evergreen, persistent for 3 seasons; 6–9" long; 3 per fascicle, fascicle sheaths ¼–½" long; stout, stiff, straight, dark green. Figure 17.

Twigs – moderately stout, greenish brown at first, becoming light brown, smooth, rough and flaky on young branchlets; buds ¾–1" long, scales reddish brown.

Bark – dark gray to almost black on young trees, becoming thick and furrowed into scaly ridges at an early age; on older trunks dark reddish brown, divided into large, flat rectangular plates. Figure 18.

Young Cones – pollen cones yellow-green, 1–1½" long, in large compact clusters at base of terminal buds; ovulate cones pale green, in pairs of 3 or 4 per cluster, slightly stalked.

Mature Cones – ovoid-conical, longer than broad, 4–5" long, cone scales prominently keeled with a stout sharp prickle, very sharp to the touch; opening at maturity, but usually falling from the tree 2–3 years later. Figure 17.

RECOGNITION DIFFICULTIES WITH OTHER TAXA: Because their needle lengths are often similar, Loblolly Pine is most commonly mistaken for Slash Pine in areas where the two species overlap. Loblolly Pine cones are dull brown and are armed with very sharp prickles, whereas those of Slash Pine are weakly armed and the face of the cone scales are glossy, chestnut brown. Slash Pine needles are usually dense all along the twig, dark green and shiny, whereas those of Loblolly Pine tend to be duller, more spreading and grouped nearer the ends of the twigs. The needles of the former are also coarser, occurring in bundles of 2s and 3s, while those of the latter occur only in fascicles of 3.

HABITAT: Loblolly Pine occurs in an extremely wide range of habitats, from moist, poorly drained floodplains to drier well-drained upland slopes and granitic outcrops. The species quickly invades abandoned fields and waste places and then forms pure stands. It is only moderately tolerant to shade and occurs in small openings or around the edges of mixed hardwood forests.

ECONOMIC, ORNAMENTAL AND OTHER USES: Loblolly Pine is one of the most widespread and valuable pines in the Southeast. In Georgia, it comprises most of the total volume of timber harvested in the Piedmont, and it is used extensively in reforestation programs because of its early rapid growth in plantations. The wood is used for lumber, construction timbers, pulp and plywood. Unlike Slash and Longleaf Pines, it produces low yields of oleoresin and is not worked for naval stores.

Pinus virginiana Miller
Virginia Pine

DESCRIPTION: Virginia Pine is commonly a small to medium-sized tree, reaching heights of 40–70' and 1–1½' in diameter. Usually the trees appear very scrubby, even in dense stands, because of numerous persistent branches that may extend to the ground. It occurs throughout much of the upper Piedmont, Ridge and Valley, and Blue Ridge Mountains.

Needles – evergreen, persistent for 3–4 seasons; 1½–3" long; 2 per fascicle, fascicle sheaths ⅛–¼" long; stout, flexible, twisted, yellowish green. Figure 19.

Twigs – slender, light green with waxy bloom, becoming light gray-brown, branchlets smooth; buds resinous, about ½" long, sharp pointed, scales red-brown.

Bark – orange-brown, thin, smooth on young stems, becoming slightly fissured and scaly on older trunks. Figure 20.

Young Cones – pollen cones yellow-green, ¼–½" long, numerous, in loose clusters; ovulate cones in clusters of 2–8, often occurring in 2–3 successive clusters in a current season; appearing March–April.

Mature Cones – ovoid-conic, reflexed downward, 1½–2 ½" long, scales thin, armed with slender, sharp prickles; opening at maturity but remaining on tree for 3–4 years, often much longer. Figure 19.

RECOGNITION DIFFICULTIES WITH OTHER TAXA: Virginia Pine is most easily confused with Shortleaf Pine. Virginia Pine commonly has a scrubby appearance because of retention of numerous dead branches, often extending to the ground even in dense stands. The needles, unlike those of Shortleaf Pine, are twisted.

HABITAT: *Pinus virginiana* occurs on a wide range of sites in northern Georgia, including well-drained upland slopes, eroded heavy clays, and dry rocky soils of ridges. It quickly invades abandoned, severely eroded farmlands or cut-over burned areas.

ECONOMIC, ORNAMENTAL AND OTHER USES: Virginia Pine is principally utilized for pulpwood, although older, larger trees on better sites are frequently harvested for lumber and paneling. It is widely cultivated in the Southeast for Christmas trees because of its dense branching habit, rapid growth and adaptability to various soils.

Tsuga–Hemlocks

KEY TO SPECIES OF *TSUGA*
1. Leaves two-ranked; seed cones less than 1″ long, cone scales about as long as broad . . . . *T. canadensis*
1. Leaves spirally arranged; seed cones 1–1½″ long, cone scales longer than wide . . . . *T. caroliniana*

Tsuga canadensis (L.) Carr.

Eastern Hemlock

DESCRIPTION: Eastern Hemlock is a medium-sized to large tree, 60–90′ tall and 2–3′ in diameter. It occurs in Georgia in the Blue Ridge Mountains and the Ridge and Valley provinces.

Needles – evergreen, persistent until the third season; ⅓–⅔″ long; 2-ranked, flattened, flexible, rounded or slightly notched at the tip; margin often minutely toothed; shiny, dark green above, 2 narrow whitish bands of stomates beneath. Figure 21.

Twigs – slender, yellow-brown, slightly pubescent at first, becoming reddish brown and smooth; buds ovoid, minute, covered with several hairy scales.

Bark – cinnamon brown, thin, scaly on young stems, becoming deeply furrowed into broad scaly ridges on older trunks; when cut alternating layers of purplish and reddish brown tissue visible. Figure 22.

Young Cones – pollen cones greenish yellow, small, less than ¼″ long, borne in axils of needles on previous year's twigs; ovulate cones light green, ¼–½″ long, solitary, terminal; appearing March–April. Figure 23, ovulate cones.

Mature Cones – oblong-ovoid, ½–¾″ long, dull light brown, scales nearly circular on end, smooth; short-stalked, opening wide at maturity, usually persistent until following spring. Figure 21.

RECOGNITION DIFFICULTIES WITH OTHER TAXA: *Tsuga canadensis* resembles *T. caroliniana*; however, the latter has needles which are arranged in numerous directions along the twigs rather than 2-ranked and the cones are 1–1½″ long rather than ½–¾″ long.

HABITAT: Eastern Hemlock occurs on moist, deep soils along streams and lower slopes, in rocky gorges and ravines, and on the upper northern slopes in the North Georgia mountains. It is found occasionally in pure stands, but more frequently in association with mixed mesic hardwoods. Hemlock is one of our most shade tolerant conifers.

ECONOMIC, ORNAMENTAL AND OTHER USES: The wood of Eastern Hemlock is soft, brittle, coarse grained and of poor quality for lumber. In colonial times, the bark was a principal source of tannin and entire stands in some localities were stripped of bark leaving the trees to die and decay. Today, it is harvested for pulp and for inexpensive crating material. The species makes a handsome ornamental tree and is widely planted. It is also frequently planted in rows and trimmed into hedges.

Tsuga caroliniana Engelm.

Carolina Hemlock

DESCRIPTION: This species is a handsome medium-sized tree, 40–60′ tall with a restricted distribution in the southern Appalachians. In Georgia, it occurs only in Rabun and Habersham Counties. It is similar to *T. canadensis* with the exception of being smaller in height at maturity, having larger cones, and needles that extend in different directions around the twigs. Carolina Hemlock occupies dry slopes, rocky cliffs and ravines in small, pure stands and in association with mixed hardwoods. It is a handsome ornamental tree, grows well in sun or shade and should be used more widely. Figure 24, foliage and mature cones; Figure 25, young pollen cones.

TAXODIACEAE–TAXODIUM FAMILY

The Taxodiaceae is a small family with three genera in North America, including *Sequoia* (Coastal Redwood), *Sequoidendron* (Giant Redwoods) and *Taxodium* (Bald Cypress). Several Asiatic genera are cultivated as ornamentals, including *Cryptomeria, Metasequoia,* and *Cunninghamia.* Members of this family are large (or gigantic) trees with narrow, thin leaves and red, decay resistant wood. The two species of Bald Cypress native to Georgia, are deciduous, with needle-like or flat-linear leaves occurring on slender twigs which drop with the leaves in autumn.

Taxodium–Bald Cypress

KEY TO SPECIES OF *TAXODIUM*
1. Deciduous twigs ascending; leaves appressed to twig or curving upwards; spirally arranged........................ *T. ascendens*
1. Deciduous twigs spreading from larger branches; leaves spreading, appearing 2-ranked .... *T. distichum*

Taxodium ascendens Brongr.

[*T. distichum* var. *nutans* (Aiton) Sweet]

Pond Cypress

DESCRIPTION: Pond Cypress is a small to medium-sized tree, 40–80' tall and 1–2' in diameter, often with an abruptly tapered buttressed trunk and broad, bluntly round knees. The crowns of young trees are cylindrical, becoming flat-topped with age. It is frequent throughout the Coastal Plain.

Needles – deciduous, along with supporting branchlets; $1/8$–$1/4$" long; awl-shaped, or acicular, keeled, spirally arranged, appressed along ascending branchlets. Figure 26.

Twigs – slender, light green-tan, becoming reddish brown; buds small, nearly globular, covered with several overlapping, pointed scales.

Bark – ashy gray to reddish brown, moderately thick, coarsely fissured into scaly plates, peeling off in fibrous strips. Figure 27.

Young Cones – pollen cones produced in catkins, catkins elongated, drooping, 3–5" long; ovulate cones about $1/4$" long, solitary or in clusters of 2–3 near ends of previous year's twigs, composed of several green, overlapping scales fused at base; appearing in March before the leaves. Similar to *T. distichum*, see Figure 30 of ovulate cones.

Mature Cones – globular, ¾–1″ in diameter, cone scales peltate, leathery; maturing in one year, opening at maturity, usually disintegrating; maturing September–October. Similar to *T. distichum*, see Figure 31.

RECOGNITION DIFFICULTIES WITH OTHER TAXA: Pond Cypress is distinguished from Bald Cypress by its awl-shaped, appressed needles and strongly ascending branchlets in contrast to the leaves of Bald Cypress which appear 2-ranked with spreading branchlets. Pond Cypress is treated by some authorities as a variety of Bald Cypress, *T. distichum* var. *nutans* (Aiton) Sweet. See also discussion of habitat differences for each species.

HABITAT: Pond Cypress occurs in shallow ponds, wet depressions in flatwoods, and along stream margins throughout the Coastal Plain.

ECONOMIC, ORNAMENTAL AND OTHER USES: Pond Cypress commonly does not attain the size and form of Bald Cypress and the quality of the lumber is inferior since the trunk is often twisted. Pond Cypress is occasionally planted as an ornamental tree because of its interesting form and cinnamon-red autumn coloration. It grows quite well on moist, well-drained sites and is hardy as far north as New England.

Taxodium distichum (L.) Rich.

Bald Cypress

DESCRIPTION: Bald Cypress is a large, long-lived tree reaching heights of 70–100′ and diameters of 3–5′ or more. It occurs throughout the Coastal Plain in Georgia.

Needles – deciduous, along with the branchlets on which they are borne; ¼–½″ long; linear, flat, spirally arranged, but appearing 2-ranked in one plane on either side of the branchlets, feather-like. Figure 28.

Twigs – similar to *T. ascendens*.

Bark – grayish to reddish brown, moderately thin, shallowly furrowed and divided into flat, longitudinal ridges, peeling off in long, narrow strips. Figure 29, shows a buttressed and fluted base of a single tree with numerous knees.

Young Cones – similar to *T. ascendens*. Figure 30, ovulate cones.

Mature Cones – similar to *T. ascendens*. Figure 31.

RECOGNITION DIFFICULTIES WITH OTHER TAXA: Bald Cypress differs from Pond Cypress in the shape and arrangement of the leaves. The leaves of Bald Cypress are linear, flat and 2-ranked, whereas those of Pond Cypress are mostly keeled, spirally appressed and not in a single plane. The knees of Bald Cypress differ from those of Pond Cypress by being more narrowly conical and sharp pointed than the flattened, dome-shaped knees of Pond Cypress. See Figure 29.

HABITAT: Bald Cypress occurs in alluvial swamps with prolonged flooding and wide seasonal fluctuations in water depth, along major rivers and stream banks. It often occurs in association with *Nyssa aquatica*. It is common throughout the Coastal Plain.

ECONOMIC, ORNAMENTAL AND OTHER USES: In the original forests of the South, virgin Bald Cypress was among the most valuable and highly prized timber trees of the region because of its massive size, excellent form and wood quality. Many trees averaged over 500 years old at maturity and often reached 6–8' in diameter. The heartwood of this species is among the most resistant to decay of any conifer in North America, exceeded only by the redwoods. Therefore, the tree has always been in demand for construction timbers, docks, boats, and exterior siding. The lumber is also highly desirable for interior trim, paneling and cabinets. Bald Cypress makes a handsome ornamental tree for residential lawn and public landscapes because of its soft, feather-like, light green appearance and its bronze-red autumn coloration. It forms a narrow, conical crown, even under open conditions, giving it a stately, unique appearance in winter. It is hardy as far north as southern Canada and grows rapidly on moist, well-drained soils, much faster than in its flooded swamp habitat.

CUPRESSACEAE–**CYPRESS FAMILY**

The Cupressaceae, composed of 16 genera and about 140 species, is worldwide in distribution. In the United States, the family is represented by five genera, *Juniperus, Cupressus, Chamaecyparis, Thuja,* and *Calocedrus*. Of these, *Juniperus* and *Chamaecyparis* are native to Georgia.

Members of this family are evergreen, resinous trees and shrubs with opposite or whorled leaves, which are usually awl-shaped or scale-like and appressed against the twig. With the exception of *Juniperus*, the plants are monoecious, the small pollen and ovulate cones are borne on different branchlets. The ovulate cones are composed of fused bracts which are leathery or fleshy at maturity. Each cone bears one to several seeds.

Many species in the Cypress Family produce valuable timber and specialty products such as volatile oils. Over half of the species in this family are cultivated as ornamental specimens throughout the world.

Chamaecyparis–White-cedars

Chamaecyparis thyoides (L.) B.S.A.
Atlantic White-cedar

DESCRIPTION: Atlantic White-cedar is a medium-sized aromatic tree, 50–80' tall and 1–1½' in diameter, with a conical crown of slender, often pendulous branches. In Georgia, it is restricted to a few localities in the southwestern portion of the Coastal Plain.

Leaves – evergreen, becoming brown at end of second season, but persistent on twigs for several years; 1/16–1/8" long; opposite, scalelike, blue-green with glandular dots on dorsal side. Figure 32.

Twigs – very slender, drooping at tips, light pale green, becoming reddish brown, irregularly branched and flattened into fan-shaped sprays; buds minute, hidden by leaves.

Bark – ashy gray to reddish brown, thin, narrow fissures forming flat, interlacing, fibrous ridges. Figure 33.

Young Cones – monoecious; pollen cones minute, about ⅛" long, terminal, solitary, 10–12 anther bearing scales persistent for several months after pollination; ovulate cones pinkish green, globular with 6 fleshy scales, bearing naked ovules; appearing March–April. Figure 34, pollen cones; Figure 35, ovulate cones.

Mature Cones – globose, small, about ¼" in diameter, fleshy, bluish purple at maturity, cone scales terminating in short protuberance, becoming woody, brown, peltate after opening; maturing in one season, September–October. Figure 32.

RECOGNITION DIFFICULTIES WITH OTHER TAXA: Atlantic White-cedar superficially resembles Eastern Red-cedar. However, the twigs of Atlantic White-cedar are flattened rather than 4-angled as are those of Eastern Red-cedar, and the seed cones are larger with visible protuberances and open scales at maturity. The seed cones of the latter are less than ¼" in diameter, greenish blue, berrylike and do not open at maturity. The gray, interlacing bark ridges of Atlantic White-cedar are also quite distinct from the thinly fissured and reddish brown bark and fluted stems of Eastern Redcedar.

HABITAT: This species is restricted to wet sites around acidic, fresh water bogs and swamps. It often forms pure stands of limited extent.

ECONOMIC, ORNAMENTAL AND OTHER USES: Atlantic White-cedar was formerly a valuable timber species. It was used for shingles, piling and boat construction because of its durability to weathering and resistance to decay. It is still harvested locally for the same purposes. Because of its hardiness, it is occasionally planted as an ornamental tree on moist sites.

Juniperus–Junipers

Juniperus virginiana L.

Eastern Red-cedar

DESCRIPTION: Eastern Red-cedar is a medium-sized, aromatic tree, up to 40–60' tall and 1–2' in diameter with a compact conical-columnar shaped crown. It occurs throughout Georgia.

Leaves – evergreen, of two forms: 1) juvenile on young stems or vigorous shoots about ¼" long, pale green, awl-shaped, opposite, separated by internodes, sharp pointed, spiny to touch; 2) mature, scale-like, dark green with glandular dots, overlapping to form 4-angled twigs; both forms turning brown at end of second winter, but persistent for several years. Figure 36, mature foliage left; juvenile foliage right.

Twigs – slender, dark green, covered with compact scale-like leaves on mature trees, later becoming reddish brown; buds minute, hidden by leaves.

Bark – reddish brown, thin, fibrous, separating into longitudinal narrow strips, fluted trunks, often buttressed at base. Figure 37.

Young Cones – dioecious; pollen cones minute, about ⅛" long, terminal, numerous, 10–12 anthers borne on several distal scales; ovulate cones globular, minute, composed of several fleshy scales, each bearing 1–2 basal ovules; appearing February–March. Figure 38, pollen cones; Figure 39, ovulate cones.

Mature Cones – ovoid, about ¼" in diameter, fleshy and berrylike, greenish blue with glaucous bloom; maturing in one season, October–December. Figure 40.

RECOGNITION DIFFICULTIES WITH OTHER TAXA: Eastern Red-cedar may resemble Atlantic White-cedar (see *Chamaecyparis thyoides* for discussion of distinctive traits). Several authors recognize another taxon along the coast and in the lower Coastal Plain, Southern Red-cedar, *J. silicicola* (Small) Bailey. However, we feel that sufficient differences are not present to warrant this distinction.

HABITAT: *Juniperus virginiana* is ubiquitous in Georgia. It occurs on dry, upland, rocky soils, in particular abundance on calcareous soils. It also frequents moist floodplains or edges of swamps, abandoned fields, fencerows and other waste places. It is not shade tolerant and cannot exist long in the presence of a heavy overstory.

ECONOMIC, ORNAMENTAL AND OTHER USES: Eastern Red-cedar is the most widespread of any eastern conifer, being native to 37 States. It is still an important timber tree, although trees large enough to be harvested for lumber are not plentiful. The heartwood, because of its pleasant, aromatic odor and moth repellant properties, has long been used for closet linings, wardrobes and chests. The wood is highly decay resistent and is used for fence posts and exterior construction. Red-cedar is now widely grown in plantations for Christmas trees, although the young juvenile foliage has the disadvantage of being prickly to the touch. It is also used extensively in many areas for wind breaks and for erosion control. Many cultivars have been selected for ornamental uses in residential and public landscapes. Unfortunately, the species is the alternate host for the cedar apple rust, a fungus disease which can be quite injurious to apple trees; hence the trees are usually eradicated for some distance around commercial orchards. The mature, berrylike cones are consumed by many kinds of mammals and birds, including the cedar waxwing.

Angiosperms

ARECACEAE–PALM FAMILY

The Arecaceae is a large monocotyledonous family with about 3,000 species mostly in tropical and subtropical regions of the world. There are a number of species of economic importance including Coconut Palm, *Cocos nucifera* L., Date Palm, *Phoenix dactylifera* L., and Oil Palm, *Elaeis guineensis* Jacq. Sugars, fibers, canes, and waxes are useful products of various other species of palm. Several species are of ornamental value, in particular, the Cuban Royal Palm, *Roystonea regia* Cook.

Nine genera are native to the United States, mostly to Florida. The single species of palm that attains tree dimension in Georgia is *Sabal palmetto* (Walter) Lodd. ex Schult. & Schult.

Sabal–Palmetto

Sabal palmetto (Walter) Lodd. ex Schult. & Schult.

Cabbage Palmetto

DESCRIPTION: Cabbage Palmetto is a medium-sized tree, up to 65′ tall with a columnar, unbranched trunk with persistent petiole bases and a fanlike crown of leaves. In Georgia, it occurs only along the outer Coastal Plain.

Leaves – persistent, simple, alternate; blades 4–7′ long, often as wide as long, divided into filamentose segments, parallel-veined, midrib conspicuous; petioles 6–7′ long, stiff, flattened above, formed one at a time at the stem tip and unfurled along folds. Figure 41.

Twigs – none.

Bark – no true bark; fibrous sheath on stem; leaf sheaths persistent for indefinite period; stem roughened due to leaf scars.

Flowers – perfect; yellowish-white, small; in large, branched clusters up to 6′ tall; appearing May–July.

Fruit – drupe, black, globose, up to ½″ long; maturing October–November. Figure 42.

RECOGNITION DIFFICULTIES WITH OTHER TAXA: This distinctive species is the only native tree palm in the region.

HABITAT: Cabbage Palmetto occurs along the edges of brackish marshes and in maritime forests of the Coastal Plain.

ECONOMIC, ORNAMENTAL AND OTHER USES: Cabbage Palmetto is often cultivated and is planted as avenue trees along city streets. It grows well in a variety of soil types and light conditions.

SALICACEAE–WILLOW FAMILY

The Willow family contains four genera of trees and shrubs. Two genera are native to North America, *Salix* and *Populus*, and both are represented by species in Georgia. Hybridization between species occurs in both genera. The family is characterized by dioecious plants with simple, alternate, deciduous, stipular leaves. The flowers are borne in catkins and the fruits of all species are small capsules.

Populus–Poplars

SUMMER KEY TO SPECIES OF *POPULUS*
1. Leaves cordate at base, petioles distinctly rounded in cross section below base of leaf. . . . . *P. heterophylla*
1. Leaves triangular in shape, petioles flattened near base of leaf and along most of length . . . . *P. deltoides*

Populus deltoides Bartram ex Marshall
Eastern Cottonwood

DESCRIPTION: Eastern Cottonwood is a large tree, sometimes exceeding 100' in height and 5' in diameter. It occurs in scattered localities throughout the State, and is much more common in other areas of its range.

Leaves – deciduous, simple, alternate; blades generally triangular in shape, broadest at base, apex short acuminate or acute, 5–9" long, 4–5" broad, margins coarsely toothed, leaf stalks up to 3" long, flattened toward base of blade; turning yellow in autumn. Figure 43.

Twigs – stout, brittle, conspicuously enlarged at nodes, round in cross section or angled, yellowish-gray; terminal bud pointed, less than ¾–1" long, light green, resinous; lowermost bud scale enlarged and directly above leaf scar; leaf scar triangular to 3-lobed, bundle scars 3, stipular scars often conspicuous; pith 5-angled.

Bark – gray, smooth to lightly fissured on young trunks, becoming thick, deeply furrowed and prominently ridged with age. Figure 44.

Flowers – dioecious; small, lacking petals and sepals; male and female catkins 2–4″ long; appearing early spring prior to leaves. Figure 45, female catkin.

Fruit – capsules, light brown, elliptical, about ⅜″ long, splitting into 3 parts; borne on slender, pendant stalks about 8″ long; seeds cottony; maturing early summer. Figure 46.

RECOGNITION DIFFICULTIES WITH OTHER TAXA: Eastern Cottonwood resembles Swamp Cottonwood, but can be distinguished by its triangular shaped leaves and flattened petioles near the base, in contrast to the rounded or cordate leaf base, round petioles and tapered, blunt tips of the latter.

HABITAT: This species usually occurs in floodplain forests that are periodically inundated for short periods, however, it grows well on good upland sites.

ECONOMIC, ORNAMENTAL AND OTHER USES: The wood of Eastern Cottonwood is soft and is primarily utilized for pulp, boxes, crates, excelsior, matches and woodenware. The tree has often been planted as an ornamental because of its rapid growth, but is not particularly desirable in some situations because of its extensive root system which competes with other species, grows into septic lines and disrupts sidewalks. In addition, female trees usually produce large crops of fluffy, white, wind-blown seed which can become a nuisance on lawns and around residences.

Populus heterophylla L.

Swamp Cottonwood

DESCRIPTION: Swamp Cottonwood is a large tree which resembles *P. deltoides*, but can be distinguished by its cordate leaf bases, tapered, blunt leaf tips, petioles that are round or oval in cross section and dark, deeply fissured bark. It is usually found in wetter sites than *P. deltoides*, on soils that are wet nearly year round. It is reported infrequently in Georgia, along the Savannah River and Coastal area. Figure 47, leaves of young tree; Figure 48, male catkins; Figure 49, female catkins.

Salix–Willows

SUMMER KEY TO SPECIES OF *SALIX*

1. Leaves not glaucous on lower surface . . . . *S. nigra*
1. Leaves glaucous on lower surface 2
    2. Lower surfaces of leaves densely silky hairy; bud blunt . . . *S. sericea*
    2. Lower surfaces of leaves glabrous or pubescent, but not silky hairy; bud pointed 3
        3. Leaves lanceolate, margins finely serrate . . . . . . *S. caroliniana*
        3. Leaves elliptical, margins irregularly toothed . . . . *S. floridana*

Salix caroliniana Michaux

Coastal Plain Willow

DESCRIPTION: Coastal Plain Willow is a small tree, occasionally 25–30′ tall with many branches, distributed primarily in the Coastal Plain.

Leaves – deciduous, simple, alternate; blades variable in size and shape, usually lance-shaped, tips long acuminate, base rounded, up to 7″ long and 1″ wide, margins finely toothed, teeth with yellowish-glands on tip; both surfaces glabrous when mature, lower surface white and glaucous; stipules wing-like. Figure 50.

Twigs – slender, yellowish, becoming reddish brown or gray, usually hairy; terminal bud absent; lateral buds small, pointed, flattened against twig, single bud scale, cap-like; leaf scar V-shaped, bundle scars 3; flower buds larger than leaf buds.

Bark – brown or nearly black, furrowed into broad scaly ridges.

Flowers – dioecious; small, lacking petals and sepals; staminate catkins erect, pistillate catkins drooping, both 3–4″ long; appearing early spring as leaves emerge.

Fruit – capsules, 2-valved, ovate, less than ¼″; maturing in late spring when the leaves are fully expanded.

RECOGNITION DIFFICULTIES WITH OTHER TAXA: Coastal Plain Willow closely resembles Black Willow, *S. nigra*, and hybridizes with it. The leaves of Black Willow are not glaucous on the lower surface, have marginal teeth with red, rather than yellow glands, and bases that are more wedge-shaped than rounded.

HABITAT: *Salix caroliniana* occurs along streambanks, swamps, and marshes, primarily in the Coastal Plain with occasional occurrences in the Ridge and Valley and Piedmont of Georgia.

ECONOMIC, ORNAMENTAL AND OTHER USES: Coastal Plain Willow is of no commercial value.

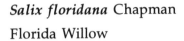

Salix floridana Chapman
Florida Willow

DESCRIPTION: Florida Willow is a small tree, most often a shrub. It is very rare, encountered only in Early and Pulaski Counties, Georgia and a few counties in Florida, on sites with calcareous soils. Florida Willow differs from the other willows in Georgia by its broad, elliptical leaves, up to 6" long and 2" broad, which are broadest near the middle rather than at the base. The lower leaf surfaces are glaucous with whitish pubescence, and the leaf margins are irregularly toothed. Figure 51.

Salix nigra Marshall
Black Willow

DESCRIPTION: Black Willow becomes a tall tree in some swampy areas, 80–100' tall, or shrubby in form along streambanks. It grows rapidly, is short-lived, and occurs throughout the State.

Leaves – deciduous, simple, alternate; blades narrowly lance-shaped, tips long acuminate, base wedge-shaped, about 7" long, and ¾" broad, margins finely serrate, teeth tipped with red glands; lower surfaces not glaucous; stipules wing-like. Figure 52.

Twigs – brittle, glabrous, otherwise similar to *S. caroliniana*.

Bark – light to dark gray or almost black, moderately fissured to form forking ridges with long scaly plates. Figure 53.

Flowers – similar to *S. caroliniana*. Figure 54, staminate catkins; Figure 55, pistillate catkins.

Fruit – similar to *S. caroliniana*. Figure 56.

RECOGNITION DIFFICULTIES WITH OTHER TAXA: See discussion under *S. caroliniana*.

HABITAT: Floodplains, streambanks, marshes and other low, moist areas.

ECONOMIC, ORNAMENTAL AND OTHER USES: The wood of Black Willow is soft and light and is used for boxes, crates, toys and rather extensively for baskets and wicker furniture. Trees are used for erosion control along streams because the root systems are dense and stabilize the soil.

Salix sericea Marshall
Silky Willow

DESCRIPTION: Silky Willow is a small tree or shrub with leaves that are glaucous and distinctly silky pubescent on the lower surface. The leaves are elliptical or lance-shaped, up to 6" in length. The fruits are also silky pubescent. In Georgia, this species is confined to a few counties in the Blue Ridge Mountains.

MYRICACEAE–WAXMYRTLE FAMILY

The Myricaceae is composed of small trees and shrubs of temperate and subtropical regions. Three species of *Myrica* attain tree size in Georgia. The leaves of these plants are alternate, simple, glandular-dotted, and (with the exception of one species) are very aromatic when crushed. The flowers are tiny and the plants are usually dioecious. The characteristic fruit is a small, wax-covered, roundish drupe.

Myrica–Waxmyrtles

SUMMER KEY TO SPECIES OF *MYRICA*
1. Leaves leathery, not reduced in size toward tip of twig; crushed twigs not fragrant; fruit more that ¼" in diameter, with conspicuous rough protuberances . . . . *M. inodora*
1. Leaves not leathery, reduced in size toward tip of twig; crushed twigs fragrant; fruit ⅛" or less in diameter, with thick blue wax 2
    2. Glands on upper leaf surface dense . . . . *M. cerifera*
    2. Glands on upper leaf surface absent or sparse . . . . . *M. heterophylla*

Myrica cerifera L.
Waxmyrtle, Southern Bayberry

DESCRIPTION: Waxmyrtle is usually shrubby in form, occasionally reaching 30' in height, often with several stems from near the base. It is most common in the Coastal Plain, but also occurs in the lower Piedmont.

Leaves – evergreen, simple, alternate; blades oblanceolate, 2–4" long, ¼–¾" wide, reduced toward the tips of branches, margins irregularly serrate near tip; yellowish glandular dots on both surfaces, dense on upper surfaces; aromatic when crushed. Figures 57, 58, 59.

Twigs – slender, reddish gray, hairy, becoming smooth with age, resinous glandular; terminal winter bud absent.

Bark – whitish to gray, thin, smooth, with conspicuous horizontal lenticels.

Flowers – dioecious, occasionally monoecious; tiny; pistillate in bracteate catkins less than ½" long; staminate in catkins less than 1". Figure 57, staminate catkins; Figure 58, pistillate catkins.

Fruit – drupe-like, covered with thick, bluish-white wax, globose, glabrous, ⅛" in diameter; maturing late summer and fall, often persistent until spring. Figure 59.

RECOGNITION DIFFICULTIES WITH OTHER TAXA: Waxmyrtle has distinctive evergreen, irregularly toothed, aromatic leaves. A variety, *M. cerifera* var. *pumila* Michaux, is a colonial shrub, less than 3' tall. Two closely related species also obtain tree size, *M. heterophylla* and *M. pensylvanica*. *Myrica heterophylla* is distinguished from *M. cerifera* by its leaves which are sparsely or not at all glandular on the upper surface and a slightly larger fruit. *Myrica pensylvanica*, which is common in northeastern states, is not documented from Georgia. The characteristics of these taxa intergrade and Houghton (1988) combines *M. heterophylla* with *M. pensylvanica*.

HABITAT: Waxmyrtle is common in the Coastal Plain on various sites including dry sandy soils, marshes, and upland forests. It is occasionally found in the Piedmont in mixed pine hardwoods.

ECONOMIC, ORNAMENTAL AND OTHER USES: Obtained from the fruits of *M. cerifera*, *M. pensylvanica*, and *M. heterophylla*, wax was used by early settlers in making candles. These species are used ornamentally for their evergreen foliage, fast growth, and shrubby or tree-like appearance. Waxmyrtle has root nodules and is known to fix nitrogen, a trait which allows it to grow in poor soils and which has proven useful in reclamation and erosion control efforts.

Myrica heterophylla Raf.

Evergreen Bayberry

DESCRIPTION: *Myrica heterophylla* differs from *M. cerifera* by the sparseness of glands on the upper leaf surface and the winter twigs which are densely hairy and dark grayish-green. The fruit is similar to *M. cerifera*, except slightly larger. This species is restricted to the Coastal Plain. Figure 60, leaves and fruit.

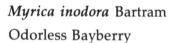

Myrica inodora Bartram

Odorless Bayberry

DESCRIPTION: Odorless Bayberry is restricted to the lower Coastal Plain and is infrequently documented in the State. It differs from other *Myrica* species by its leathery, revolute leaves which are not aromatic and not reduced in size towards the end of the twigs. The fruit is about ¼" in diameter with a rough surface and only a thin, waxy, olive-brown coating. It occurs in wet areas, around bays and swamps and in low pinelands in the southwestern part of the State. Figure 61, leaves and fruit.

LEITNERIACEAE–**CORKWOOD FAMILY**

The Leitneriaceae contains only one species, *Leitneria floridana* Chapman. The wood of this tree is noted as being the lightest of all trees in North America.

Leitneria–Corkwood

Leitneria floridana Chapman

Corkwood

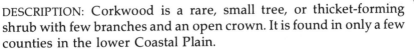

DESCRIPTION: Corkwood is a rare, small tree, or thicket-forming shrub with few branches and an open crown. It is found in only a few counties in the lower Coastal Plain.

Leaves – deciduous, simple, alternate; blades lance-elliptic, up to 6″ long, entire, leathery; venation conspicuous on both surfaces; upper surface glabrous, bright green; lower surface soft pubescent; petioles 1–2″ long. Figure 62.

Twigs – stout, densely hairy when young, becoming smooth and purplish with age; lenticels pale, conspicuous; terminal bud conical, ⅛″ long; lateral flower buds conical; staminate flower buds ½–¾″ long; pistillate flower buds up to ½″ long; leaf scars crescent shaped to 3-lobed; 3 bundle scars.

Bark – reddish brown on young stems, with prominent white lenticels; forming narrow ridges separated by shallow fissures on older stems.

Flowers – dioecious or with unisexual or bisexual flowers; pistillate flowers with 4 bractlike tepals (petals and sepals); staminate lacking calyx or corolla; both occurring in ascending catkins with brown hairy scales; appearing before or during leaf emergence. Figure 63, staminate flowers; Figure 64, pistillate flowers.

Fruit – drupes, flattened, elliptical, dry, ¾″ long and ¼″ wide; maturing early summer.

RECOGNITION DIFFICULTIES WITH OTHER TAXA: With its few, stout branches, reddish brown stems, and leathery leaves, Corkwood is very distinctive and should not be confused with other species.

HABITAT: It occurs in wet, frequently flooded sites or swamps and in brackish marshes.

ECONOMIC, ORNAMENTAL, AND OTHER USES: The soft, pale yellow

wood is the lightest of any native wood, even lighter than cork, and it has often been used for fish net floats and bottle stoppers.

JUGLANDACEAE–WALNUT FAMILY

The Juglandaceae contains about 50 species of deciduous, aromatic trees occurring mostly in north temperate America and Asia, but with a few taxa extending into the tropics. The family is represented in the United States by two economically important genera, *Carya* (hickories and pecan) and *Juglans* (Butternut and Black Walnut). Both genera possess several species of major importance for timber products and nut production.

The genera in our area are characterized by deciduous, compound leaves and a fruit which is a nut with an indehiscent or dehiscent husk. The husk is derived from the perianth and floral bracts and the nut is derived from the ovary wall which hardens before maturity. In the fruit description of *Carya* species, the fruit measurement excludes the husk, but in *Juglans* species, the measurement includes the husk.

Carya–Hickories

SUMMER KEY TO SPECIES OF *CARYA*
1. Bud scales valvate, often appearing naked; fruit with narrow wing along husk sutures 2
  2. Buds distinctly yellow; leaflets 5–9; fruit globose . . . . *C. cordiformis*
  2. Buds yellowish brown; leaflets 9–17; fruit strongly flattened. . . . . *C. aquatica*
1. Bud scales imbricate; fruit husks lacking wings 3
  3. Petioles, rachis, and lower surfaces of mature leaflets glabrous . . 4
    4. Fruit pear-shaped with a neck-like extension at the base, husks indehiscent or splitting part-way at maturity; leaflets usually 5; bark tight, not scaly . . . . *C. glabra*
    4. Fruit globose, husks tardily splitting to the base; leaflets usually 7; bark slightly shaggy or scaly . . . . *C. ovalis*
  3. Petioles, rachis, and lower surfaces of mature leaflets pubescent or with tufts of hairs on leaf margins. 5
    5. Bark with shaggy plates 6
      6. Leaves 8–14″ long; leaflets usually 5 (occasionally 7); nut about 1″ long; husk about ¼″ thick. 7
        7. Bud glabrous, scales shiny black . . . *C. ovata* var. *australis*
        7. Bud hairy, chestnut brown . . . . *C. ovata* var. *ovata*
      6. Leaves up to 20″ long; leaflets usually 7; nut 1½–2″ in length; husk about ¼″ thick. . . . . *C. laciniosa*

5. Bark without shaggy plates 8
   8. Silver to amber disklike scales on lower surface of leaflets, fruit husks and bud scales (easily visible when scratched lightly); twigs slender; fruit husks less than ⅛" thick . . .
   . . . . C. pallida
   8. Disclike scales absent; lower surface of leaflets with small glandular beads or resin; twigs stout; fruit husks ¼–⅓" thick. . . . . C. tomentosa

Carya aquatica (Michaux f.) Nutt.

Water Hickory

DESCRIPTION: Water Hickory is a large tree, 70–100' tall, with numerous slender, upright branches resembling Pecan. In Georgia, it is restricted to wet sites of the lower Coastal Plain.

Leaves – deciduous, pinnately compound, alternate, 9–15" long; leaflets 9–17, scythe-shaped, 2–5" long, margins finely serrate; lower surfaces rusty pubescent. Figure 65.

Twigs – slender, lenticels numerous, terminal bud elongated, ¼–½" long, bud scales valvate, 4–6, yellowish brown, scurfy pubescent; leaf scars heart-shaped to 3-lobed; bundle scars many.

Bark – light gray to brown, smooth when young, becoming scaly, shredding into small plates. Figure 66.

Flowers – monoecious; female small, less than ¼" long, solitary or 2–10 in a spikelike cluster; male in cylindrical prominent catkins, 3 catkins per cluster. Figure 67, female flower; Figure 68, male catkins.

Fruit – nut, elliptical and flattened, ¾–1¼" long; husks 1/16" thick, yellow scales, split entire length, with narrow wing along husk sutures; seed bitter. Figure 69.

RECOGNITION DIFFICULTIES WITH OTHER TAXA: *Carya aquatica* most closely resembles the cultivated Pecan, *C. illinoensis* (Wangenh.) K. Koch, but can be distinguished by its pubescent leaflets and flattened nut. Pecan has glabrous leaves and a nut rounded in cross section. *Carya aquatica* usually has more leaflets than *C. cordiformis* but can have as few as seven to nine. The winter buds of *C. cordiformis* are also valvate, but are a brighter orange-yellow color rather than the yellow-brown color of *C. aquatica*. The fruits of *C. cordiformis* are not flattened and the bark is not scaly.

HABITAT: The species is common in the Coastal Plain in periodically inundated river floodplains and natural levees.

ECONOMIC, ORNAMENTAL AND OTHER USES: Water Hickory is of minor economic importance. The wood is hard and brittle and is used mostly for fuel wood. The nuts of this species are the least preferred by mammals, although water fowl and wood ducks consume considerable quantities.

Carya cordiformis (Wangenh.) K. Koch

Bitternut Hickory

DESCRIPTION: Bitternut Hickory is a medium-sized tree, 50–80' tall, with stout, spreading branches forming a large, open crown. It is found scattered throughout the State.

Leaves – deciduous, pinnately compound, alternate; leaflets 5–9; lance-shaped to obovate, margins sharply toothed; surfaces with resinous scales, lower surfaces pubescent. Figure 70.

Twigs – slender; terminal bud slightly flattened, elongated, ½" or longer, bud scales valvate, bright orange-yellow; leaf scars and bundle scars similar to other hickories.

Bark – gray to brown, shallowly furrowed, tight; does not become scaly or shaggy.

Flowers – similar to other hickories.

Fruit – nut, globose, slightly flattened, beaked, about 1–1¼" long; husks 1/16" thick or less, with yellowish hairs on surface, narrowly winged along husk sutures, splitting part way; seed bitter. Figure 71.

RECOGNITION DIFFICULTIES WITH OTHER TAXA: *Carya cordiformis* might be confused with *C. aquatica* which also occurs in low woods of the Coastal Plain. The two can be separated by bud, bark and fruit: *C. cordiformis* has conspicuous, bright yellow buds, furrowed, but not scaly bark, and round (or only slightly flattened) nuts.

HABITAT: Bitternut Hickory is common in moist soils of valleys and slopes in the mountains and along streams, river bottoms and flood plains in the Piedmont and Coastal Plain.

ECONOMIC, ORNAMENTAL AND OTHER USES: The wood is hard and heavy, but rather brittle and inferior to other hickories. It is frequently harvested for fuelwood and is especially good for smoking meats. It burns with an intense flame and leaves little ash. Although the seed kernels are bitter and unpalatable to humans, they are consumed by rodents. Bitternut Hickory is one of the fastest growing hickories in the State and makes a handsome, long-lived shade tree when planted on moist, well-drained sites.

Carya glabra (Miller) Sweet
Pignut Hickory

DESCRIPTION: Pignut Hickory is a tree that reaches 70–80' in height. It is commonly found throughout the State, most frequently in the Piedmont.

Leaves – deciduous, pinnately compound, alternate; 8–12" long; leaflets usually 5, 3–6" long, glabrous; turning yellow in autumn; petioles glabrous. Figure 72.

Twigs – moderately slender, reddish brown; terminal bud ovoid, ¼–⅜" long, bud scales 6–8, imbricate, glabrous, exposed inner scales tawny; leaf scars and bundle scars similar to other hickories.

Bark – gray, almost smooth when young, tight, not scaly, becoming shallowly fissured with a close, firm, irregular diamond-shaped pattern. Figure 73.

Flowers – similar to other hickories.

Fruit – nut, subglobose, about ¾–1¼" in diameter; with husks appearing pear-shaped, often with neck at base; husk ⅛" or less thick, indehiscent or splitting only part way, lacks wings; seed sweet. Figure 74.

RECOGNITION DIFFICULTIES WITH OTHER TAXA: Pignut Hickory and False Pignut Hickory, *Carya ovalis*, are the only hickory taxa in our range with glabrous leaves. The nut of Pignut Hickory, enclosed by husks, is usually pear-shaped with a neck at the base and the husks splitting only part way or not at all at maturity. The fruit of False Pignut is globose with husks splitting tardily to the base. The bark of Pignut Hickory has low, lacy, diamond-like ridges, while that of False Pignut Hickory becomes more deeply furrowed and broken transversely to become somewhat scaly or shaggy on larger trunks.

HABITAT: Pignut Hickory is common on moist to drier upland sites in association with oaks and other hickories. It occurs throughout most of the State.

ECONOMIC, ORNAMENTAL AND OTHER USES: Pignut Hickory is an important source of timber. The wood is hard and strong, used mainly for tool handles, farm implements and fuel. The nuts are consumed in quantity by small mammals.

Carya laciniosa (Michaux f.) Loudon

Shellbark Hickory

DESCRIPTION: This is a large, long-lived tree reaching heights of 70–100' with stout, fairly uniform branches forming an oblong crown. Shellbark Hickory has the largest leaves and nuts of our native hickories. It occurs infrequently in the northwestern part of the State.

Leaves – deciduous, pinnately compound, alternate; 12–20" long; leaflets 7–9 (usually 7), lance-shaped to obovate, 3–8" long, margins finely serrate; lower surfaces soft pubescent; petioles pubescent.

Twigs – stout, pale orange-brown, hairy, with prominent lenticels; terminal bud brown, ¾–1" long, pubescent, bud scales imbricate; lateral buds divergent; leaf scars and bundle scars similar to other hickories.

Bark – light gray, becoming rough and shaggy with age, separating into long, loosely attached plates.

Flowers – similar to other hickories.

Fruit – nut, oblong, 1½–2" long, shell ribbed; husks about ¼" thick, lacking wings; seeds edible and sweet. Figure 75.

RECOGNITION DIFFICULTIES WITH OTHER TAXA: Shellbark Hickory is very similar to Shagbark Hickory, *C. ovata*. The leaves and nuts of *C. laciniosa* are generally larger than Shagbark Hickory. It also differs by its orange to buff twigs and larger terminal buds.

HABITAT: Shellbark Hickory is documented in Georgia in northwestern counties of the Ridge and Valley on deep, rich, moist alluvial soils along streams or bottomlands.

ECONOMIC, ORNAMENTAL OR OTHER USES: Shellbark Hickory produces some of the best quality lumber of the native hickories. It is used for tool handles, implements, furniture and heavy construction timbers. The large sweet nuts were formerly marketed and they are consumed in quantity by wildlife.

Carya ovalis (Wangenh.) Sarg.

[*Carya glabra* var. *odorata*
(Marshall) Little]

False Pignut Hickory, Red Hickory

DESCRIPTION: This taxon is considered by some authorities to be a separate species as listed here, i.e., *C. ovalis* (Wangenh.) Sarg. Other workers do not consider it as meriting even varietal status and simply include it under *C. glabra*, while still others consider it as a variety of *C. glabra*. Young trees have a weakly shaggy, or scaly bark which becomes broken transversely into short, loose plates with age, but not nearly as shaggy as the bark of Shagbark Hickory, *C. ovata*. The leaves of *C. ovalis* are glabrous and very spicy aromatic when crushed, whereas leafstalks of *C. ovata* are pubescent and the leaves have only a faint apple smell. *Carya ovalis* fruits are smaller, globose, and have much thinner husks than those of *C. ovata* which have fruit husks ¼–⅜" thick. Figure 76, leaves; Figure 77, bark; Figure 78, fruit.

Carya ovata (Miller) K. Koch var. *ovata*

Shagbark Hickory

DESCRIPTION: Shagbark Hickory is a large tree, 70–90' tall, with stout ascending branches forming an irregular crown. The species is found frequently in the highlands and Piedmont and extends into south-western Georgia in the Coastal Plain.

Leaves – deciduous, pinnately compound, alternate; 8–14" long; leaflets usually 5, 3–7" long, margins serrate with persistent tufts of hairs on teeth; lower surfaces sometimes pubescent when young, but becoming essentially glabrous with age; petiole pubescent, petiole and leaf rachis persistent into fall; crushed leaves have faint apple smell rather than astringent odor of other hickories. Figure 79.

Twigs – stout, dark brown, lenticels long, pale; terminal bud chestnut brown, ¾" long, hairy; bud scales imbricate; leaf scars and bundle scars similar to other hickories.

Bark – dark gray, exfoliating in long, narrow plates which are often detached at both ends, resulting in a conspicuously shaggy appearance. Figure 80.

Flowers – similar to other hickories.

Fruit – nut, nearly round, 1–1½″ in diameter, sometimes flattened at tip, shell angled; husk ¼–⅜″ thick, splitting to base; seed edible. Figure 81.

RECOGNITION DIFFICULTIES WITH OTHER TAXA: Shagbark Hickory is quite distinctive in all seasons because of its bark characteristics. In this respect, it is similar to *C. laciniosa*, but where these two species overlap in distribution they may be separated by leaf and fruit characteristics. See *C. laciniosa* description.

HABITAT: Shagbark Hickory attains best development on moist, alluvial river or valley soils, although it frequently occurs on adjacent slopes and ridges.

ECONOMIC, ORNAMENTAL AND OTHER USES: The wood of Shagbark Hickory is of very good quality and is used for the same purposes as that of *C. laciniosa*. It is valuable economically because of its more widespread occurrence and abundance throughout the eastern United States. The shaggy bark makes a picturesque ornamental tree, but the slow growth and large fruit crops detract from its widespread use as a lawn or street tree. The large nuts are sweet and edible, and are consumed by squirrels and other small mammals.

Carya ovata var. *australis* (Ashe) Little

(*C. carolinae-septentrionalis* Ashe)

Southern Shagbark Hickory

DESCRIPTION: *Carya ovata* var. *australis* differs from var. *ovata* by its smaller leaves and fruit and the glabrous and shiny, black, outer bud scales. The twigs are slender, glabrous, dark brown and lustrous. Southern Shagbark Hickory is commonly found in low, flat moist woods and river bottoms or along streams. It occurs infrequently in the Piedmont and mountains in association with bottomland oaks and other hickories. The wood is used for the same purposes as *C. ovata* var. *ovata*.

Carya pallida (Ashe) Engelm. & Graebner

Sand Hickory

DESCRIPTION: This is usually a small to medium-sized tree, but occasionally attains heights of 80–90' on richer sites. Sand Hickory is scattered throughout the State, less frequently in the Coastal Plain than in the highlands or Piedmont.

Leaves – deciduous, pinnately compound, alternate; 7–15" long; leaflets 7–9, lance-shaped to elliptical, margins serrate; lower surfaces finely pubescent, with silvery scales; rachis densely pubescent. Figure 82.

Twigs – moderately slender; terminal buds reddish brown to dark brown, ¼–⅓" long, imbricate bud scales with silvery scales; leaf scars and bundle scars similar to other hickories.

Bark – light gray, tight and slightly furrowed on young trees; older trees on poor sites gray to almost black and deeply furrowed; similar to the bark of *C. glabra*. Figure 83.

Flowers – similar to other hickories.

Fruit – nut, ¾–1" in diameter, shell round, slightly ridged; husks less than ⅛" thick, tardily splitting to base, lacking suture wings, yellow scales, hairy; seed small, but edible. Figure 84.

RECOGNITION DIFFICULTIES WITH OTHER TAXA: Sand Hickory is most easily distinguished from other hickories by the numerous silvery-yellow scales on the underside of its leaflets and fruit husks, and by the dense pubescence of the rachis. The fruit is also smaller than other Hickories and the husk splits tardily to the base.

HABITAT: This species is most often found on drier, sandy or rocky upland sites in association with other hickories and upland oaks. It is common in the Piedmont, particularly on soils of granitic origin.

ECONOMIC, ORNAMENTAL AND OTHER USES: Sand Hickory is of little economic importance except as a source of fuel wood. The small, sweet nuts are consumed in quantity by squirrels and other wildlife.

Carya tomentosa (Poiret) Nutt.

Mockernut Hickory

DESCRIPTION: Mockernut Hickory is a large tree, up to 90' tall with distinctively stout, ascending branches. It is common throughout the State.

Leaves – deciduous, pinnately compound, alternate; 8–15" long; leaflets usually 7, variable in size, margins coarsely or finely toothed, lower surfaces pubescent, with fascicles of hairs; petioles pubescent; aromatic when crushed. Figure 85.

Twigs – stout, reddish brown, often pubescent, numerous lenticels; terminal buds ovoid, ½–¾" long, hairy, bud scales imbricate, outer pair of reddish brown bud scales shed early, exposing inner, silky, buff-colored scales; leaf scars and bundle scars similar to other hickories.

Bark – tight with shallow furrows when young, becoming deeply furrowed with pronounced interlacing ridges which form a diamond-like pattern. Figure 86.

Flowers – similar to other hickories.

Fruit – nut, about 1–1½" long, shell rounded or elliptical, angled; husk ¼–⅓" thick, hard, freely splitting to base, lacks glands, lacks suture wing; seed edible. Figure 87.

RECOGNITION DIFFICULTIES WITH OTHER TAXA: Mockernut Hickory is easily recognized by the hairy leaves, the thick fruit husks, and the lacy, diamond-pattern of the bark. In winter condition, the stout twig and large terminal bud are distinctive. Sand Hickory also has pubescent leaves, but has silvery-yellow, disk-like scales on the lower surfaces of the leaflets; slender twigs, and fruit husks less than ⅛" thick. Other hickories with large terminal buds include Shagbark Hickory and Southern Shagbark Hickory, but these taxa both have distinctive bark exfoliating in shaggy plates, a characteristic never found in Mockernut Hickory.

HABITAT: Mockernut is the most common hickory in the State. It is found in upland forests throughout all physiographic provinces.

ECONOMIC, ORNAMENTAL AND OTHER USES: Similar to Shagbark and Shellbark Hickories.

Juglans–Walnuts

SUMMER KEY TO SPECIES OF *JUGLANS*

1. Fruits (including husk) ellipsoid to ovoid with pointed end; leaf scars with hairy fringes; bark light gray, broad ridges . . . . *J. cinerea*
1. Fruits (including husk) globose; leaf scars without hairy fringes; bark dark brown, lacy ridges . . . . *J. nigra*

Juglans cinerea L.
Butternut, White Walnut

DESCRIPTION: Butternut is a medium-sized tree, 50–70' tall, somewhat smaller in stature than the familiar Black Walnut. In Georgia, it occurs only in the mountains.

Leaves – deciduous, pinnately compound, alternate; leaflets 11–17, lance-shaped, up to 4″ long, margins toothed; lower surfaces pubescent; aromatic when crushed; turning yellow in autumn. Figure 88.

Twigs – stout, reddish brown-gray, pale lenticels; terminal bud ½–¾″ long, lateral buds smaller, often superposed; leaf scars inversely triangular, large, raised, upper margin with a hairy tuft; bundle scar in each lobe of leaf scar in U-shaped clusters; pith dark, chambered (chambering develops at the end of the growing season).

Bark – light gray and smooth on young trunks, becoming broken into broad, gray ridges separated by darker fissures.

Flowers – monoecious; staminate in 3–5″ catkins; pistillate in 6–8 flowered spikes, ½″ long with bright red, plumose pistils; appearing in April.

Fruit – nut, shell of nut ribbed; indehiscent husk, oblong, fleshy, sticky, hairy, green, becoming light brown at maturity, often angular, 1 ½–2″ long; solitary or in clusters of 2–5. Figure 89 shows differences in shape and size of mature fruits with indehiscent husks, Black Walnut (top) Butternut (bottom).

RECOGNITION DIFFICULTIES WITH OTHER TAXA: Butternut can be distinguished from hickories by the presence of a chambered pith, an indehiscent fruit husk, and irregularly furrowed shell surface. Butternut differs from Black Walnut by its elliptical to ovoid fruit, an unnotched leaf scar with hairy tuft on upper margin, and a terminal bud ½″ long or greater. Black Walnut has a globose fruit, notched leaf scar without a tuft of hair, and terminal buds about ⅓″ long. There are also differences in bark characteristics between the two species. The bark of Butternut is usually light to medium gray with broad ridges separated by darker fissures while the bark of Black Walnut is dark brown and possesses long, vertical interlacing ridges.

HABITAT: Butternut occurs on rich, moist well-drained soils; however, it is also found on drier, rocky slopes especially on soils of limestone origin.

ECONOMIC, ORNAMENTAL AND OTHER USES: The wood of Butternut is much softer and lighter in color than Black Walnut, but is sometimes used as a substitute. The nuts are edible. An orange-yellow dye can be obtained from the inner bark and fruit husks.

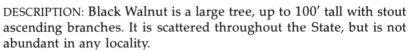

Juglans nigra L.
Black Walnut

DESCRIPTION: Black Walnut is a large tree, up to 100' tall with stout ascending branches. It is scattered throughout the State, but is not abundant in any locality.

Leaves – deciduous, pinnately compound, alternate, 12–24" long; leaflets 9–21, terminal leaflet often aborted, lance-shaped, long pointed, margins finely toothed; lower surfaces pubescent; pungent odor when crushed; turning yellow in autumn. Figure 90.

Twigs – stout, brown; terminal bud about ⅓" long; leaf scar notched, tuft of hair lacking on upper margin; bundle scar in each lobe of leaf scar in U-shaped cluster; pith chambered, light to dark brown.

Bark – dark gray to brown, sometimes almost black, deeply furrowed and forming distinctive, anastomosing ridges. Figure 91.

Flowers – similar to *J. cinerea*. Figure 92.

Fruit – nut, shell irregularly ridged; with indehiscent husk, globose, up to 2½" in diameter, green, turning dark brown-black; seed oily, edible. Figure 93.

RECOGNITION DIFFICULTIES WITH OTHER TAXA: See description of *J. cinerea* to distinguish Black Walnut from hickories. Another species which has a large, pinnately compound leaf is the exotic and naturalized weedy tree, *Ailanthus altissima* (Miller) Swingle. The leaflets of this tree are coarsely toothed and glandular tipped at the base. Also, the unchambered pith is yellowish.

HABITAT: Black Walnut is scattered throughout the State in rich woods, on moist, well-drained soils. Trees often grow around old homesites where they were planted.

ECONOMIC, ORNAMENTAL AND OTHER USES: Black Walnut is one of the most valuable trees in North America due to its strong, durable, and rich-grained wood. It is in great demand for veneers, cabinet making, and gunstocks. The bark is used in tanning and a yellow-brown dye is made from the fruit husks. Other plant species often do not survive within the root zone of large walnut trees due to the root production of juglone, which inhibits growth or kills the roots of neighboring plants.

BETULACEAE–BIRCH FAMILY

The Betulaceae comprise six genera, five of which are found in North America and which include about 28 tree or shrub species. In Georgia, all five genera are represented by eight species. Both species in the genus *Corylus* are colonial shrubs, whereas species of *Betula, Carpinus, Ostrya,* and *Alnus* attain tree size.

Two of the birch species, *Betula lenta* L. and *B. alleghaniensis* Britton, provide wood for furniture, doors, paneling, floors, and numerous other products.

Alnus–Alder

Alnus serrulata (Aiton) Willd.
Hazel Alder, Tag Alder

DESCRIPTION: Hazel Alder occasionally becomes a small tree, but most often it forms a large shrub with multiple stems. It is found throughout the State.

Leaves – deciduous, simple, alternate; elliptic to obovate, 3–5″ long, margins finely toothed and occasionally slightly wavy; lower surfaces glabrous to hairy. Figure 94.

Twigs – brown to gray, rusty pubescent when young; terminal bud absent; lateral buds stalked, up to ½″ long, valvate bud scales; leaf scars raised, half-round to triangular, bundle scars 3, U-shaped; pith triangular, greenish brown.

Bark – brown to gray; smooth, frequently fluted and twisted, similar to that of *Carpinus caroliniana*.

Flowers – monoecious; tiny; staminate in slender, pendulous, elongate catkins; pistillate in erect, short, ovoid, conelike spikes and located below the male catkins; both inflorescence types appear in fall, but flowers open in early spring, mostly before leaves appear. Figure 95, pistillate and staminate catkins.

Fruit – nutlet, small, narrowly winged, in persistent semiwoody cone-like structures; cones about ½″ long; maturing in late summer or fall. Figure 96, persistent cones.

RECOGNITION DIFFICULTIES WITH OTHER TAXA: Hazel Alder is usually distinctive in winter or summer condition because of the persistent inflorescences and fruit cones, and should not be easily confused with any other species. However, the leaves somewhat resemble those of Witch-hazel, *Hamamelis virginiana* L., another small tree, or those of the Hazelnuts, *Corylus cornuta* Marshall and *Corylus americana* Walter, colonial shrubs. The leaf margins of Witch-hazel are wavy and not toothed; those of *C. cornuta* and *C. americana* are doubly serrate. Hazel Alder has a finely serrate leaf margin and is occasionally wavy along the margins.

HABITAT: The species commonly occurs along streambanks, pond margins and marshes throughout the State.

ECONOMIC, ORNAMENTAL AND OTHER USES: Hazel Alder is known to be a nitrogen fixer, as are the western North American species in the genus.

Betula – Birches

SUMMER KEY TO SPECIES OF *BETULA*

1. Leaf bases oblique to cordate; twigs and foliage aromatic 2
    2. Bark reddish brown to black, breaking into scaly plates; bracts of pistillate spikes glabrous or essentially so . . . . *B. lenta*
    2. Bark yellow to bronze-gray, exfoliating into large, horizontal papery sheets; bracts of pistillate spikes ciliate . . . . *B. alleghaniensis*
1. Leaf bases angularly wedge-shaped or truncate; twigs and foliage not aromatic . . . . *B. nigra*

Betula alleghaniensis Britton

(*Betula lutea* Michaux f.)

Yellow Birch

DESCRIPTION: Yellow Birch is a medium to large-sized tree from 70–100' tall, restricted in Georgia to mountain slopes 3–4500' elevation.

Leaves – deciduous, simple, alternate, 2-ranked; blades ovate, 3–4½" long, margins weakly doubly serrate, apex acute to acuminate, base rounded to cordate or oblique; lower surfaces pubescent along veins, or tufts in axils of veins; petioles slender, pubescent. Figure 97.

Twigs – slender, zigzag, greenish brown, lenticels on young stems horizontally elongated, occasionally pubescent; terminal buds absent; lateral buds ovate, sharply pointed, with overlapping, chestnut-brown, ciliated scales; wintergreen taste and aroma when crushed; spur shoots common on older twigs.

Bark – shiny golden-gray to bronze-gray, peeling into thin, horizontal papery layers; young stems with long horizontally elongated lenticels; larger trunks become fissured to form reddish brown, scaly plates. Figure 98.

Flowers – monoecious; tiny; male in drooping catkins near tip of twigs, 1½–2½" long; female in short erect catkins about ¾" long, below the male; appearing March–April.

Fruit – nutlets, small, winged, ⅛–¼", subtended by 3-lobed, ciliate bracts; in upright conelike cluster ¾–1¼" long; maturing in late spring or early summer; tardily deciduous. Figure 99.

RECOGNITION DIFFICULTIES WITH OTHER TAXA: *Betula alleghaniensis* and *B. lenta* can be separated most easily by bark characteristics. Bark of *B. alleghaniensis* is shiny golden to bronze-gray and separates into thin, papery layers; in contrast the smoother, reddish brown to nearly black bark of *B. lenta* breaks into irregular plates. The pistillate bracts of *B. alleghaniensis* are ciliate while those of *B. lenta* are essentially glabrous. Some authors maintain that the shape of the fruit clusters of these two species differ, however, we have seen considerable variation in this trait and feel that it is not a reliable key characteristic. The leaves of Yellow Birch are frequently (but not always) more prominently double serrate than those of Black Birch, *B. lenta*, which tend to be singly serrate.

HABITAT: Yellow Birch occurs in moist, well-drained soils in several Northeast Georgia counties of the Blue Ridge Mountains between 3–4500' elevation. The species grows slowly and reproduces prolifically. Seeds often germinate on decomposing logs and roots grow out over the log. With time the log completely decomposes, leaving the tree standing as though on stilts.

ECONOMIC, ORNAMENTAL AND OTHER USES: Yellow Birch is one of the most valuable hardwoods of the northeastern United States. The wood is used primarily for furniture, veneer, paneling, cabinets, flooring and toys. The papery bark curls are highly flammable and may be used, even when wet, to start a campfire. Oil of wintergreen can be obtained by distillation of young twigs and inner bark, but the practice is no longer economically feasible because synthetic oil can be produced more cheaply.

Betula lenta L.

Black Birch, Sweet Birch

DESCRIPTION: Black Birch is a medium-sized tree attaining heights of 50–80'. It is found in Georgia in the mountainous areas of the Blue Ridge and Ridge and Valley Provinces.

Leaves – deciduous, simple, alternate, 2-ranked; blades elliptical,

2½–5″ long, margins singly or irregularly doubly serrate, apex acute to acuminate, base cordate or rounded, lower surfaces pubescent on veins; strong wintergreen fragrance when crushed. Figure 100.

Twigs – slender, zigzag, brown, usually glabrous, lenticels conspicuous; terminal bud absent; lateral buds ovoid, sharply pointed, divergent, chestnut brown, about ¼″ long, with several imbricated scales; spur twigs on older growth; three bundle scars; wintergreen odor and taste when crushed.

Bark – dark reddish brown to almost black on young trees, smooth, shiny, with prominent horizontal lenticels, breaking into fissures with scaly plates with age; somewhat resembling Pin Cherry, *Prunus pensylvanica* L. Figure 101.

Flowers – monoecious; tiny; staminate in drooping catkins near tip of twigs, 1–2½″ long; pistillate glabrous, in short erect catkins ¾–1 ½″ long, below the male; appearing March–April.

Fruit – similar to *B. alleghaniensis*, except that the bracts of the cone-like cluster are glabrous or only slightly ciliate. In general, the cones appear slightly more elongate and smaller in diameter than those of Yellow Birch.

RECOGNITION DIFFICULTIES WITH OTHER TAXA: *Betula lenta* and *Betula alleghaniensis* can be separated most easily by bark characteristics (see *B. alleghaniensis*). In winter, young trees of *B. lenta* might be confused with Pin Cherry, *Prunus pensylvanica*, both occurring at high elevations. However, *B. lenta* has fewer bud scales and the cut twigs have a wintergreen aroma.

HABITAT: Black Birch usually occurs on deep, fertile, well-drained soils, but also on drier, rocky soils in mountainous regions of the State.

ECONOMIC, ORNAMENTAL AND OTHER USES: Its uses are similar to those of *B. alleghaniensis*, although the trunks seldom reach the large merchantable size and quality of Yellow Birch.

Betula nigra L.

River Birch

DESCRIPTION: River Birch is a medium-sized tree, often 60–80′ in height, usually with a short trunk and forked spreading crown. It occurs throughout the State, but is less frequent in the Coastal Plain.

Leaves – deciduous, simple, alternate, 2-ranked; blades triangularly ovate, base truncated or angularly wedge-shaped, margins doubly serrate; lower surfaces densely pubescent when young, glabrous or pubescent on veins at maturity; petioles densely pubescent. Figure 102.

Twigs – slender, zigzag, red-brown, lenticels horizontally elongated; terminal bud absent; winter lateral buds ¼" long, ovoid, acute, with 3 visible scales, usually hooked; spur twigs on older growth; leaf scars crescent to triangular; bundle scars 3, not aromatic.

Bark – reddish to gray-brown, often pinkish, peeling into thin papery layers on young trees; older bark darker grayish brown, dividing into coarser, shreddy plates. Figure 103.

Flowers – monoecious; tiny; staminate catkins elongate and drooping, about 1½" long; pistillate catkins cylindric and upright, about ½" long; appearing in the fall, opening in early spring. Figure 104, pistillate catkins.

Fruit – nutlet, about ¼–½" long, with ciliate wings; in upright, cone-like clusters of pubescent bracts; clusters oblong, up to 1½" in length.

RECOGNITION DIFFICULTIES WITH OTHER TAXA: River Birch can usually be easily distinguished by its bark. The leaves of River Birch are deeply doubly serrate and have a distinct truncate or angular base which gives the leaves a rhombic appearance.

HABITAT: River Birch is typically a flood plain species occurring along streams, rivers and wet bottomlands, but occasionally occurs along moist roadsides. It is common throughout the State, but is most prevalent in the Piedmont.

ECONOMIC, ORNAMENTAL AND OTHER USES: The wood is used for furniture, veneer, and cabinets. River Birch is frequently used as a specimen tree in landscaping. It is well suited to drainage areas that stay moist during part of the year. The tree grows well on well-drained upland sites once established.

Carpinus–Hornbeam

Carpinus caroliniana Walter
American Hornbeam, Ironwood,

Musclewood

DESCRIPTION: American Hornbeam is a small tree up to 35' tall and 8–10" in diameter, with an irregularly fluted and commonly twisted trunk. It occurs throughout the State.

Leaves – deciduous, simple, alternate; 2-ranked; blades elliptic to ovate, 1½–3" long, doubly serrate, base rounded; upper surfaces dark green, glabrous; lower surfaces pale green with pubescent veins; petioles usually pubescent. Figure 105.

Twigs – slender, variably pubescent or hairy, zigzag; terminal bud absent; lateral buds brown, pointed, four angled (squarish in cross section); leaf scars crescent-shaped to oval; bundle scars three, often indistinct.

Bark – blue-gray, smooth, trunk twisted and fluted giving a muscular appearing form. Figure 106.

Flowers – monoecious; tiny; male flowers in drooping catkins 1–1½" long; female catkins reddish green, about ½" long; appearing in early spring with emergence of leaves. Figure 107.

Fruit – nutlets, ovoid, each subtended by a conspicuously 3-lobed, leaf-like bract; in clusters 2–4" long. Figure 108.

RECOGNITION DIFFICULTIES WITH OTHER TAXA: American Hornbeam leaves resemble those of *Ostrya virginiana*, Eastern Hophornbeam; however, they are darker bluish green above and not finely hairy below. The buds of American Hornbeam are angled instead of rounded and the bark is smooth instead of shreddy as in *O. virginiana*. American Hornbeam leaves differ from those of River Birch, *Betula nigra*, by their rounded bases and lack of dense pubescence beneath; in contrast to the truncated bases and pubescent leaves of River Birch.

HABITAT: *Carpinus caroliniana* is a shade tolerant, understory tree found on a variety of sites, most frequently along streams, ravines and moist bottomlands, but it also occurs on lower, well-drained slopes throughout most of the State.

ECONOMIC, ORNAMENTAL AND OTHER USES: The wood of American Hornbeam is extremely hard and tough. In the past, it was frequently used for mallets, golf club heads, tool handles and wooden ware. The autumn foliage ranges from yellow to brown, but is frequently discolored by pests and mildews. The nutlets are eaten by squirrels and song birds.

Ostrya–Hophornbeam

Ostrya virginiana (Miller) K. Koch
Eastern Hophornbeam

DESCRIPTION: Eastern Hophornbeam is a small tree occasionally reaching 35–50' in height and 10" in diameter. It is frequent in the Piedmont and mountains, but less prevalent in the Coastal Plain.

Leaves – deciduous, simple, alternate, 2-ranked; blades oblong to elliptical, bases rounded to subcordate or oblique, apices acute to acuminate, 2–5" long, 1½–2½" wide, margins singly or doubly serrate; lower surfaces finely pubescent. Figure 109.

Twigs – slender, zigzag, reddish brown; terminal bud absent; lateral buds red-brown, ⅛–¼" long, sharp pointed; leaf scars small, crescent-shaped to oval; bundle scars 3.

Bark – reddish brown, thin, finely fissured into narrow plates with loose scales; often shreddy in appearance. Figure 110.

Flowers – monoecious; staminate catkins 1–1½" long; female catkins inconspicuous, about ¼" long; staminate catkins develop in late summer and overwinter, both pistillate and staminate flowers mature in early spring as leaves emerge. Figure 111.

Fruit – nutlets, small, brown, about ¼" long, enclosed in a papery sac; mature cluster of nutlets 1–3" long, with bracts nearly ½" long; maturing in late summer, and persisting into early fall. Figure 112.

RECOGNITION DIFFICULTIES WITH OTHER TAXA: See *Carpinus caroliniana.*

HABITAT: Eastern Hophornbeam occurs on moist soils in upland forests throughout the State.

ECONOMIC, ORNAMENTAL AND OTHER USES: The wood of Eastern Hophornbeam is hard and tough and has been used for the same purposes as *Carpinus caroliniana.* Occasionally, it is planted as an ornamental because of its attractive foliage, bark, and fruit clusters, although it is a slow growing tree. The nutlets are eaten by many birds and rodents.

FAGACEAE–BEECH FAMILY

The Fagaceae is distributed worldwide in temperate and tropical regions and contains approximately eight genera and 100 species. Forest dominants in the family are beeches, oaks and chestnuts. Some species, particularly the oaks, are important timber trees worldwide. The timber has a wide range of uses from furniture, construction, flooring, to whiskey and wine barrels. Commercial cork is obtained from Cork Oak, *Quercus suber* L. Several species are planted as shade trees.

In eastern North America, three important genera occur: *Quercus*, *Castanea*, and *Fagus*. These trees are monoecious, have alternate, simple leaves, and may be deciduous or evergreen. Species of *Quercus* characteristically have lateral buds clustered at the tip of the twig. The fruits provide a significant source of food for wildlife.

Castanea–Chestnuts

SUMMER KEY TO SPECIES OF *CASTANEA*

1. Leaves more than 6" long, glabrous on both surfaces; nut flattened on one side, more than 1 per bur; bur 2–3" in diameter. . . . *C. dentata*
1. Leaves usually less than 6" long, hairy beneath, often densely so; nuts not flattened; single nut in a bur; bur 1–1½" in diameter . . . . *C. pumila*

Castanea dentata (Marshall) Borkh.

American Chestnut

DESCRIPTION: Formerly, these large trees were dominant in the Piedmont and mountain regions. In the early 1900s the virulent chestnut blight, *Endothia parasitica*, was introduced and resulted in the death of vast stands of trees. Today, small trees may develop from stump sprouts of the original trees and may even attain reproductive maturity. However, these sprouts eventually succumb to the blight by the time they reach 20–25' in height.

Leaves – deciduous, simple, alternate; blades thin and papery, elliptical to oblong, tip acuminate, up to 11" long and 3½" wide, margins coarsely serrate, teeth glandular, curved, bristle-tipped; lower surface glabrous with age; leafstalks slightly angled. Figure 113.

Twigs – usually zigzag, gray to shiny chestnut brown, glabrous; lenticels numerous, white; terminal bud usually absent; lateral buds ovoid, about ¼" long, scales 2–3, dark brown, glabrous; leaf scars half-round, bundle scars 3 or more; pith 5-angled.

Bark – gray to brown, smooth on sprouts, thick with shallow furrows separating, flattened plates on small trunks.

Flowers – monoecious; lacking petals; staminate in upright catkins 6–8" long; pistillate in clusters of 2–3; appearing May–June. Figure 113.

Fruit – nut, shiny brown, flattened on 1 side, sweet edible kernel; 2 or more nuts enclosed in spiny bur, 2–3" across; maturing September–October. Figure 114, immature, green bur in late July.

RECOGNITION DIFFICULTIES WITH OTHER TAXA: The long, sharply toothed leaves of this species should make it distinctive. The Allegheny Chinquapin is similar, but the leaves are shorter and are hairy. Chinese Chestnut, *C. mollissima* Blume, has been introduced into this country and is resistant to the blight. This Asiatic species differs from American Chestnut by leaves which are whitish tomentose beneath and by greenish gray twigs and buds covered with long spreading hairs.

HABITAT: Prior to the chestnut blight, American Chestnut occurred abundantly on rocky, well-drained slopes of the mountains and Piedmont.

ECONOMIC, ORNAMENTAL AND OTHER USES: Formerly, this tree was valuable for its lumber which was used for furniture, fences, and caskets. The reddish gold wood is quite durable. At one time Chestnut wood was the major source of tannin used in the United States. The nuts are edible and were once a staple for American Indians and wildlife.

Castanea pumila Miller
Allegheny Chinquapin

DESCRIPTION: Allegheny Chinquapin is a shrub which occasionally attains tree size. It occurs sporadically throughout Georgia.

Leaves – deciduous, simple, alternate; blades elliptical, base often unequal, up to 6″ long, 2″ wide, margins serrate, teeth bristle-tipped; lower surface densely pubescent; petiole hairy, flattened on upper surface. Figure 115.

Twigs – slender, gray, woolly pubescent when young, becoming glabrous with age; terminal bud usually absent; lateral buds reddish, hairy; pith 5-angled.

Bark – light red-brown, shallowly furrowed with flattened plates.

Flowers – monoecious; staminate flowers in upright catkins, 4–6″ long; female flowers inconspicuous, near the base of some male catkins; appearing early summer.

Fruit – nut, shiny brown, not flattened on one side; occurs singly in a spiny bur; maturing September–October. Figure 116.

RECOGNITION DIFFICULTIES WITH OTHER TAXA: The leaves of Allegheny Chinquapin somewhat resemble American Chestnut; however, the leaves of the latter are longer and are not densely hairy. Another chinquapin, *C. alnifolia* Nutt., is a shrubby species of the Coastal Plain. The characteristics used to separate this taxon from *C. pumila* intergrade and recognition of the two can be confusing, suggesting a need for taxonomic study.

HABITAT: Allegheny Chinquapin is widespread throughout the State in dry, deciduous forests.

ECONOMIC, ORNAMENTAL AND OTHER USES: The wood of Allegheny Chinquapin has been used for fence posts, although the small size of this species prohibits it from being economically important. The sweet nut is edible and is occasionally marketed in some localities. It is consumed by many small mammals.

Fagus–Beech

Fagus grandifolia Ehrh.
American Beech

DESCRIPTION: American Beech is a slow growing tree, up to 100' in height and often over 3' in diameter. It is common throughout the Piedmont and mountainous regions, but less prevalent in the lower Coastal Plain.

Leaves – deciduous, simple, alternate; blades papery thin to leathery, broadly elliptical, up to 5½" long, margins bluntly serrate, principal lateral veins prominent and parallel to each other; upper surfaces dark green; lower surfaces paler, becoming glabrous; turns yellow-brown in autumn and persists on lower branches into the winter. Figure 117.

Twigs – slender, zigzag, gray; buds 1" long, lance shaped, very sharp pointed, scales 10–24, lustrous, tan; leaf scars half-round, not directly below bud; bundle scars 3 or sometimes more; stipular scars nearly encircle twig.

Bark – bluish gray, sometimes mottled, thin, smooth, showing little change in texture with age; a favorite tree trunk for initial carving. Figure 118.

Flowers – monoecious; minute, lacking petals; staminate in densely clustered drooping heads, about ¾" across, suspended on a 2" stalk; pistillate paired on stout, 1" stalk; appearing March–April. Figure 119.

Fruit – nut, yellowish brown, unevenly triangular, enclosed in spiny bur; bur less than 1" long; maturing September–October. Large fruit production occurs every 2–3 years. Figure 117.

RECOGNITION DIFFICULTIES WITH OTHER TAXA: The smooth steel-gray bark and long pointed winter buds are distinctive characters of American Beech in winter. The leaves of Chinquapin are somewhat similar, but have more sharply serrated margins.

HABITAT: *Fagus grandifolia* is common on rich, mesic hardwood slopes throughout the State, and is most prevalent in the mountains and Piedmont regions.

ECONOMIC, ORNAMENTAL AND OTHER USES: The wood of American Beech is hard and strong and is widely used for toys, furniture, wooden cookware and for barrels to age beer. It is an excellent fuel wood and was formerly used for charcoal. As a shade tree, American Beech is quite handsome, and although a slow grower, it is relatively disease-free and long-lived. The nuts are important for squirrels, turkey, wood ducks and ruffed grouse.

Quercus–Oaks

SUMMER KEY TO SPECIES OF *QUERCUS*

Note: With some species the presence or absence of bristle tips can be misleading because there are exceptions; if in question, key both ways, i.e., Key I and II. Many oak species hybridize resulting in highly variable specimens which may present difficulties in identification.

1. Leaves entire, toothed or lobed, without bristle tips, acorns maturing at end of first season; inner surface of acorn shell glabrous (use knife to open shell) .... White Oaks—Key I
1. Leaves entire, toothed or lobed, with bristle tips; acorns maturing in second season; inner surface of acorn shell pubescent (use knife to open shell) .... Red Oaks—Key II

Key I (White Oaks)
1. Leaves unlobed... 2
  2. Leaves evergreen 3
    3. Leaf margins distinctly revolute, lower surface wrinkled with conspicuous raised veins .... *Q. geminata*
    3. Leaf margins sometimes thickened, but not distinctly revolute, lower surface without conspicuously raised veins ....
    .... *Q. virginiana*
  2. Leaves deciduous (sometimes tardily deciduous) 4
    4. Leaves coarsely toothed.............................. 5
      5. Marginal teeth sharply pointed, callous tipped ....
      .... *Q. muehlenbergii*
      5. Marginal teeth blunt, not callous tipped or only minutely so 6
        6. Bark dark gray to brown, deeply fissured with pronounced ridges, but not scaly; acorn cup thin, narrowed at base .... *Q. prinus*
        6. Bark light gray to silver-gray, with scales resembling White Oak; acorn cup thick, broadened at base......
        .... *Q. michauxii*
    4. Leaves entire, or nearly so............................ 7
      7. Leaves leathery, often broadest near the tip............
      .... *Q. chapmanii*
      7. Leaves not leathery, broader at the middle or uniformly wide .... *Q. oglethorpensis*

1. Leaves lobed 8
  8. Mature leaves mostly glabrous beneath 9
    9. Leaves with 7–10 shallow to deep, but regularly spaced lobes;
      whitish beneath . . . . *Q. alba*
    9. Leaves with 3–5 shallow lobes that tend to point toward the
      apex of blade, often irregularly spaced; greenish beneath . . . . .
      . . . . *Q. austrina*
  8. Mature leaves slightly to densely pubescent beneath 10
    10. Leaves not densely stellate-pubescent below, 5–9 acute lobes;
      acorn cup nearly enclosing entire nut. . . . . *Q. lyrata*
    10. Leaves densely stellate pubescent, 3–5 deep spreading lobes,
      some resembling a crucifix; acorn cup enclosing less than half
      the nut. 11
      11. Leaves 4–6″ long; twigs densely pubescent; buds
        pubescent. . . . . *Q. stellata*
      11. Leaves 3½″ long; twigs glabrous; buds not pubescent. . . .
        . . . . *Q. margaretta*

Key II (Red Oaks)

1. Leaves evergreen 2
  2. Leaves less than 2″ long, margins revolute, apex rounded, usually
    lacking bristle tip; usually shrubby. . . . . *Q. myrtifolia*
  2. Leaves 1–5″ long, margins not revolute, apex usually pointed and
    bristle-tipped; tree. . . . . *Q. hemisphaerica*
1. Leaves not evergreen (sometimes tardily deciduous) 3
  3. Leaves entire or somewhat 3-lobed at tip. 4
    4. Leaves much broader at apex than at base. 5
      5. Leaves densely rusty tomentose beneath, coriaceous,
        abruptly narrowed at base; twigs stout. . . . *Q. marilandica*
      5. Leaves glabrous, thinnish texture and somewhat pliable,
        gradually narrowed at base; twigs slender 6
        6. Leaves ½ as wide as long . . . . *Q. nigra*
        6. Leaves almost as wide as long . . . . *Q. arkansana*
    4. Some leaves broadest at midpoint or gradually widened at
      apex 7
      7. Leaves narrowly elliptic to lanceolate, bristle-tipped at
        apex . . . . *Q. phellos*
      7. Leaves diamond-shaped or obovate, usually lacking
        bristle tip . . . . *Q. laurifolia*
  3. Leaves distinctly lobed. 8
    8. Mature leaves with yellowish to rusty hairs beneath; buds
      rounded and slightly hairy 9
      9. Terminal leaf lobe elongated, base U-shaped; bark not
        scaly (may be rough and deeply fissured), nearly
        black . . . . *Q. falcata*
      9. Terminal leaf lobe not conspicuously elongated, base
        broadly wedge-shaped or gradually narrowed; bark
        scaly, reddish brown . . . . *Q. pagoda*

8. Leaves lacking pubescence except in leaf axils, or if pubescent on lower surface, the buds angular and woolly pubescent 10
  10. Base of leaves tapered to a point 11
    11. Leaf blades 3–12" long; petioles twisted so that the flattened blade hangs perpendicular to the ground; margin of acorn cup rolled inward against nut. . . . .
    . . . . *Q. laevis*
    11. Leaf blades 4" long or less; petioles not twisted as above; margin of acorn cup not rolled inward . . . . .
    . . . . *Q. georgiana*
  10. Base of leaves rounded, truncate, or very shortly tapered 12
    12. Leaves with 5–7 lobes; buds woolly, distinctly angled . . . . *Q. velutina*
    12. Leaves with 7–9 (or 11) lobes; buds nearly glabrous, not distinctly angled 13
      13. Sinuses of leaves less than ½ the distance to midrib; acorn cup saucer-like, enclosing only the base . . . . *Q. rubra*
      13. Sinuses of leaves more than ½ the distance to midrib; acorn cup bowl-like, enclosing ⅓–½ of nut 14
        14. Leaves usually 7-lobed, lobes not spreading wider at tips; apex of nut usually with concentric circles; bark on upper trunk with shiny vertical streaks . . . .
        . . . . *Q. coccinea*
        14. Leaves with 7–9 (or 11) lobes, lobes spreading wider at tips; apex of nut without concentric rings; bark without shiny vertical streaks . . . . *Q. shumardii*

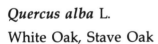

Quercus alba L.

White Oak, Stave Oak

DESCRIPTION: White Oak is a large, long-lived tree, frequently 80–100' tall and 3–4' in diameter. It occurs throughout the State.

Leaves – deciduous, simple, alternate; blades usually widest above the middle, 7–10 rounded lobes, sinuses deep to shallow, 5–9" long, 2–4" wide, margins entire; surfaces hairy when young, but smooth with age; lower surface whitish; turning red to purplish in autumn. Figure 120.

Twigs – moderately stout, dark red-brown; buds small, globose, clustered near end of twig, bud scales smooth, reddish; leaf scars half-round; bundle scars numerous.

Bark – light gray, thick, shallow lengthwise fissures separating into long, broad scaly plates, often loose and flaky. Figure 121.

Flowers – monoecious; staminate in pendulous catkins near base of current year twig; pistillate with 3-lobed stigmas, subtended by numerous scales which form the acorn cup, sessile, solitary or in few-flowered spikes; appearing in April. See Figures 128 and 129 for staminate and pistillate flowers of *Quercus coccinea* which are similar to those of other oaks.

Fruit – acorn, about ¾" long; cup bowl-like, enclosing the lower ¼ of the nut, scales knobby, tightly appressed; maturing in one season and germinating in the fall after they drop from tree. Figure 120.

RECOGNITION DIFFICULTIES WITH OTHER TAXA: White Oak reportedly hybridizes with *Q. michauxii, Q. prinoides, Q. stellata,* and *Q. prinus.* The leaves of Bluff Oak, *Q. austrina,* may sometimes resemble White Oak, but have broader and fewer lobes.

HABITAT: White Oak is common throughout the State in a variety of habitats. It most frequently occurs in deep, rich, well-drained soils in association with other oaks and hickories.

ECONOMIC, ORNAMENTAL AND OTHER USES: White Oak is one of the most important woods of North America. The wood is hard and strong and is utilized for furniture, flooring and interior finishing and numerous specialty products. It is often referred to as "Stave Oak" because the wood has been utilized for whiskey and wine barrels. It is an attractive, long-lived, shade tree, although slow growing.

Quercus arkansana Sarg.

Arkansas Oak

DESCRIPTION: In Georgia, this is a small to medium-sized tree, reaching 40–50' in height and often with a crooked trunk. It occurs in several localities in southwestern Georgia.

Leaves – deciduous, simple, alternate; blades variable in shape from broadly obovate to slightly 3-lobed at apex with bristle tips, base wedge-shaped, 3–5" long and 2–4" broad at widest part; lower surface pubescent until mature, then essentially glabrous except for tufts of hairs in the axils of the veins beneath. Figure 122.

Twigs – grayish-brown, pubescent until late in season, becoming darker and glabrous; buds ovoid to acute, slightly pubescent, bud scales light brown; leaf scars half round; bundle scars numerous.

Bark – dark brown to black, thick, deeply fissured into narrow ridges with scaly plates.

Flowers – similar to other oaks.

Fruit – acorn, subglobose, about ½" long, pubescent; cup saucer-shaped, enclosing only the base of the nut; maturing second season. Figure 122.

RECOGNITION DIFFICULTIES WITH OTHER TAXA: The leaves are similar to Blackjack Oak. Arkansas Oak has a rounded general leaf outline and the lower surfaces are essentially glabrous, whereas Blackjack Oak tends to have a more abruptly narrowed base and the leaf undersides are rusty pubescent. The acorns of the latter enclose ½ or slightly more of the nut rather than only the base.

HABITAT: Arkansas Oak is restricted to sandy soils in mesic pine forests in the Coastal Plain of Georgia. The small, localized stands documented in several southwestern counties are the easternmost extension of the range of this species.

ECONOMIC, ORNAMENTAL AND OTHER USES: Due to its scarcity and scrubby form, Arkansas Oak is of little economical importance.

Quercus austrina Small
Bluff Oak, Bastard White Oak

DESCRIPTION: Bluff Oak is a medium-sized tree, attaining heights of up to 80' and a diameter of about 2'. The grayish, scaly bark gives it a general appearance like White Oak. However, the leaves of *Q. austrina* have 3–5 rounded, irregularly spaced lobes which are broader than those of *Q. alba* and the lower leaf surfaces are green rather than white. The acorns of Bluff Oak are usually ½–¾" in length and are widest near the base, acorn cup scales are thin and the cup encloses ¼–⅓ of the nut. *Quercus austrina* occurs in scattered localities in the lower Coastal Plain in well-drained bottomland soils and along river bluffs. Some recent authors (Little 1979, Elias 1980, Duncan and Duncan, 1988) include *Q. durandii* as a species which occurs in Georgia. However, our field observations concur with those of Godfrey (1988) that specimens from this area do not appear to be *Q. durandii*. Figure 123, leaves; Figure 124 acorns.

Quercus chapmanii Sarg.
Chapman Oak

DESCRIPTION: Chapman Oak is a small tree, seldom over 30' tall, with a rounded crown of tardily deciduous leaves which persist into the winter or early spring. It is not very common in Georgia, occurring locally in sandy scrub oak areas of the lower Coastal Plain. Chapman Oak is characterized by light gray bark which exfoliates into scaly plates similar to White Oak. The leaves are alternate, simple, leathery, up to 3½" long and 1–1½" wide, broadest beyond the middle, varying from unlobed to somewhat 3-lobed toward the apex, entire, and are shiny dark green above. The acorn is up to ¾" long and is enclosed to almost half its length by the cup. Acorns mature in one season. Figure 125, leaves and acorns.

Quercus coccinea Muenchh.
Scarlet Oak

DESCRIPTION: Scarlet Oak is a medium-sized, fast growing tree, often reaching 70–80' tall, typically occurring in the mountains and Piedmont regions of Georgia, often as a dominant in the canopy.

Leaves – deciduous, simple, alternate; blades with usually 7 (sometimes 9) rounded sinuses, extending more than ½ the distance to the midrib, lobes coarsely toothed at tip, base rounded, truncate or shortly tapered, up to 8" long, 5" wide; occasionally with tufts of hair in axils of main veins beneath; turning scarlet in autumn. Figures 126 and 128.

Twigs – slender, finely pubescent when young, smooth with age; terminal buds ⅛–¼" long, blunt, angular in cross section; bud scales brown-gray, whitish hairs at tips; leaf scars half round; bundle scars numerous.

Bark – light to dark gray with lighter streaks on upper trunk, dark brown to nearly black at base on mature trees, with shallow fissures and irregular ridges, often very rough and blocky at base. Figure 127.

Flowers – similar to other oaks. Figure 128, staminate catkins at base of current year's twig; Figure 129, pistillate flowers in axils of young developing leaves.

Fruit – acorn, up to 1" long, oval, with concentric rings near the apex; cup bowl-like, enclosing ½–⅓ of nut, edge of cup clasping nut; solitary or paired; maturing second season. Figure 126, mature fruit; Figure 130, the young developing acorns at the end of the first season typical of the Red Oak group which require two seasons for acorns to mature.

RECOGNITION DIFFICULTIES WITH OTHER TAXA: Scarlet Oak leaves resemble those of Black Oak, Northern Red Oak, and Shumard Oak, but are distinguished by the lobing pattern. In Black Oak and Northern Red Oak, the leaf lobes are not nearly as deep. Black Oak leaves are often tawny pubescent beneath, with tufts of hairs in leaf axils. The acorn cup of Black Oak has loose hairy scales. Also, the distinctive buds of Black Oak are angular and woolly, whereas buds of Scarlet Oak are white hairy only near the tip and are not angular. Northern Red Oak acorn cups enclose the nut only at the base. The upper trunk of Scarlet Oak is usually streaked with light gray longitudinal stripes and is often confused with Northern Red Oak bark. However, Scarlet Oak characteristically has numerous, dead, persistent, lateral branches remaining along the mid- to upper bole. This characteristic significantly lowers the quality of the wood for lumber because of knots and decay. Shumard Oak is predominantly a bottomland species (except in limestone areas) and does not usually overlap in habitat with Scarlet Oak. Its leaves are generally larger than Scarlet Oak, with 7–11 lobes that have more spreading, bristle-tipped teeth, with largest lobes toward the ends. Shumard Oak acorns are finely hairy and the cups enclose only the base of the nut. Pin Oak, *Quercus palustris* Muenchh., is a commonly planted shade tree with leaves resembling Scarlet Oak. Pin Oak has shiny, dark green leaves with 5–7 bristle-tipped lobes, and the lower surface has conspicuous tufts of hairs in the axils of the veins. However, the bark of Pin Oak is nearly smooth and the acorns are about ½" long with saucer-shaped cups. Pin Oak occurs natively in abundance in mid-Atlantic and central States in bottomlands and swampy habitats. It has been reported as native to Georgia in one or two locations in the Ridge and Valley Province (Duncan and Duncan, 1988).

HABITAT: Scarlet Oak is common on poor, dry, upland ridges and slopes of the mountains and Piedmont.

ECONOMIC, ORNAMENTAL AND OTHER USES: Scarlet Oak is a handsome tree with shiny green foliage that turns a spectacular, scarlet red in autumn. It is fast growing with average longevity and is often used as a landscape tree. Although the reddish brown, hard, strong wood has poorer quality than Northern Red or Black Oak, it is used for similar purposes.

Quercus falcata Michaux

Southern Red Oak, Spanish Oak

DESCRIPTION: Southern Red Oak is a medium to large tree, up to 100' tall. It is common throughout the State.

Leaves – deciduous, simple, alternate; blades with highly variable lobing pattern with 3–5 lobes, lobes prominently bristle-tipped, often terminal lobe elongated and sub-lobed, sinuses wide, leaf base conspicuously U-shaped; frequently up to 9" long, 5" wide; upper surfaces shiny green; lower surfaces yellowish to rusty to gray pubescent. Figure 131 shows variation in leaf shape.

Twigs – gray, with rust-colored hairs, becoming reddish brown and glabrous with age; terminal bud ¼" long, pointed, scales hairy, chestnut brown; leaf scars half round; bundle scars numerous.

Bark – dark brown to black, thick, deeply fissured, becoming ridged and rough plated near base, not scaly. Figure 132.

Flowers – similar to other oaks.

Fruit – acorn, about ½" long, subglobose; cup enclosing about ⅓ of the nut, strongly tapering toward base; scales densely gray hairy; inner surface of nut shell hairy; borne singly on short stalk; maturing second season. Figure 133.

RECOGNITION DIFFICULTIES WITH OTHER TAXA: The 3-pronged terminal lobe and U-shaped base are distinctive. Turkey Oak has deeply lobed leaves, but with more prominent basal lobes and a longer, more slender bud. Cherrybark Oak, sometimes considered a variety of *Q. falcata*, has flaky bark and the leaf bases are not U-shaped but abruptly truncated or short-tapered. A distinct diagnostic trait of Southern Red Oak is the droopy, wilted appearance of the mature leaves throughout the crown during the summer months.

HABITAT: Southern Red Oak is typical of forests of drier, less fertile upland soils throughout the State. Occasionally it occurs on more mesic sites.

ECONOMIC, ORNAMENTAL AND OTHER USES: The wood of Southern Red Oak, although not as good in quality as Northern Red or Cherrybark Oak, is marketed in quantity for furniture, flooring and heavy construction along with other Red Oak species. It is often planted around homes for shade because it grows well on drier sites and is a fairly long-lived tree.

Quercus geminata Small

[*Q. virginiana* var. *geminata* (Small) Sarg.]

Sand Live Oak

DESCRIPTION: Sand Live Oak is a small to medium-sized evergreen tree that often forms shrubby thickets. This species is considered a variety of Live Oak by some authorities. It occurs in the State in dry, sandy woods of the lower Coastal Plain. Sand Live Oak leaves differ from Live Oak by leaf margins which are decidedly revolute and by down-curving leaves. The leaves are conspicuously tomentose and the veins below are prominent. Acorns of these two taxa are similar. Two other shrubby oak species, *Q. pumila* and *Q. minima*, occur in Georgia which should not be confused with Sand Live Oak. These dwarf oaks rarely exceed 3' in height, whereas the thicket forming stands of Sand Live Oak usually have several stems exceeding 3' in height. Figure 134.

Quercus georgiana M. A. Curtis

Georgia Oak

DESCRIPTION: Georgia Oak is a small tree, up to 40' tall and often shrub-like. It is restricted to a few localities in the State, primarily associated with granitic rock outcrops in the Piedmont. The oak is of no economic value. It is distinguished by its bright green, shiny, small leaves (up to 4" long and 2½" wide) with 3–5 lobes. The sinuses are often obliquely angular and the leaf base is broadly wedge-shaped. The acorns are globular with a shallow cup enclosing ¼ of the nut, the margin not rolled inward. The bark is thin, almost smooth, and grayish brown on young trees, becoming furrowed and rougher near the ground with age. Figure 135.

Quercus hemisphaerica Bartram ex Willd.

Laurel Oak, Darlington Oak

DESCRIPTION: Laurel Oak may be a large tree, often 80–90' tall, but in dune areas it is a small shrubby tree. It is common throughout the Coastal Plain.

Leaves – persistent until new foliage appears, simple, alternate; blade elliptic or lance-shaped, bases pointed or rounded, occasionally wavy or lobed, apex acute and bristle-tipped or blunt and lacking bristles, 1–5" long, 1–2" wide; surfaces smooth and lustrous. Figure 136.

Twigs – slender, reddish brown, glabrous; buds small, ovoid, acute; leaf scars half round; bundle scars numerous.

Bark – dark gray, smooth at first, older trees somewhat irregularly furrowed with broad, flat ridges.

Flowers – similar to other oaks.

Fruit – acorn, about ½" long, inner surface of nut shell pubescent; cup enclosing less than ¼ of the nut; maturing in second season. Figure 136.

RECOGNITION DIFFICULTIES WITH OTHER TAXA: Some authors do not recognize *Q. hemisphaerica* and *Q. laurifolia* as separate species, hence the confusion in the common name Laurel Oak. If both species are recognized, the common name of *Q. laurifolia* should be Diamond Leaf Oak. Leaves of Laurel Oak are similar to Willow and Diamond Leaf Oaks and the species readily hybridize. The leaves of Laurel Oak are usually wider above the middle and those of Willow Oak taper at both ends. The leaves of Diamond Leaf Oak are rounded, with tufts of hairs in the midribs beneath and not bristle-tipped.

HABITAT: Laurel Oak occurs naturally on upland sites on dry sandy soils, dune areas and scrub oak sandhills.

ECONOMIC, ORNAMENTAL AND OTHER USES: The wood of Laurel Oak is used for hardwood pulp and fuelwood. This species is often planted as a shade tree in cities and yards, although it is rather short-lived.

Quercus incana Bartram
Bluejack Oak

DESCRIPTION: Bluejack Oak is a small tree, reaching 30–40' in height, sometimes shrub-like and forming thickets from underground lateral root sprouts. It is common in dry habitats of the Coastal Plain.

Leaves – deciduous, simple, alternate; blade leathery, oblong or elliptic, apex blunt and bristle-tipped, up to 5" long, 1½" wide; both surfaces bluish gray in color; upper surface becoming glabrous; lower surface with grayish pubescence. Figure 137.

Twigs – slender, reddish brown when young, becoming darker with age; pubescent; terminal buds ¼" long, pointed, bud scales reddish brown and hairy; leaf scars half round; bundle scars numerous.

Bark – thick, gray to black, becoming rough and furrowed into rectangular or square plates.

Flowers – similar to other oaks.

Fruit – acorn, ½" long, broadest near the base and slightly flattened, finely pubescent, inner surfaces of nut shell pubescent; cup enclosing about ¼ of the nut at the base; maturing in second season. Figure 137.

RECOGNITION DIFFICULTIES WITH OTHER TAXA: *Quercus incana* has distinctive bristle-tipped leaves which are bluish, entire and pubescent beneath.

HABITAT: Bluejack Oak is most commonly found in the sandhills in association with Longleaf Pine, Turkey Oak and Sand Post Oak. However, it may be scattered in other localities on dry, sandy or rocky soils in the Piedmont and throughout the lower Coastal Plain.

ECONOMIC, ORNAMENTAL AND OTHER USES: Although Bluejack Oak is occasionally harvested for fuel and pulpwood, it is not of economic importance. The acorns of this species are a valuable food source for whitetail deer, raccoons, squirrel and other rodents and cover is provided by the dense thickets often produced.

Quercus laevis Walter
Turkey Oak

DESCRIPTION: Turkey Oak is a small, distinctive tree up to 30 or 40' tall, with crooked branches, and is often shrubby. It is common in the Coastal Plain. Three-lobed leaves of Turkey Oak are thought to resemble a turkey foot, hence the common name.

Leaves – deciduous, simple, alternate; blades variable in size and lobing, leathery, base gradually tapered to a point, lobes 3, 5, or 7, sinuses broad, open, 3–12" long and 1–8" wide; upper surface yellow-green, shiny, smooth; lower surface hairy only in axils of veins; petioles twisted so that blades are positioned with their flattened surfaces in a vertical rather than horizontal plane. Figure 138.

Twigs – stout, reddish, becoming smooth; terminal buds ½" long or more, sharply pointed; bud scales reddish, hairy; leaf scars half round; bundle scars numerous.

Bark – thick, deeply furrowed, dark brown to nearly black, forming rough, blocky, irregular ridges.

Flowers – similar to other oaks.

Fruit – acorn, 1" long, inner surface of nut shell hairy; cup enclosing ⅓ of nut, scales distinctly rolled inward along edge; maturing in second season. Figure 138.

RECOGNITION DIFFICULTIES WITH OTHER TAXA: Turkey Oak and Southern Red Oak habitat can overlap in some areas of the Coastal Plain. The leaves of Turkey Oak have a tapered base and are hairy only in the axils of the leaves, whereas those of Southern Red Oak have a U-shaped base and are pubescent beneath. The acorns of Turkey Oak differ in that the scales of the edge of the cup are rolled inward against the nut.

HABITAT: Turkey Oak is common throughout the sandhills of the upper Coastal Plain and is associated with Longleaf Pine, Bluejack Oak and Sand Post Oak. This species is well adapted to drought stress and fire.

ECONOMIC, ORNAMENTAL AND OTHER USES: Turkey Oak has no commercial value, but provides excellent fuel. The acorns are an important food source for deer, turkey and small rodents.

Quercus laurifolia Michaux
Diamond Leaf Oak, Swamp Laurel Oak

DESCRIPTION: Diamond Leaf Oak is a rapidly growing, large tree, often reaching 80–90' in height and 2–3' in diameter. It is common in the Coastal Plain and occasional in the Piedmont.

Leaves – tardily deciduous, simple, alternate; blades variable in shape even on same tree, usually gradually widened near apex, but often some leaves decidedly wider at the middle in a diamond shape, apex blunt, usually without a bristle-tip, 2–5" long, ½–2" wide; upper and lower surfaces glabrous except for tufts of hairs around veins. Figure 139.

Twigs – slender, grayish with age, smooth; terminal buds pointed, bud scales reddish brown; leaf scars half round; bundle scars numerous.

Bark – dark gray, shallowly ridged and furrowed, becoming rough at base of older trunks.

Flowers – similar to other oaks.

Fruit – acorn, about ¾" long, nearly round; cup enclosing ¼" of the nut, margins ciliate; maturing second year. Figure 139.

RECOGNITION DIFFICULTIES WITH OTHER TAXA: Diamond Leaf Oak resembles Laurel Oak and is distinguished by the blunt apex and diamond-like shape. See Laurel Oak. The habitats of these two species also differ, that of Laurel Oak predominantly dry, sandy uplands. This species hybridizes with Water Oak.

HABITAT: This species is common in floodplain forests, river and stream banks, and margins of swamps throughout the Coastal Plain. It occurs occasionally in stream bottom localities in the Piedmont.

ECONOMIC, ORNAMENTAL AND OTHER USES: *Quercus laurifolia* is an attractive tree, sometimes planted as a street or shade tree, although it is short-lived. The wood is used locally for fuel and hardwood pulp.

Quercus lyrata Walter
Overcup Oak

DESCRIPTION: Overcup Oak is a medium-sized tree, 60–80' tall, frequently with epicormic branching. It occurs most commonly in the Coastal Plain, but is occasional in the Piedmont and the Ridge and Valley in floodplains and poorly drained soils.

Leaves – deciduous, simple, alternate; blades broadest above the middle, base narrow, 5–9 (usually 7) lobed and sometimes sublobed, upper 3 lobes often squarish and basal lobes are much reduced, sinuses broad, 6–8" long; lower surfaces of young leaves hairy but not densely stellate, becoming smooth with age. Figure 140.

Twigs – slender, gray-brown with age, glabrous; winter buds ⅛" long, almost rounded, scales chestnut colored and pubescent; leaf scars half round; bundle scars numerous.

Bark – somewhat similar to *Q. alba*, but thinner with less scaly plates; trunk usually possesses numerous epicormic branches. Figure 141.

Flowers – similar to other White Oaks.

Fruit – acorn, solitary or in pairs, ½–1" long, usually wider than long, nut sometimes silky hairy; cup nearly encloses entire nut, often fringed on edge; matures in fall and germinates in following spring; seed production varies, usually heavier every 3–4 years. Figure 140.

RECOGNITION DIFFICULTIES WITH OTHER TAXA: The nearly complete enclosure of the nut by the cup is distinctive. White Oak, although with similar bark, has leaves that are wider and more evenly lobed than Overcup Oak. In winter, the buds of White Oak are not pubescent. Generally, the two species do not occupy similar habitats.

HABITAT: Overcup Oak occurs in poorly drained clay soils of bottomlands, sloughs, and river floodplains. It is most common in the Coastal Plain.

ECONOMIC, ORNAMENTAL AND OTHER USES: The wood of Overcup Oak is poorer in quality than that of White Oak, but is usually harvested and sold for some of the same uses. The acorns are eaten by deer, hogs, turkeys and squirrels.

Quercus margaretta Ashe

[*Q. stellata* var. *margaretta* (Ashe) Sarg.]

Sand Post Oak, Scrub Post Oak

DESCRIPTION: This is a small tree with an irregular growth form. It occurs in the fall line region and occasionally in the Piedmont.

Leaves – deciduous, simple, alternate; blades 2–4½" long, up to 3" wide, 3-lobed or upper three lobes cross-like, lobes rounded; lower surfaces usually stellate-pubescent. Figure 142.

Twigs – red-brown, glabrous; buds similar to Post Oak; leaf scars half round; bundle scars numerous.

Bark – reddish brown to gray, similar to *Q. stellata*.

Flowers – similar to other oaks.

Fruit – acorn, similar to Post Oak. Figure 142.

RECOGNITION DIFFICULTIES WITH OTHER TAXA: Sand Post Oak and Post Oak can sometimes be difficult to distinguish. Sand Post Oak has glabrous twigs, and smaller leaves than Post Oak. The leaves of Sand Post Oak also have more rounded lobes than the decidedly squarish lobes of Post Oak.

HABITAT: Sand Post Oak occurs in xeric, sandy soils of the Coastal Plain and along the fall line in the Sandhills regions. It is usually associated with other scrubby Oaks, *Quercus incana*, *Quercus laevis* and Longleaf Pine, *Pinus palustris*. Usually Post Oak would not be found in the same habitat.

ECONOMIC, ORNAMENTAL AND OTHER USES: This species is not of economic or ornamental value. Occasionally it is used for fuel wood, and the acorns are consumed by wildlife and game birds, especially wild turkeys.

Quercus marilandica Muenchh.

Blackjack Oak

DESCRIPTION: Blackjack Oak is usually a small scrubby tree, 30–40' tall, with a characteristic round, compact crown. It occurs throughout the State.

Leaves – deciduous, simple, alternate; blades leathery, abruptly broadened at tip with 3 lobes or unlobed in overall T- or triangular shape, abruptly narrowed at base, bristle-tipped, 4–8" long, 2–6" wide; upper surface dark green, shiny above; lower surface densely rusty-yellow hairy. Figure 143.

Twigs – stout, ashy gray, slightly pubescent; terminal buds ¼" long; buds angular; bud scales rusty pubescent; leaf scars half round; bundle scars numerous.

Bark – thick, black, rough, deeply fissured into broad, nearly square plates. Figure 144.

Flowers – similar to other oaks.

Fruit – acorn, about ¾" long, downy, ending in stout point, inner nut shell pubescent; cup turbinate, enclosing ½ or more of nut; maturing second season. Figure 145.

RECOGNITION DIFFICULTIES WITH OTHER TAXA: Blackjack Oak is distinctive by its broadly triangular leaf shape, rusty-yellow pubescence on lower leaf surfaces, scraggly habit, and characteristic bark. It should not be confused with any other native species.

HABITAT: Blackjack Oak occurs on dry, rocky or sandy woodlands throughout the State. It often invades following fire or other disturbances and forms almost pure stands.

ECONOMIC, ORNAMENTAL AND OTHER USES: Blackjack Oak is generally not considered a commercial species, although the wood has been used for railroad ties and fence posts. The compact form of the tree and the shiny dark green foliage are traits that would make this tree useful in the landscape, however, it is infrequently planted. These trees are slow growing and short-lived.

Quercus michauxii Nutt.

(*Q. prinus* L.
misapplied, see *Q. prinus* description)

Swamp Chestnut Oak, Basket Oak

DESCRIPTION: Swamp Chestnut Oak is a medium-sized to large tree, 70–90' tall, in scattered localities throughout the State, particularly in the Piedmont and Coastal Plain.

Leaves – deciduous, simple, alternate; blades usually wider above the middle, up to 9" long and 6" broad, margins with regular, rounded or sometimes sharp teeth or margins sometimes merely wavy; lower surface sparsely hairy. Figure 146.

Twigs – moderately stout, reddish brown to straw colored; terminal buds ¼" long, pointed; bud scales red-brown, sparsely hairy;

leaf scars half round; bundle scars numerous.

Bark – thick, light gray, scaly plates, very similar to *Q. alba*.

Flowers – similar to other White Oaks.

Fruit – acorn, up to 1½" long, broadest near the base, rounded tip; cup enclosing nut ⅓–½ length, hairy, scales attached only at base and overlapping; stalkless or short stalked. Figure 146.

RECOGNITION DIFFICULTIES WITH OTHER TAXA: This species is similar to *Q. prinus*, an upland species. Generally, the leaves of Swamp Chestnut Oak are broader relative to length than those of Chestnut Oak and the cup scales of Chestnut Oak do not overlap and are free only at the tip. The bark of Swamp Chestnut Oak resembles that of *Q. alba* in contrast to Chestnut Oak which is dark, deeply furrowed and not scaly.

HABITAT: Swamp Chestnut Oak is common in bottomlands and floodplains of streams primarily in the Piedmont and Coastal Plain.

ECONOMIC, ORNAMENTAL AND OTHER USES: Another common name for *Quercus michauxii* is Basket Oak, because baskets were woven from strips of the wood. The wood is of excellent quality, similar to that of *Q. alba*, and is used for the same purposes. The sweet, large acorns can be eaten raw or boiled. They are a preferred food of livestock and small mammals.

Quercus muehlenbergii Engelm.

(*Q. prinoides* Willd.)

Chinquapin Oak

DESCRIPTION: Chinquapin Oak is a small to medium-sized deciduous tree which occurs on limestone outcrops. It is not common in the State, and the scattered localities are concentrated in the northwestern and southwestern counties. It is distinguished by leaves that rarely exceed 5" and are toothed similarly to Chestnut Oak. However, the marginal teeth are sharply pointed and callous tipped and the lower surfaces are pubescent. The acorns are oval, less than ¾" long and the thin cup encloses about ½ of the nut. It has no economic value.

Quercus myrtifolia Willd.
Myrtle Oak

DESCRIPTION: Myrtle Oak is usually a thicket-forming shrub, occasionally forming a small tree with a much branched, crooked trunk. It is occasional along the outer Coastal Plain and scattered localities inland.

Leaves – evergreen, simple, alternate; blades leathery, variable in shape from oval to elliptic, apex rounded, occasionally bristle-tipped, less than 2" long and 1" wide, leaf margins entire, revolute; upper and lower surfaces smooth, except for tufts of hairs in axils of veins, both surfaces dark green and shiny. Figure 147.

Twigs – slender, reddish brown, weakly pubescent; buds pointed, dark chestnut brown; leaf scars half round; bundle scars numerous.

Bark – smooth, brown.

Flowers – similar to other oaks.

Fruit – acorn, about ½" long, nearly round; cup enclosing about ¼ of the nut; maturing in second season. Figure 147.

RECOGNITION DIFFICULTIES WITH OTHER TAXA: Myrtle Oak may occur in similar habitats as *Q. chapmanii* and *Q. geminata*. It is distinguished from those species by its leaves which are shiny dark green on both surfaces. The leaves of *Q. chapmanii* are nonlustrous below, and usually some leaves are 3-lobed at the apices. The lower leaf surfaces of *Q. geminata* are conspicuously veiny and hairy.

HABITAT: *Quercus myrtifolia* is frequent along coastal dunes and sandy ridges of the lower Coastal Plain, and inland on upper sandy terraces of rivers.

ECONOMIC, ORNAMENTAL AND OTHER USES: Myrtle Oak is not of economic importance. Presently, it is offered by a few nurseries as a small, slow-growing accent specimen for dry, severe areas in residential landscapes.

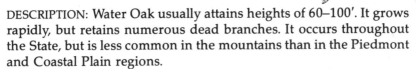

Quercus nigra L.
Water Oak

DESCRIPTION: Water Oak usually attains heights of 60–100'. It grows rapidly, but retains numerous dead branches. It occurs throughout the State, but is less common in the mountains than in the Piedmont and Coastal Plain regions.

Leaves – tardily deciduous, simple, alternate; blades thinnish and somewhat pliable, variable in size and shape, broadest near the tip, tapering to a long narrow base, sometimes lobed (young trees and sprouts varying from deeply lobed to long elliptical), bristle-tipped, up to 4" long and 2" wide; upper surface smooth, dull green; lower surface smooth except for tufts of hairs in axils of veins. Figure 148.

Twigs – slender, grayish brown, smooth, dull; terminal buds about ¼" long, pointed, strongly angled, bud scales reddish brown, hairy; leaf scars half round; bundle scars numerous.

Bark – smooth, gray; becoming shallowly furrowed on older trunks. Figure 149.

Flowers – similar to other oaks.

Fruit – acorn, oval to nearly round, about ½" or less; cup saucer-shaped, enclosing only the base of the nut; maturing second year. Figure 148.

RECOGNITION DIFFICULTIES WITH OTHER TAXA: Water Oak often occurs with Diamond Leaf Oak and has some leaf similarities. In general, Water Oak leaves are shorter and broader at the tip and sometimes 3- or more lobed. The bark is grayer and smoother than Diamond Leaf Oak.

HABITAT: Water Oak occupies a wide range of habitats including floodplains, bottomlands, fence rows, mixed forests, and well-drained uplands throughout the State.

ECONOMIC, ORNAMENTAL AND OTHER USES: The wood is utilized as oak lumber, but is generally of poorer quality because of numerous knots. It is planted as a shade and street tree because of its early rapid growth, but it is rather short-lived and retains numerous dead limbs in the crown. The dropping of dead branches, the prolific crops of acorns and small, persistent leaves which are difficult to remove from a lawn are undesirable attributes for a yard tree. The annual heavy acorn crop is a major food source for deer, turkeys, ducks, quail, raccoons, and other small mammals.

Quercus oglethorpensis W. Duncan

Oglethorpe Oak

DESCRIPTION: Oglethorpe Oak is a rare, small to medium-sized tree, up to 70' tall, restricted to a few counties in the Piedmont of Georgia and South Carolina and disjunctly in Louisiana and Mississippi. It was first described in 1940 and is named for Oglethorpe County, Georgia, where it was discovered. It is listed as a Georgia Protected species.

Leaves – deciduous, simple, alternate; blades quite variable in size, shape, and degree of pubescence, not leathery, narrowly elliptic to somewhat broader at the middle, blunt tipped, generally to 5" in length and 1½" broad, margins entire, shallowly wavy, or shallowly lobed distally; lower surface velvety with yellowish stellate hairs to nearly glabrous. Figure 150.

Twigs – reddish or purplish when young, grayish with age, glabrous; buds small; leaf scars half round; bundle scars numerous.

Bark – light gray to whitish, broken into thin, loosely appressed plates, similar to *Q. lyrata*, occasionally with scattered epicormic shoots along the trunk.

Flowers – similar to other oaks.

Fruit – acorn, globose, pubescent apically, up to ½" long; cups bowl-like, enclosing about ⅓ of the acorn; sessile or stalked; maturing in one season. Figure 150.

RECOGNITION DIFFICULTIES WITH OTHER TAXA: The combination of narrowly elliptic leaves with yellowish pubescence and whitish scaly bark is rather distinctive. Willow Oak could occur in similar habitats, but differs by its elliptical leaf with an acute apex and bristle tip, blade surfaces with hairs only in the axils of veins, and dark gray bark with shallow, irregular fissures. Kral (1983) suggests that this taxon is closely related to *Q. durandii* Buckley and may be a variant form of it.

HABITAT: Oglethorpe Oak occurs in a few localities in Piedmont bottomlands along streams, often in heavy soils which are poorly drained and occasionally on adjacent slopes. This species is subject to chestnut blight and most trees are afflicted with cankers of this disease.

ECONOMIC, ORNAMENTAL AND OTHER USES: *Quercus oglethorpensis* is a rare tree, although locally abundant in some localities. Acorn crops are usually light and seed viability is often low.

Quercus pagoda Raf.
(*Q. falcata* var. *pagodifolia* Elliott)
Cherrybark Oak

DESCRIPTION: Cherrybark Oak is a large tree, often 100' or more in height and 4–5' in diameter with a better formed trunk than *Quercus falcata*. It is usually associated with bottomlands of streams and rivers in the Piedmont and Coastal Plain. Cherrybark Oak differs from Southern Red Oak by its leaves which are more regularly lobed, with prominent basal lobes and with the base broadly wedge-shaped or tapered, rather than U-shaped. The bark on older trees becomes scaly with age, and somewhat resembles that of large Black Cherry trees, hence the common name. It is valuable as a timber tree, the wood of better quality than that of *Quercus falcata*. Figure 151, leaves; Figure 152, bark.

Quercus phellos L.
Willow Oak

DESCRIPTION: Willow Oak is a tall, fast growing tree with a straight trunk, frequently reaching 90–100' in height. It occurs throughout the State, but is infrequent in the mountains.

Leaves – deciduous, simple, alternate; blade narrowly elliptic to lanceolate, small bristle-tip, up to 5" long and 1" wide, margins entire; surfaces smooth, occasionally with tufts of hairs along the lower midrib; short leafstalk. Figure 153.

Twigs – dark brown and graying with age, smooth; terminal buds ⅛" long, pointed, bud scales brownish, paler along margins; leaf scars half round; bundle scars numerous.

Bark – grayish brown, smooth when young, becoming dark gray, roughened and shallowly fissured with age.

Flowers – similar to other oaks.

Fruit – acorn, roundish, about ¼–½" long; saucer-shaped cups enclosing just the base of the nut, scales slightly hairy; maturing second season. Figure 153.

RECOGNITION DIFFICULTIES WITH OTHER TAXA: Willow Oak can occur in the same habitat as Diamond Leaf Oak. Usually the leaves of

Willow Oak are narrower and taper gradually to both ends, whereas those of Diamond Leaf Oak are usually wider, and widest above the middle, or diamond shaped.

HABITAT: *Quercus phellos* is common in low, wet sites of river flood-plains, bottomlands or richer upland soils.

ECONOMIC, ORNAMENTAL AND OTHER USES: Willow Oak is marketed as a Red Oak and used similarly. Trees are often planted as a shade and street tree because of their fast growth. It produces abundant crops of acorns that are important to wildlife.

Quercus prinus L.

(*Q. montana* Willd.)

Chestnut Oak, Rock Chestnut Oak

DESCRIPTION: Chestnut Oak is a medium-sized tree that occasionally reaches heights of 80'. It readily sprouts from stumps or root collar following disturbance. This species occurs in the mountains and upper Piedmont.

Leaves – deciduous, simple, alternate; blades nearly elliptical, up to 10" long, 3" wide, margins coarsely and irregularly toothed and not callous tipped (or only minutely so); lower surface thinly pubescent. Figure 154.

Twigs – stout, red-brown, smooth; buds acute, ½" long, bud scales shiny brown, silky pubescent; leaf scars half round; bundle scars numerous.

Bark – dark gray to brown, becoming deeply furrowed with pronounced, non-scaly ridges. Figure 155.

Flowers – similar to other oaks.

Fruit – acorn, 1–1½" long, rounded or pointed at tip; cup deeply bowl-shaped, thin, narrowed at the base, enclosing about ½ of the nut; short stalked; maturing in one season. Figure 156.

RECOGNITION DIFFICULTIES WITH OTHER TAXA: Chestnut Oak resembles Swamp Chestnut Oak, but is morphologically and ecologically distinct. Swamp Chestnut Oak has more obovate leaves, and thick acorn cups that are broad at the base with scales that are knobby. The bark of Swamp Chestnut Oak is gray and scaly. A discussion of the inconsistent use of the name *Q. prinus* for over 175 years is provided by Hardin (1979). Since the type specimen cannot be identified conclusively, there are several interpretations as to whether the name, *Q. prinus* applies to Chestnut Oak or Swamp Chestnut Oak. Unfortunately, the name has been applied to both species by various authors. We follow Little (1979) who chose to use *Q. prinus* for Chestnut Oak rather than the alternately used name *Q. montana* Willd. It is helpful in this case to also use the common name when referencing *Q. prinus*.

HABITAT: Chestnut Oak occurs on dry, upland slopes in deciduous forests throughout the mountains and upper Piedmont.

ECONOMIC, ORNAMENTAL AND OTHER USES: The wood is heavy, hard and durable in contact with the soil, hence it was formerly used for fence posts, railroad ties and fuel. Although a slow growing tree, this handsome species should be used more as an ornamental shade tree. Its autumn coloration varies from yellow to brown.

Quercus rubra L.

Northern Red Oak

DESCRIPTION: Northern Red Oak is a medium to large, moderately fast growing tree, often 90–100' tall on moist, fertile sites. It is common in the Piedmont and mountains.

   Leaves – deciduous, simple, alternate; blades often widest above the middle, usually 7–11 shallow lobes (extending less than halfway to the midrib), base rounded, truncate or shortly tapered, up to 9" long, 5" wide; surfaces glabrous except for inconspicuous tufts of hair in axils of veins beneath. Figure 157.

   Twigs – stout, brown, glabrous; terminal buds ¼" long, round in cross section, bud scales shiny, reddish brown, sometimes slightly hairy on tips; leaf scars half round; bundle scars numerous.

   Bark – dark gray to blackish, shallow vertical furrows giving rise to narrow scaly plates; the upper trunk lightly fissured, dark gray with conspicuous lighter gray vertical streaks. Figure 158.

   Flowers – similar to other oaks.

   Fruit – acorn, large, often over 1" in length, oblong to ovoid; cup shallow, enclosing only the base, edge of cup slightly rolled inward; solitary or in pairs; maturing in 2 seasons. Figure 159.

RECOGNITION DIFFICULTIES WITH OTHER TAXA: The leaves of Northern Red Oak are similar to lower, immature leaves of Black Oak, and the two species often occur together and reportedly hybridize. The leaves of Northern Red Oak are hairless and generally more papery in texture. The terminal buds of Northern Red Oak are essentially hairless, not angled and smaller than buds of Black Oak which are woolly, conspicuously angled and up to ½″ long. Black Oak bark lacks the shiny vertical streaks of Northern Red Oak. The acorn cup of Northern Red Oak encloses only the base while that of Black Oak encloses ⅓–¼ of the nut. The bark of Northern Red Oak is often confused with that of Scarlet Oak, which can have whitish streaks in the upper trunk. The leaves of Scarlet Oak are usually smaller and the sinuses extend more than halfway to the midrib, whereas the leaf sinuses of Northern Red Oak extend about halfway to the midrib. Scarlet Oak acorn cups enclose ½–⅓ of the nut.

HABITAT: Northern Red Oak occurs in rich, moist, hardwood forests of the mountains and Piedmont.

ECONOMIC, ORNAMENTAL AND OTHER USES: Northern Red Oak is the most important lumber producing species among the Red Oak group because of its high quality wood. It is used for flooring, furniture and heavy construction timbers. Northern Red Oak is often used as an ornamental tree because of its symmetrical growth form, moderate growth rate and autumn coloration. It transplants easily and is generally pest-free. This species has been widely cultivated in Europe as a landscape specimen.

Quercus shumardii Buckley
Shumard Oak

DESCRIPTION: Shumard Oak is a large tree, often 80–90′ tall, with a well-formed trunk and broad, open crown. It is most common in the Coastal Plain lowlands, but also occurs in the lower Piedmont and in limestone soils of the Ridge and Valley of Georgia.

Leaves – deciduous, simple, alternate; blades lustrous, 7–11 lobed, lobes extending halfway to midrib, often subdivided into secondary lobes with up to 13 spreading bristle tips, bases cut squarely across, up to 8″ long, 5″ wide; lower surface with tufts of hair in vein axils. Figure 160.

Twigs – stout to slender, becoming brown, smooth with age; terminal buds ¼″ long, angular, bud scales light brown; leaf scars half round; bundle scars numerous.

Bark – thick, smooth, dark gray becoming shallowly furrowed, with scaly ridges.

Flowers – similar to other oaks.

Fruit – acorn, up to 1″ long; cup enclosing only the base of the nut, cup scales hairy and closely appressed; resembles *Q. rubra*; maturing in 2 seasons. Figure 161.

RECOGNITION DIFFICULTIES WITH OTHER TAXA: The leaves of Shumard Oak resemble those of Black Oak and Northern Red Oak. Black Oak differs in having fewer (usually 5), shallower lobes, and broadly rounded leaf bases. The acorn cup of Black Oak is deeper. The leaves of Northern Red Oak are not as deeply lobed as those of Shumard Oak and the latter possesses many more bristle tips and flattened, almost truncate, leaf bases.

HABITAT: Shumard Oak occurs in rich woods and bottomlands of the Piedmont and Coastal Plain in scattered localities, and also in limestone soils of northwest Georgia in the Ridge and Valley region.

ECONOMIC, ORNAMENTAL AND OTHER USES: Shumard Oak wood is of good quality and is marketed as other Red Oaks for flooring, furniture and construction timbers. It is under-utilized as an ornamental. Its shiny, dark green foliage is striking and it is moderately fast growing.

Quercus stellata Wangenh.

Post Oak

DESCRIPTION: Post Oak is a small to medium-sized tree, occasionally 70–80' tall. It is widespread throughout the State.

    Leaves – deciduous, simple, alternate; blades 3–5-lobed, deeply spreading, the middle lobes largest and usually opposite each other in a crucifix shape, 4–6" long, 3–4" wide, upper surface dark green, rough with scattered hairs; lower surface light gray-green, densely stellate pubescent. Figure 162.

    Twigs – stout, tawny, becoming gray with age, usually densely pubescent; terminal buds about ⅛" long, rounded, bud scales chestnut to dark brown and hairy; leaf scars half round; bundle scars numerous.

    Bark – somewhat similar to White Oak, except gray-brown and with irregular fissures and narrow, thick plates. Figure 163.

    Flowers – similar to other oaks.

    Fruit – acorn, ½–1" long, broadest at the base, slightly striped or minutely pubescent; cup enclosing about ⅓ of the nut, scales thin; stalkless or with a short stalk.

RECOGNITION DIFFICULTIES WITH OTHER TAXA: The leaf shape and tawny, stellate pubescence on the leaf surface are distinctive features. Sand Post Oak, *Q. margaretta*, is similar in appearance to Post Oak and is sometimes considered a variety. Sand Post Oak is a small tree with an irregular growth form that occurs predominantly on dry sandhills in association with Turkey Oak and Longleaf Pine. The leaves are more variable in shape than those of Post Oak, and are smaller.

HABITAT: Post Oak is common in dry woodlands, in rocky or sandy soils throughout.

ECONOMIC, ORNAMENTAL AND OTHER USES: Post Oak wood is strong and durable and is used similarly to White Oak, although wood quality is poorer. This species is drought tolerant and can be utilized on drier sites in the landscape, although it is a slow growing tree and is occasionally susceptible to chestnut blight.

Quercus velutina Lam.

Black Oak

DESCRIPTION: Black Oak is a medium to large-sized tree, frequently 70–90' tall which occurs throughout the State.

   Leaves – deciduous, simple, alternate; blades with leathery texture, highly variable in shape from lower to upper crown, 5–7 large lobes, base rounded, truncate or shortly tapered, up to 8" long, 5" wide; upper surface shiny; lower surface yellowish tawny, tawny hairs along the veins of lower surface; turning reddish brown in autumn. Figure 165.

   Twigs – stout, dark reddish brown, shiny; terminal buds ¼–½" long, sharp-pointed, distinctly angled, woolly; leaf scars half round; bundle scars numerous.

   Bark – thick, nearly black; deep irregular fissures; inner bark bright orange. Figure 166.

   Flowers – similar to other oaks.

   Fruit – acorn, ½–¾" long, inner surfaces of nut shell pubescent; cup enclosing ⅓–½ of nut, scales with fringed border of loose, rusty-brown, hairy scales; borne singly or in pairs; matures second season. Figure 165.

RECOGNITION DIFFICULTIES WITH OTHER TAXA: Black Oak has similarities with several other Red Oaks previously described. See discussion of Scarlet Oak, Northern Red Oak, and Shumard Oak. Black Oak hybridizes with many other species of oak, including Northern Red Oak, Southern Red Oak, Bluejack Oak, Blackjack Oak, and Willow Oak.

HABITAT: *Quercus velutina* occurs on dry, well-drained upland slopes and ridges in association with other oaks and hickories. It is less common at high mountain elevations and in the lower Coastal Plain.

ECONOMIC, ORNAMENTAL AND OTHER USES: Tannins extracted from the bark were once used to tan leather. The wood is an important source of lumber and is marketed for use similar to other Red Oaks.

Quercus virginiana Miller
Live Oak

DESCRIPTION: Live Oak is a large, spreading, evergreen tree, commonly with a short, massive trunk and large, horizontally spreading branches. It is common in the Coastal Plain.

Leaves – evergreen, simple, alternate; blades thickened, variable in shape, widest near or above the middle, tapering at the base, rounded to short-pointed at the tip, up to 4" long and 1½" wide, margins usually entire, sometimes slightly wavy, occasionally with a few teeth; upper surface dark green, shiny; lower surface pale, hairy. Figure 167.

Twigs – slender, rigid, smooth with age; terminal buds less than ⅛" long, almost round; bud scales dark brown; leaf scars half round; bundle scars numerous.

Bark – thick, grayish dark brown, rough, deeply furrowed and separating into pronounced scaly ridges. Figure 168.

Flowers – similar to other oaks.

Fruit – acorn, up to 1" long, narrow, oblong, dark brown, shiny; cup enclosing ¼ or more of nut; stalked; maturing in one season on current year twigs. See Figure 134 of *Q. geminata* for an essentially identical acorn.

RECOGNITION DIFFICULTIES WITH OTHER TAXA: Sand Live Oak (*Q. geminata*) occasionally forms a thicket, although it will form a small to medium-sized tree, and its leaf margins are decidedly revolute and leaves curve downward. Live Oak leaves may roll downward, and the margins may be thickened, but they are not revolute. The lower surface of the leaves are hairy, but not conspicuously tomentose and the veins are not markedly raised. These taxa frequently intergrade.

HABITAT: Live Oak is common in dry, sandy woods and occasionally occurs in moist deciduous forests, roadsides, and borders of salt marshes.

ECONOMIC, ORNAMENTAL AND OTHER USES: The wood of Live Oak is one of the heaviest native hardwoods, making it a significant fuel wood. Previously, the strong, tough wood was used for ship building, and in the days of sailing ships, the nation's first publicly owned timber lands were Live Oak forests purchased for the Navy's shipyards. The Live Oak is the official State tree of Georgia. It is often planted in cities, yards and parks for its massive spreading form.

ULMACEAE–ELM FAMILY

The Ulmaceae, consisting primarily of trees and shrubs, contains about 200 species distributed worldwide. In Georgia, three genera containing arborescent species occur: *Ulmus*, *Planera*, and *Celtis*.

The family is characterized by alternate, simple leaves. Flowers are either bisexual or unisexual, typically green, rather inconspicuous, lacking petals and borne in clusters. The fruit of *Ulmus* is a samara, that of *Celtis* and *Planera*, a drupe. The leaves of these trees are two-ranked, and the twigs are zigzag to varying degrees. All abort their shoot tips during the latter part of the season, hence they lack true terminal buds.

Species in both *Ulmus* and *Celtis* often present identification and separation difficulties in the field. Elms show considerable variability in vegetative traits and intermediate forms are found. The overlapping vegetative and reproductive traits used to distinguish species of *Celtis* suggest that this genus needs additional taxonomic study.

Celtis–Hackberries

SUMMER KEY TO SPECIES OF *CELTIS*
Note: Generally, leaf characteristics and fruit characteristics have been used to separate species of *Celtis*, and these often intergrade.
1. Leaves mostly lance-shaped; drupes beakless . . . . *C. laevigata*
1. Leaves mostly ovate; drupes thick-beaked 2
    2. Leaves mostly less than 2" long, very rough above, entire or sparingly toothed (except sprout leaves) . . . . *C. tenuifolia*
    2. Leaves greater than 2" long, glabrous or nearly so above, serrate with 10 to 40 teeth. . . . . *C. occidentalis*

Celtis laevigata Willd.

Sugarberry

DESCRIPTION: Sugarberry is a medium-sized tree up to 80' tall with a well-formed, straight trunk occasionally reaching 3' in diameter, terminating in a rounded, open crown. It occurs throughout most of Georgia, but is more prevalent in the Coastal plain and lower Piedmont.

Leaves – deciduous, simple, alternate; extremely variable: blades ovate to lanceolate, bases vary from subcordate to abruptly acute, often oblique, apex varies from long acuminate to abruptly acuminate, 2–6" long, 1–2½" wide, margins entire to wavy or sparsely serrate, lower lateral veins more prominent than upper lateral veins; upper surfaces smooth or rarely rough. Figure 169.

Twigs – slender, zigzag, brown, lenticels pale, numerous, slightly raised; terminal bud absent; lateral buds ovoid, sharply pointed, small, less than ⅛" long with 4 visible scales; leaf scars oval to crescent-shaped, bundle scars 3; pith white, chambered at nodes.

Bark – gray, smooth with irregular, prominent corky outgrowths. Figure 170.

Flowers – monoecious; greenish, petals absent, small; pistillate in pairs or solitary in axils of emerging leaves toward tip of twig; staminate in fascicles lower on twig. Figure 171.

Fruit – drupes, orange to brownish red, globose, beakless, ¼–⅓" in diameter. September–October.

RECOGNITION DIFFICULTIES WITH OTHER TAXA: Positive identification of *Celtis* species in areas where their ranges overlap is difficult because leaf, twig, fruit and bark characteristics intergrade. In general, *C. laevigata* is recognized by nearly entire leaves, whereas, the leaves of *C. occidentalis* are coarsely serrated. *Celtis tenuifolia* has leaves that are usually less than twice as long as wide, in contrast to *C. laevigata* which are usually twice as long as wide. Also, *C. tenuifolia* is a small scraggly tree, unlike the habit of *C. laevigata*. *C. laevigata* can occur in the same habitat with *Planera aquatica*. The bark of *C. laevigata* is smooth, gray, with warty outgrowths or corky ridges, whereas that of *Planera* is reddish brown and conspicuously flaky. The leaves of *C. laevigata* are variably serrated and have translucent veinlets when viewed in bright light, while those of *P. aquatica* are always serrate, and the veinlets are not translucent.

HABITAT: Sugarberry is common along moist stream banks and in alluvial forests throughout most of Georgia, predominantly in the Coastal Plain and lower Piedmont.

ECONOMIC, ORNAMENTAL AND OTHER USES: Sugarberry is included by the wood-using industries as elm because the wood is very similar and is used for essentially the same purposes, e.g., furniture, veneer, and plywood. The species is often used as a shade or street tree because it adapts to a wide range of conditions. The fruit is a food source for song and game birds.

Celtis occidentalis L.

Hackberry

DESCRIPTION: Hackberry is a medium to large-sized tree, occasionally reaching 90' tall and 2–3' in diameter, with a rounded crown of spreading, evenly drooping branches. It is often disfigured by witches broom caused by the mite *Eriophyes*. It is found most frequently in the Piedmont and northwestern part of the State, occasionally in the Coastal Plain.

Leaves – deciduous, simple, alternate; variable: blades ovate to lanceolate, base obliquely rounded, tip acuminate, 2½–5" long, 1½–2½" wide, usually coarsely serrate; upper surfaces glabrous or slightly scabrous; lower surfaces sparsely hairy on veins. Figure 172.

Twigs – similar to *C. laevigata*, except buds about ¼" long.

Bark – gray to light brown, smooth with corky outgrowths, on older trees becoming fissured into thick warty plates.

Flowers – similar to *C. laevigata*.

Fruit – drupes, dark red or purple, subglobose, ⅓" in diameter; style persistent on young or often mature fruit; maturing in September and October.

RECOGNITION DIFFICULTIES WITH OTHER TAXA: See comments under *C. laevigata*.

HABITAT: Hackberry is frequently found on moist, alluvial soils, but occurs on a wide range of sites and is often found on drier upland rocky slopes or limestone outcrops.

ECONOMIC, ORNAMENTAL AND OTHER USES: Similar to those of *C. laevigata*.

Celtis tenuifolia Nutt.

Georgia Hackberry

DESCRIPTION: This species is a small irregularly shaped tree, seldom reaching heights of over 30' or diameters over 8–10". The leaves are 1–2 (3)" long, usually less than twice their width, entire or sparingly toothed, and usually scabrous on the upper surface. Other characteristics resemble those of *C. laevigata* or *C. occidentalis*. Georgia Hackberry occurs along slopes on drier, often rocky sites throughout the State. It has no commercial value and little ornamental appeal because of its scraggly, irregular, and slow growth habit. Figure 173, leaves and fruit.

Planera–Water-elm

Planera aquatica (Walter) J. Gmelin.

Water-elm, Planer-tree

DESCRIPTION: Water-elm is a small tree, usually less than 40–50' tall and 1–1½' in diameter. The trunk is often short giving rise to ascending branches which form an open, fan-like crown similar to the elms.

Leaves – deciduous, simple, alternate, two-ranked; blades ovate to deltoid-ovate, base sometimes unequally wedge-shaped or rounded, 1–3½" long, ½–1" wide, margins irregularly serrate to doubly-serrate with glandular teeth; upper surfaces dark green, glabrous or roughened; lower surfaces glabrous or sparsely pubescent. Figure 174, young immature leaves.

Twigs – red-brown and hairy in early spring, becoming grayish and glabrous; terminal winter buds absent; lateral buds minute; leaf scars circular to triangular; bundle scars 3.

Bark – gray-brown, thin, loose scales, exfoliating to expose distinctive, red-brown areas of bark.

Flowers – bisexual or unisexual, usually on the same plant; greenish, inconspicuous, small, ⅛"; staminate in the axils of bud scales; pistillate in axils of new leaves; appearing February–April.

Fruit – drupes, dry, with numerous irregular, fleshy, projections ⅓" long; maturing in April–May. Figure 174, immature green fruits which turn brown at maturity.

RECOGNITION DIFFICULTIES WITH OTHER TAXA: Water-elm can be distinguished from species of elms by the flaky bark with reddish brown inner bark on older trees. The leaves of *Celtis* have pronounced lower lateral veins not found in Water-elm.

HABITAT: Water-elm occurs in alluvial floodplains subject to temporary, periodic flooding.

ECONOMIC, ORNAMENTAL AND OTHER USES: *Planera aquatica* has little commercial value. The wood is soft, light and weak, but it is sometimes harvested with other hardwoods for pulpwood. This tree is the only extant species in the monotypic genus, although closely related taxa are found in the fossil record from Eurasia.

Ulmus–Elms

SUMMER KEY TO SPECIES OF *ULMUS*
1. Leaves less than 4" long; some twigs with corky ridges 2
  2. Leaves usually less than 2" long; flowering in spring; twigs usually with corky ridges . . . . *U. alata*
  2. Leaves usually more than 2" long; flowering in fall; corky ridges typically on older wood, when present. . . . . *U. serotina*
1. Leaves more than 4" long; twigs without corky ridges. 3
  3. Buds with rusty hairs, blunt; fruit pubescent on the seed body, glabrous on margin; leaves extremely scabrous on upper surfaces, lower surfaces tomentose . . . . *U. rubra*
  3. Buds glabrous or essentially so, pointed; fruit body glabrous, margins ciliate; leaves glabrous to somewhat scabrous. . . . .
  . . . . *U. americana*

Ulmus alata Michaux

Winged Elm

DESCRIPTION: This is a medium-sized tree up to 70–80' in height and occasionally 2' in diameter with ascending branches producing an open crown. It is common throughout the State but occurs less frequently at higher elevations in the mountains.

  Leaves – deciduous, simple, alternate; blades oblong-ovate to elliptical, often asymmetrical, apex acute to slightly acuminate, base oblique or cordate, 1½–3½" long, margins doubly serrate; upper surfaces smooth to scabrous; lower surfaces pubescent; dark green, turning yellow in autumn. Figure 176.

Twigs – slender, 2nd year or older twigs usually form corky ridges on two sides, grayish brown to reddish brown, pubescent when young, glabrous with age, lenticels minute, orange; terminal buds absent; lateral buds ovoid, acute, about ⅛" long; leaf scars elevated by a corky layer, semicircular, positioned to side of bud; 3 bundle scars.

Bark – light brown to gray, with narrow, shallow fissures producing irregular, scaly ridges.

Flowers – perfect; petals lacking, calyx brownish-green; in pendulous racemes; appearing before leaf emergence in February–March.

Fruit – samaras, about ⅓" long, elliptical, deeply notched at the apex, downy pubescent; maturing March–April as the leaves appear. Figure 177.

RECOGNITION DIFFICULTIES WITH OTHER TAXA: Only two other native species in the State produce prominent corky wings on the twigs: September Elm, *Ulmus serotina*, and Sweetgum, *Liquidambar styraciflua*. The leaves of Winged Elm are usually less than 2" long and those of September Elm are 2–3½" long. In winter condition, the buds of Winged Elm are about ⅛" long and those of September Elm are up to ½" long. In winter, Winged Elm can be distinguished from Sweetgum because Winged Elm lacks a terminal bud and the bud scales of lateral buds are not fringed.

HABITAT: Winged Elm is found occasionally along streams and flood-plains, even wet areas, but is more common on drier, upland, or rocky soils. It frequently invades old fields, and is usually a minor deciduous forest component.

ECONOMIC, ORNAMENTAL AND OTHER USES: When large enough, Winged Elm is harvested and used in the manufacture of inexpensive furniture and as a filler in the veneer industry. The wood is hard, heavy and, because of interlocked grain, is difficult to split. Winged Elm is frequently used as a street and shade tree throughout the South on drier, upland sites. It grows rapidly when young, and is relatively free of insect and other pests, although there are some recent reports of susceptibility to Dutch Elm disease. When grown in the open, the tree possesses an attractive pyramidal crown in early life and an open, rounded crown of fine branches at maturity. Autumn coloration varies from yellow to light brown and is not particularly showy.

Ulmus americana L.

American Elm

DESCRIPTION: American Elm is a large, long-lived, distinctive and attractive tree, reaching heights of over 100' and 3–4' in diameter. The trunk usually divides into many large spreading branches in open-grown trees to form a wide spreading crown with a fan-like appearance. It occurs throughout the State, but is more prevalent in the Piedmont and Coastal Plain than in the higher mountains.

Leaves – deciduous, simple, alternate; blades oblong-ovate to elliptical, asymmetrical, bases unequal, acuminate tip, variable in size, up to 6" long, coarsely doubly serrate; upper surfaces smooth to scabrous; lower surfaces glabrous or pubescent with tufts of hairs in axils of veins; bright yellow in autumn. Figure 178.

Twigs – slender, without corky wings, red-brown, hairless or sparsely hairy, pale lenticels; terminal winter buds absent; lateral buds ovoid, acute, about ¼" long, nearly glabrous, scales light brown with dark-edged scales; leaf scars elevated with corky layer, often positioned to side of bud.

Bark – light to medium gray, moderately fissured to form interlacing, reticulate scaly ridges. Figure 179.

Flowers – perfect; greenish, small, about ⅛"; borne in fascicles; February or March.

Fruit – samaras, elliptical, flattened, about ½" in diameter, deeply notched at apex, densely ciliate; maturing in March–April. Figure 180.

RECOGNITION DIFFICULTIES WITH OTHER TAXA: *Ulmus americana* is often mistaken for *U. rubra* when the leaves are scabrous above. The most distinguishing characteristic between the two species is the bud. Typically, the bud of *U. americana* is chestnut brown, nearly glabrous and pointed, whereas that of *U. rubra* is purplish-brown to black, prominently red hairy and blunt.

HABITAT: This species occurs in flood plains, margins of wet areas, moist fertile slopes and drier uplands throughout the State.

ECONOMIC, ORNAMENTAL AND OTHER USES: American Elm is a valuable timber tree and is an ornamental shade and street tree. The wood is hard, strong, and difficult to split. When steamed, it can be bent easily into various shapes and was once prized for barrel and wheel hoops, veneer, basketry, etc. Now the wood is chiefly used in the furniture industry and in the production of various wooden wares for home use. This species is subject to Dutch Elm disease and phloem necrosis and is rapidly declining in many parts of the United States; however, these diseases have not spread as extensively in the Southeast as in the northeastern part of its range.

Ulmus rubra Muhlenb.

Slippery Elm

DESCRIPTION: This is a medium-sized tree, usually 70–80' tall with a form similar to that of American Elm, but smaller, with a more open, and frequently flatter crown. It occurs throughout the State, but it is most prevalent in the Piedmont and Coastal Plain and the limestone areas of northwestern Georgia.

Leaves – deciduous, simple, alternate; blades variable in shape from ovate to broadly elliptical, asymmetrical, bases rounded to oblique, apex abruptly acuminate, 5–7" long; upper surfaces very scabrous, lower surfaces densely covered with soft hairs; turning dull yellow in autumn. Figure 181.

Twigs – stout, brownish to ashy gray, bark slightly shreddy, with exceptional tensile strength due to phloem fibers which prevent breaking of twigs by hand without cutting the "stringy" bark, hairy; terminal buds absent; lateral buds purplish brown to black, covered with prominent reddish woolly hairs; leaf scars elevated with corky layer, often positioned to side of bud.

Bark – dark reddish brown, moderately fissured into wavy, lacy appearing scaly ridges; inner bark red-brown, somewhat fragrant and mucilaginous. Figure 182.

Flowers – perfect; greenish, small, about ⅛" across, stamens long exerted, pistils reddish; numerous in compact fascicles; appearing in February–March before leaf emergence.

Fruit – samaras, nearly round, flat, ½–¾" across; slightly notched at tip; wing lacking hairs; maturing in March–April before or with the unfolding of the leaves. Figure 183.

RECOGNITION DIFFICULTIES WITH OTHER TAXA: No other elm has rough-hairy twigs and red-hairy buds. Some texts use scabrous upper leaf surface as a key character to identify this species; however, American Elm can also have quite scabrous leaves. There appears to be considerable variability in the characteristics used to separate the two species.

HABITAT: Slippery Elm is found on moist sites, deep soils of lower slopes, floodplains and occasionally on drier upland sites, especially on limestone soils.

ECONOMIC, ORNAMENTAL AND OTHER USES: The wood of Slippery Elm is similar to that of American Elm and is used for the same purposes. The common name of this tree comes from the slimy inner bark which was once used as a scurvy preventive by chewing or grinding it into a flour. The species is seldom used as an ornamental, although it grows rapidly and provides excellent, heavy shade. The leaves are highly susceptible to numerous insects and mildews in late summer, as are most other elms.

Ulmus serotina Sarg.
September Elm

DESCRIPTION: September Elm is a medium-sized tree, up to 70' tall and 2' in diameter with stout, spreading branches forming a broad, open crown. It is called September Elm because it flowers in the fall. The species is rare in Georgia, although once planted as a shade and street tree. It has only been reported from a single locality in Floyd County along the Coosa River.

Leaves – deciduous, simple, alternate; blades oblong to obovate, acuminate, oblique bases, 3–4" long, up to 2" wide, doubly serrate; pale pubescent below with conspicuous tufts in the axils of the veins. Figure 184.

Twigs – corky-winged on older branches, older twigs with white lenticels; buds about ⅓" long, elongated, bud scales nearly glabrous.

Bark – gray to reddish-brown, shallowly fissured into flat scaly ridges.

Flowers – perfect; greenish, ⅛" long, deeply divided calyx; in drooping racemes; stalks conspicuously jointed; appearing in autumn.

Fruit – samaras, elliptical, flattened, ⅜–½" long, ciliate with white hairs; maturing in October and November. Figure 184.

RECOGNITION DIFFICULTIES WITH OTHER TAXA: In overall appearance September Elm resembles American Elm, but can be distinguished by its corky winged twigs and leaves less than 4" long. When the tree is not in fruit or flower, September Elm may also be confused with Winged Elm, however, the leaves of Winged Elm are even smaller, usually less than 2" long. September Elm can be distinguished from Winged Elm in the winter by its larger buds which are about ⅓" long, whereas those of Winged Elm are about ⅛" long.

HABITAT: September Elm is reported from a single locality in Georgia, in Floyd County along the Coosa River. Although this species ranges from Kentucky and Southern Illinois southward to Oklahoma, Arkansas, and northern Alabama, it occurs infrequently in scattered localities of moist soils along streams and on limestone hills. Reports indicate it was formerly more prevalent in Georgia than it is today, and the species was once widely planted in several towns and cities in Northwest Georgia (Sargent, 1965). It is known to be susceptible to the Dutch Elm disease.

ECONOMIC, ORNAMENTAL AND OTHER USES: September Elm is of little commercial importance because of its sparse occurrence.

MORACEAE–MULBERRY FAMILY

The Moraceae is a large economically important family of predominantly tropical and subtropical trees and shrubs comprising 73 genera and over 1000 species. Most notable are the Fig, *Ficus*, Mulberry, *Morus*, and Jackfruit, *Artocarpus*. Osage Orange, *Maclura*, and Oroko-wood, *Chlorophora*, are important timber genera. Some species of *Ficus* were formerly used as latex sources in rubber manufacture. In fact, one of the most distinctive characteristics of the family is the presence of milky sap containing latex.

In Georgia, the only native tree species of this family is *Morus rubra* L., although several introduced and naturalized species also occur, including Paper Mulberry, *Broussonetia papyrifera* (L.) Vent., White Mulberry, *Morus alba* L., and Osage Orange, *Maclura pomifera* (Raf.) C. Schneider.

Morus–Mulberry

Morus rubra L.

Red Mulberry

DESCRIPTION: Red Mulberry is a medium-size tree reaching heights of 60–70'. It usually possesses a short trunk which divides into stout, spreading branches to form a dense crown. It is sporadic in occurrence throughout the State.

Leaves – deciduous, simple, alternate; blades ovate, often with 1–3 lobes on sprouts or young twigs, long acuminate tip, heart-shaped or blunt straight across at the base, 3–5" long, margins coarsely serrate; smooth or rough above. Figure 185.

Twigs – slender, zigzag, yellowish brown, pubescent when young; terminal winter bud absent; lateral buds ovoid, about ¼" long, 6–7 bud scales; leaf scars half-round to elliptical; bundle scars numerous; exudes milky sap when cut.

Bark – light gray to dark reddish brown, smooth on young stems becoming moderately fissured into thin, long, and narrow scaly plates.

Flowers – unisexual, monoecious or dioecious; small, ⅛" long, green, petals absent; staminate flowers loosely arranged in spikes, pistillate in dense spikes; appearing in April with leaves. Figure 186.

Fruit – a multiple of drupes, resembling a blackberry; dark red to black, cylindrical, 1–2" long, edible; May–June. Figure 187.

RECOGNITION DIFFICULTIES WITH OTHER TAXA: Red Mulberry is closely related to the naturalized White Mulberry (*M. alba*), which was introduced in colonial times as a source of food for silkworms in an unsuccessful attempt to establish a silkworm industry. The two species frequently hybridize. In general, the leaves of White Mulberry are glabrous or occasionally pubescent on the larger veins beneath and the fruit is white to pink when mature. Red Mulberry leaves can be scabrous above and are pubescent on the underside, and the fruit is dark red to black. Sterile and unlobed specimens of Red Mulberry might be confused with Paper Mulberry (*Broussonetia papyrifera*), an introduced species from Asia, which differs in having extremely sandpapery upper leaf surfaces, heavily pubescent twigs and slightly shield-shaped leaves. Red Mulberry, without lobed leaves, might also be mistaken for Basswood (*Tilia americana*). Basswood does not have milky sap and usually has asymmetrical leaves that are also unequal at the base.

HABITAT: This tree sporadically occurs on moist, well-drained sites in bottomlands and valleys, as well as drier upland slopes throughout the State.

ECONOMIC, ORNAMENTAL AND OTHER USES: Mulberry wood is light and soft, but the heartwood is very durable and it was once in much demand for fence posts. It is sometimes planted for its edible fruit and autumn coloration, but is generally not recognized as a desirable ornamental tree because of its short-lived nature and susceptibility to breakage in wind and ice storms, and the messy fruits. However, the fruit is relished by many song and game birds, squirrels, raccoons and opossum.

Fig. 1   *Torreya taxifolia* × 1/5

Fig. 2   *Pinus echinata* × 1/7

Fig. 3   *Pinus echinata* × 1/4

Fig. 4   *Pinus elliottii* × 1/8

Fig. 5   *Pinus elliottii* × 1/12

PLATE 1

Fig. 6 *Pinus elliottii* × 1/4

Fig. 7 *Pinus glabra* × 1/7

Fig. 8 *Pinus glabra* × 1/14

Fig. 9 *Pinus palustris* × 1/10

Fig. 10 *Pinus palustris* × 1/5

PLATE 2

Fig. 11   *Pinus palustris* × 1/4

Fig. 12   *Pinus pungens* × 1/4

Fig. 13   *Pinus rigida* × 1/6

Fig. 14   *Pinus serotina* × 1/4

Fig. 15   *Pinus strobus* × 1/8

PLATE 3

Fig. 16   *Pinus strobus* × 1/16

Fig. 17   *Pinus taeda* × 1/7

Fig. 18   *Pinus taeda* × 1/8

Fig. 19   *Pinus virginiana* × 1/9

Fig. 20   *Pinus virginiana* × 1/10

PLATE 4

Fig. 21   *Tsuga canadensis* × 1/4

Fig. 22   *Tsuga canadensis* × 1/12

Fig. 23   *Tsuga canadensis* × 1/3

Fig. 24   *Tsuga caroliniana* × 1/2

Fig. 25   *Tsuga caroliniana* × 1/3

PLATE 5

Fig. 26   *Taxodium ascendens* × 1/3

Fig. 27   *Taxodium ascendens* × 1/15

Fig. 28   *Taxodium distichum* × 1/4

Fig. 29   *Taxodium distichum* × 1/100

Fig. 30   *Taxodium distichum* × 1¼

PLATE 6

Fig. 31   *Taxodium distichum* × 1/5

Fig. 32   *Chamaecyparis thyoides* × 1/2

Fig. 33   *Chamaecyparis thyoides* × 1/10

Fig. 34   *Chamaecyparis thyoides* × 1/2

Fig. 35   *Chamaecyparis thyoides* × 1/4

PLATE 7

Fig. 36 *Juniperus virginiana* × 1/4

Fig. 37 *Juniperus virginiana* × 1/10

Fig. 38 *Juniperus virginiana* × 1¼

Fig. 39 *Juniperus virginiana* × 1/2

Fig. 40 *Juniperus virginiana* × 1/6

PLATE 8

Fig. 41   *Sabal palmetto* × 1/125

Fig. 42   *Sabal palmetto* × 1/25

Fig. 43   *Populus deltoides* × 1/7

Fig. 44   *Populus deltoides* × 1/15

Fig. 45   *Populus deltoides* × 1/3

Fig. 46   *Populus deltoides* × 1/4

PLATE 9

Fig. 47 *Populus heterophylla* × 1/8

Fig. 48 *Populus heterophylla* × 1/3

Fig. 49 *Populus heterophylla* × 1/3

Fig. 50 *Salix caroliniana* × 1/4

Fig. 51 *Salix floridana* × 1/4

Fig. 52 *Salix nigra* × 1/5

PLATE 10

Fig. 53   *Salix nigra* × 1/12

Fig. 54   *Salix nigra* × 1/2

Fig. 55   *Salix nigra* × 1/3

Fig. 56   *Salix nigra* × 1/3

Fig. 57   *Myrica cerifera* × 1/4

Fig. 58   *Myrica cerifera* × 1/4

PLATE 11

Fig. 59   *Myrica cerifera* × 1/6

Fig. 60   *Myrica heterophylla* × 1/7

Fig. 61   *Myrica inodora* × 1/2

Fig. 62   *Leitneria floridana* × 1/6

Fig. 63   *Leitneria floridana* × 1/3

Fig. 64   *Leitneria floridana* × 1/2

PLATE 12

Fig. 65 *Carya aquatica* × 1/6

Fig. 66 *Carya aquatica* × 1/17

Fig. 67 *Carya aquatica* × 1

Fig. 68 *Carya aquatica* × 1/3

Fig. 69 *Carya aquatica* × 1/3

Fig. 70 *Carya cordiformis* × 1/5

PLATE 13

Fig. 71   *Carya cordiformis* × 1/4

Fig. 72   *Carya glabra* × 1/6

Fig. 73   *Carya glabra* ×

Fig. 74   *Carya glabra* × 1/3

Fig. 75   *Carya laciniosa* × 1/2

Fig. 76   *Carya ovalis* × 1/6

PLATE 14

Fig. 77 *Carya ovalis* × 1/14

Fig. 78 *Carya ovalis* × 1/3

Fig. 79 *Carya ovata* × 1/8

Fig. 80 *Carya ovata* × 1/10

Fig. 81 *Carya ovata* × 1/3

Fig. 82 *Carya pallida* × 1/8

PLATE 15

Fig. 83 *Carya pallida* × 1/12

Fig. 84 *Carya pallida* × 1/5

Fig. 85 *Carya tomentosa* × 1/7

Fig. 86 *Carya tomentosa* × 1/12

Fig. 87 *Carya tomentosa* × 1/3

Fig. 88 *Juglans cinerea* × 1/5

PLATE 16

Fig. 89 *Juglans nigra* (top)
Juglans cinerea (bottom) × 1/4

Fig. 90 *Juglans nigra* × 1/8

Fig. 91 *Juglans nigra* × 1/16

Fig. 92 *Juglans nigra* × 1

Fig. 93 *Juglans nigra* × 1/4

Fig. 94 *Alnus serrulata* × 1/6

PLATE 17

Fig. 95   *Alnus serrulata* × 1/2

Fig. 96   *Alnus serrulata* × 1/2

Fig. 97   *Betula alleghaniensis* × 1/4

Fig. 98   *Betula alleghaniensis* × 1/15

Fig. 99   *Betula alleghaniensis* × 2/3

Fig. 100   *Betula lenta* × 1/4

PLATE 18

Fig. 101 *Betula lenta* × 1/12

Fig. 102 *Betula nigra* × 1/5

Fig. 103 *Betula nigra* × 1/12

Fig. 104 *Betula nigra* × 1

Fig. 105 *Carpinus caroliniana* × 1/5

Fig. 106 *Carpinus caroliniana* × 1/12

PLATE 19

Fig. 107   *Carpinus caroliniana* × 1/2

Fig. 108   *Carpinus caroliniana* × 1/5

Fig. 109   *Ostrya virginiana* × 1/8

Fig. 110   *Ostrya virginiana* × 1/12

Fig. 111   *Ostrya virginiana* × 1

Fig. 112   *Ostrya virginiana* × 1/4

PLATE 20

Fig. 113   *Castanea dentata* × 1/4

Fig. 114   *Castanea dentata* × 1/3

PLATE 21

Fig. 115   *Castanea pumila* × 1/4

Fig. 116   *Castanea pumila* × 1/2

Fig. 117   *Fagus grandifolia* × 1/3

Fig. 118   *Fagus grandifolia* × 1/20

Fig. 119   *Fagus grandifolia* × 1/4

Fig. 120   *Quercus alba* × 1/6

PLATE 22

Fig. 121 *Quercus alba* × 1/12

Fig. 122 *Quercus arkansana* × 1/3

Fig. 123 *Quercus austrina* × 1/4

PLATE 23

Fig. 124 *Quercus austrina* × 1

Fig. 125 *Quercus chapmanii* × 1/2

Fig. 126 *Quercus coccinea* × 1/4

PLATE 24

Fig. 127 *Quercus coccinea* × 1/15

Fig. 128 *Quercus coccinea* × 1/3

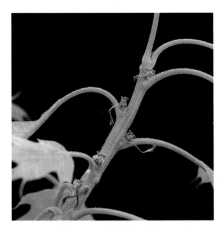

Fig. 129 *Quercus coccinea* × 1

Fig. 130 *Quercus coccinea* × 1/2

Fig. 131 *Quercus falcata* × 1/5

Fig. 132 *Quercus falcata* × 1/16

PLATE 25

Fig. 133　*Quercus falcata* × 1/3

Fig. 134　*Quercus geminata* × 1/4

Fig. 135　*Quercus georgiana* × 1/5

Fig. 136　*Quercus hemisphaerica* × 1/5

Fig. 137　*Quercus incana* × 1/4

Fig. 138　*Quercus laevis* × 1/3

PLATE 26

Fig. 139   *Quercus laurifolia* × 1/5

Fig. 140   *Quercus lyrata* × 1/2

Fig. 141   *Quercus lyrata* × 1/15

PLATE 27

Fig. 142   *Quercus margaretta* × 1/2

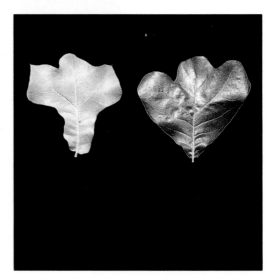

Fig. 143   *Quercus marilandica* × 1/5

Fig. 144   *Quercus marilandica* × 1/12

PLATE 28

Fig. 145   *Quercus marilandica* × 1/2

Fig. 146   *Quercus michauxii* × 1/4

Fig. 147   *Quercus myrtifolia* × 2/3

Fig. 148   *Quercus nigra* × 1/5

Fig. 149   *Quercus nigra* × 1/12

Fig. 150   *Quercus oglethorpensis* × 1/3

PLATE 29

Fig. 151   *Quercus pagoda* × 1/5

Fig. 152   *Quercus pagoda* × 1/12

Fig. 153   *Quercus phellos* × 1/3

Fig. 154   *Quercus prinus* × 1/5

Fig. 155   *Quercus prinus* × 1/12

Fig. 156   *Quercus prinus* × 1/4

PLATE 30

Fig. 157   *Quercus rubra* × 1/8

Fig. 158   *Quercus rubra* × 1/15

Fig. 159   *Quercus rubra* × 3/8

Fig. 160   *Quercus shumardii* × 1/8

Fig. 161   *Quercus shumardii* × 1/4

Fig. 162   *Quercus stellata* × 1/5

PLATE 31

Fig. 163   *Quercus stellata* × 1/12

Fig. 164   *Quercus stellata* × 1/4

Fig. 165   *Quercus velutina* × 1/3

Fig. 166   *Quercus velutina* × 1/12

Fig. 167   *Quercus virginiana* × 1/8

Fig. 168   *Quercus virginiana* × 1/15

PLATE 32

Fig. 169　*Celtis laevigata* × 1/5

Fig. 170　*Celtis laevigata* × 1/15

Fig. 171　*Celtis laevigata* × 1/2

Fig. 172　*Celtis occidentalis* × 1/10

Fig. 173　*Celtis tenuifolia* × 1/6

PLATE 33

Fig. 174   *Planera aquatica* × 1/2

Fig. 175   *Planera aquatica* × 1¼

Fig. 176   *Ulmus alata* × 1/4

Fig. 177   *Ulmus alata* × 1

Fig. 178   *Ulmus americana* × 1/4

PLATE 34

Fig. 179　*Ulmus americana* × 1/12　　　Fig. 180　*Ulmus americana* × 1/2

Fig. 181　*Ulmus rubra* × 1/6　　　Fig. 182　*Ulmus rubra* × 1/12

Fig. 183　*Ulmus rubra* × 1/4

PLATE 35

Fig. 184   *Ulmus serotina* × 1/5

Fig. 185   *Morus rubra* × 1/5

Fig. 186   *Morus rubra* × 1/2

Fig. 187   *Morus rubra* × 1/3

Fig. 188   *Liriodendron tulipifera* × 1/3

PLATE 36

Fig. 189   *Liriodendron tulipifera* × 1/15

Fig. 190   *Liriodendron tulipifera* × 1/3

Fig. 191   *Magnolia acuminata* × 1/5

Fig. 192   *Magnolia acuminata* × 1/15

Fig. 193   *Magnolia acuminata* var. *subcordata* × 1/3

PLATE 37

Fig. 194   *Magnolia acuminata* × 1/3

Fig. 195   *Magnolia fraseri* × 1/10

Fig. 196   *Magnolia fraseri* × 1/6

Fig. 197   *Magnolia fraseri* × 1/2

Fig. 198   *Magnolia grandiflora* × 1/7

PLATE 38

Fig. 199   *Magnolia grandiflora* × 1/4

Fig. 200   *Magnolia grandiflora* × 1/3

Fig. 201   *Magnolia macrophylla* × 1/16

Fig. 202   *Magnolia macrophylla* × 1/5

Fig. 203   *Magnolia macrophylla* × 1/5

PLATE 39

Fig. 204 *Magnolia tripetala* × 1/12

Fig. 205 *Magnolia tripetala* × 1/6

Fig. 206 *Magnolia virginiana* × 1/3

Fig. 207 *Illicium floridanum* × 1/2

Fig. 208 *Illicium floridanum* × 1/2

PLATE 40

Fig. 209   *Asimina triloba* × 1/8

Fig. 210   *Asimina triloba* × 1/2

Fig. 211   *Asimina triloba* × 1/4

Fig. 212   *Persea borbonia* **var.** *pubescens* × 1

Fig. 213   *Persea borbonia* × 1/5

Fig. 214   *Persea borbonia* × 1/12

PLATE 41

Fig. 215   *Sassafras albidum* × 1/5

Fig. 216   *Sassafras albidum* × 1/12

Fig. 217   *Sassafras albidum* × 1/2

Fig. 218   *Sassafras albidum* × 1/2

Fig. 219   *Hamamelis virginiana* × 1/2

Fig. 220   *Hamamelis virginiana* × 1/5

PLATE 42

Fig. 221   *Liquidambar styraciflua* × 1/7

Fig. 222   *Liquidambar styraciflua* × 1/10

Fig. 223   *Liquidambar styraciflua* × 1/2

Fig. 224   *Liquidambar styraciflua* × 1/4

Fig. 225   *Platanus occidentalis* × 1/6

Fig. 226   *Platanus occidentalis* × 1/12

PLATE 43

Fig. 227　*Platanus occidentalis* × 3/4

Fig. 228　*Platanus occidentalis* × 3/8

Fig. 229　*Amelanchier arborea* × 1/2

Fig. 230　*Amelanchier arborea* × 1/3

Fig. 231　*Crataegus flabellata* × 1/7

Fig. 232　*Crataegus spathulata* × 1/3

PLATE 44

Fig. 233   *Crataegus flava* × 2/3

Fig. 234   *Malus angustifolia* × 1/3

Fig. 235   *Malus angustifolia* × 1/2

Fig. 236   *Malus angustifolia* × 1/6

Fig. 237   *Prunus americana* × 1/2

Fig. 238   *Prunus angustifolia* × 1/3

PLATE 45

Fig. 239　*Prunus angustifolia* × 1/2

Fig. 240　*Prunus caroliniana* × 1/4

Fig. 241　*Prunus caroliniana* × 1/5

Fig. 242　*Prunus pensylvanica* × 1/2

Fig. 243　*Prunus pensylvanica* × 1/15

Fig. 244　*Prunus pensylvanica* × 1/6

PLATE 46

Fig. 245   *Prunus serotina* × 1/7

Fig. 246   *Prunus serotina* × 1/17

Fig. 247   *Prunus serotina* × 1/4

Fig. 248   *Prunus serotina* **var.** *alabamensis* × 1/2

Fig. 249   *Prunus umbellata* × 1/4

Fig. 250   *Prunus umbellata* × 1/2

PLATE 47

Fig. 251 *Sorbus americana* × 1/10

Fig. 252 *Sorbus americana* × 1/3

Fig. 253 *Sorbus americana* × 1/2

Fig. 254 *Cercis canadensis* × 1/5

Fig. 255 *Cercis canadensis* × 1/3

Fig. 256 *Cercis canadensis* × 1/4

PLATE 48

Fig. 257　*Cladrastis kentukea* × 1/6

Fig. 258　*Cladrastis kentukea* × 1/6

Fig. 259　*Gleditsia aquatica* × 1/2

Fig. 260　*Gleditsia triacanthos* × 1/6

Fig. 261　*Gleditsia triacanthos* × 1/12

PLATE 49

Fig. 262   *Gleditsia triacanthos* × 1

Fig. 263   *Gleditsia triacanthos* × 1/8

Fig. 264   *Robinia pseudoacacia* × 1/10

Fig. 265   *Robinia pseudoacacia* × 1/12

Fig. 266   *Robinia pseudoacacia* × 1/2

PLATE 50

Fig. 267   *Robinia pseudoacacia* × 1/6

Fig. 268   *Ptelea trifoliata* × 1/2

Fig. 269   *Ptelea trifoliata* × 1/3

Fig. 270   *Zanthoxylum americanum* × 1/4

Fig. 271   *Zanthoxylum clava-herculis* × 1/8

PLATE 51

Fig. 272 *Zanthoxylum clava-herculis* × 1/6   Fig. 273 *Zanthoxylum clava-herculis* × 1/4

Fig. 274 *Rhus copallina* × 1/5

Fig. 275 *Rhus copallina* × 1/7   Fig. 276 *Rhus copallina* × 1/8

PLATE 52

Fig. 277　*Rhus glabra* × 1/10

Fig. 278　*Rhus glabra* × 1/6

Fig. 279　*Rhus typhina* × 1/6

Fig. 280　*Toxicodendron vernix* × 1/6

Fig. 281　*Toxicodendron vernix* × 1/10

PLATE 53

Fig. 282   *Toxicodendron vernix* × 1/4

Fig. 283   *Cliftonia monophylla* × 1/3

Fig. 284   *Cliftonia monophylla* × 1/4

Fig. 285   *Cyrilla racemiflora* × 1/5

Fig. 286   *Cyrilla racemiflora* var. *parvifolia* Sarg. × 1/5

PLATE 54

Fig. 287   *Ilex ambigua* × 1/3

Fig. 288   *Ilex amelanchier* × 1/4

Fig. 289   *Ilex cassine* × 1/5

Fig. 290   *Ilex decidua* × 1/12

Fig. 291   *Ilex montana* × 1/8

PLATE 55

Fig. 292   *Ilex myrtifolia* × 1/3

Fig. 293   *Ilex opaca* × 1/4

Fig. 294   *Ilex opaca* × 1/12

Fig. 295   *Ilex verticillata* × 1/4

Fig. 296   *Ilex vomitoria* × 1/4

PLATE 56

Fig. 297   *Euonymus atropurpureus* × 1/5

Fig. 298   *Staphylea trifolia* × 1/4

Fig. 299   *Staphylea trifolia* × 1/3

Fig. 300   *Staphylea trifolia* × 1/4

Fig. 301   *Acer barbatum* × 1/6

Fig. 302   *Acer barbatum* × 1/10

PLATE 57

Fig. 303 *Acer barbatum* × 1/4

Fig. 304 *Acer barbatum* × 1/6

Fig. 305 *Acer leucoderme* × 1/5

Fig. 306 *Acer leucoderme* × 1/15

Fig. 307 *Acer negundo* × 1/4

Fig. 308 *Acer negundo* × 1/10

PLATE 58

Fig. 309 *Acer nigrum* × 1/4

Fig. 310 *Acer pensylvanicum* × 1/4

Fig. 311 *Acer pensylvanicum* × 1/3

Fig. 312 *Acer rubrum* × 1/4

Fig. 313 *Acer rubrum* × 1/12

Fig. 314 *Acer rubrum* × 1/2

PLATE 59

Fig. 315 *Acer rubrum* × 1/2

Fig. 316 *Acer saccharinum* × 1/4

Fig. 317 *Acer saccharum* × 1/5

Fig. 318 *Acer spicatum* × 1/4

Fig. 319 *Aesculus flava* × 1/5

Fig. 320 *Aesculus flava* × 1/12

PLATE 60

Fig. 321   *Aesculus flava* × 1/4

Fig. 322   *Aesculus flava* × 1/3

Fig. 323   *Aesculus glabra* × 1/3

Fig. 324   *Aesculus parviflora* × 1/5

Fig. 325   *Aesculus parviflora* × 1/5

Fig. 326   *Aesculus pavia* × 1/5

PLATE 61

Fig. 327   *Aesculus sylvatica* × 1/5

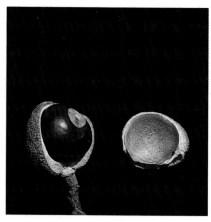

Fig. 328   *Aesculus sylvatica* × 1/2

Fig. 329   *Sapindus marginatus* × 1/6

Fig. 330   *Sapindus marginatus* × 1/2

Fig. 331   *Rhamnus caroliniana* × 1/2

Fig. 332   *Rhamnus caroliniana* × 1/5

PLATE 62

Fig. 333 *Tilia americana* × 1/6

Fig. 334 *Tilia americana* × 1/5

Fig. 335 *Tilia americana* × 1/5

Fig. 336 *Franklinia alatamaha* × 1/3

Fig. 337 *Gordonia lasianthus* × 1/3

Fig. 338 *Gordonia lasianthus* × 1/15

PLATE 63

Fig. 339   *Gordonia lasianthus* × 1/3

Fig. 340   *Stewartia malacodendron* × 1/2

Fig. 341   *Stewartia ovata* × 1/5

Fig. 342   *Aralia spinosa* × 1/10

Fig. 343   *Aralia spinosa* × 1/4

Fig. 344   *Aralia spinosa* × 1/4

PLATE 64

Fig. 345   *Nyssa aquatica* × 1/8

Fig. 346   *Nyssa aquatica* × 1/16

Fig. 347   *Nyssa aquatica* × 1/2

Fig. 348   *Nyssa aquatica* × 1/2

Fig. 349   *Nyssa ogeche* × 1/5

Fig. 350   *Nyssa ogeche* × 1/2

PLATE 65

Fig. 351   *Nyssa sylvatica* × 1/5

Fig. 352   *Nyssa sylvatica* × 1/14

Fig. 353   *Nyssa sylvatica* × 1/2

Fig. 354   *Nyssa sylvatica* × 1/5

Fig. 355   *Nyssa sylvatica* var. *biflora* × 1/5

Fig. 356   *Cornus alternifolia* × 1/3

PLATE 66

Fig. 357   *Cornus alternifolia* × 1/3

Fig. 358   *Cornus florida* × 1/4

Fig. 359   *Cornus florida* × 1/12

Fig. 360   *Cornus florida* × 1/6

Fig. 361   *Cornus florida* × 1/4

Fig. 362   *Cornus stricta* × 1/4

PLATE 67

Fig. 363 *Cornus stricta* × 1

Fig. 364 *Clethra acuminata* × 1/3

Fig. 365 *Clethra acuminata* × 1/2

Fig. 366 *Elliottia racemosa* × 1/5

Fig. 367 *Elliottia racemosa* × 1/8

Fig. 368 *Elliottia racemosa* × 1/2

PLATE 68

Fig. 369   *Kalmia latifolia* × 1/4

Fig. 370   *Lyonia ferruginea* × 1/3

Fig. 371   *Oxydendrum arboreum* × 1/6

Fig. 372   *Oxydendrum arboreum* × 1/10

Fig. 373   *Oxydendrum arboreum* × 1/6

Fig. 374   *Rhododendron catawbiense* × 1/10

PLATE 69

Fig. 375   *Rhododendron maximum* × 1/5

Fig. 376   *Vaccinium arboreum* × 1/3

Fig. 377   *Vaccinium arboreum* × 1/4

Fig. 378   *Bumelia lanuginosa* × 2/3

Fig. 379   *Bumelia lycioides* × 1/5

Fig. 380   *Bumelia lycioides* × 1/6

PLATE 70

Fig. 381   *Bumelia lycioides* × 1/5

Fig. 382   *Bumelia tenax* × 1/2

Fig. 383   *Diospyros virginiana* × 1/4

Fig. 384   *Diospyros virginiana* × 1/12

Fig. 385   *Diospyros virginiana* × 1/3

Fig. 386   *Diospyros virginiana* × 1/4

PLATE 71

Fig. 387   *Halesia carolina* × 1/4

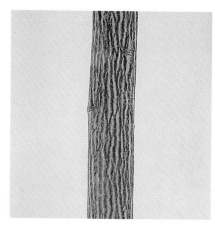

Fig. 388   *Halesia carolina* × 1/5

Fig. 389   *Halesia carolina* × 3/8

Fig. 390   *Halesia carolina* × 1/3

Fig. 391   *Halesia diptera* × 1/5

Fig. 392   *Styrax americanus* × 1/3

PLATE 72

Fig. 393　*Styrax grandifolius* × 1/3

Fig. 394　*Symplocos tinctoria* × 1/3

Fig. 395　*Chionanthus virginicus* × 1/5

Fig. 396　*Chionanthus virginicus* × 1/6

Fig. 397　*Chionanthus virginicus* × 1/5

PLATE 73

Fig. 398   *Foresteria acuminata* × 1/3

Fig. 399   *Foresteria acuminata* × 1/4

Fig. 400   *Foresteria acuminata* × 1⅓

Fig. 401   *Fraxinus americana* × 1/6

Fig. 402   *Fraxinus americana* × 1/12

PLATE 74

Fig. 403 *Fraxinus americana* × 1/2

Fig. 404 *Fraxinus caroliniana* × 1/7

Fig. 405 *Fraxinus caroliniana* × 1/12

Fig. 406 *Fraxinus caroliniana* × 1/4

Fig. 407 *Fraxinus pennsylvanica* × 1/4

PLATE 75

Fig. 408   *Fraxinus pennsylvanica* × 1/15

Fig. 409   *Fraxinus pennsylvanica* × 1

Fig. 410   *Fraxinus pennsylvanica* × 3/4

Fig. 411   *Fraxinus quadrangulata* × 1/6

Fig. 412   *Fraxinus quadrangulata* × 1/2

PLATE 76

Fig. 413   *Osmanthus americanus* × 1/6

Fig. 414   *Catalpa bignonioides* × 1/6

Fig. 415   *Catalpa bignonioides* × 1/4

Fig. 416   *Catalpa bignonioides* × 1/10

Fig. 417   *Cephalanthus occidentalis* × 1/5

PLATE 77

Fig. 418   *Cephalanthus occidentalis* × 1/3

Fig. 419   *Cephalanthus occidentalis* × 1/3

Fig. 420   *Pinckneya bracteata* × 1/6

Fig. 421   *Pinckneya bracteata* × 1/3

Fig. 422   *Pinckneya bracteata* × 1/3

PLATE 78

Fig. 423 *Sambucus canadensis* × 1/5

Fig. 424 *Sambucus canadensis* × 1/4

Fig. 425 *Sambucus canadensis* × 1/3

Fig. 426 *Viburnum nudum* × 1/3

Fig. 427 *Viburnum nudum* × 1/4

PLATE 79

Fig. 428   *Viburnum obovatum* × 1/3   Fig. 429   *Viburnum prunifolium* × 1/5

Fig. 430   *Viburnum rufidulum* × 1/3

Fig. 431   *Viburnum rufidulum* × 1/3   Fig. 432   *Viburnum rufidulum* × 1/3

PLATE 80

MAGNOLIACEAE–MAGNOLIA FAMILY

Of the 12 genera in the family Magnoliaceae in temperate and tropical regions, only two North American arborescent genera are represented in Georgia. *Liriodendron* has a single native species and *Magnolia* has eight native taxa.

The native species of *Magnolia* are trees or shrubs with large showy flowers, several of which are used ornamentally. All native species produce flowers after the leaves appear. Two well-known non-native cultivated magnolias are the Star Magnolia (*Magnolia stellata* Siebold. & Zucc. Maxim) and Saucer Magnolia (*Magnolia* × *soulangeana* Soul. Bod.). The flowers of these ornamentals appear before the leaves in early spring. The fruit, which is characteristic of the family, is a cone-like aggregate of follicles. When the follicles open, the released seeds are suspended by long slender threads. Twigs characteristically have a stipular scar encircling the twig.

Liriodendron–Yellow-Poplar

Liriodendron tulipifera L.
Yellow-poplar, Tulip-poplar

DESCRIPTION: This large tree has a well-pruned, straight trunk and characteristic conical crown. It reaches heights of over 100' and diameters of 3–4', or larger, on moist, fertile sites. Yellow-poplar is one of the most distinctive and valuable hardwoods in the eastern United States. It occurs throughout Georgia.

Leaves – deciduous, simple, alternate; blades with 4–6 lobes, apex abruptly truncated or with broad shallow sinus, 5–6" long; turning bright yellow in autumn. Figure 188.

Twigs – red-brown, lenticels pale, circular to elongated; terminal buds flattened, valvate, with 2 scales, about ½" long, buds dark, covered by a glaucous bloom; leaf scars large, nearly circular; bundle scars several; stipular scars conspicuous, encircling twig; pith diaphragmed.

Bark – light gray and smooth on young trunks with black V markings below branches; older bark gray, thick and deeply furrowed. Figure 189.

Flowers – perfect; greenish yellow, blotched with orange, tulip-shaped, petals 5, 2–3" across; sepals 3; many stamens and pistils spirally arranged; appearing after the leaves in April–May. Figure 188.

Fruit – cone consisting of numerous dry, winged samaras, narrow, light brown, upright; maturing early autumn, the lowermost scales persistent through winter. Figure 190.

RECOGNITION DIFFICULTIES WITH OTHER TAXA: Yellow-poplar should not be confused with any other species, due to its distinctive broadly notched 4–6 lobed leaves, the tulip-shaped, greenish yellow flowers and the scaly, persistent cones of fruits.

HABITAT: This species is common throughout the State on moist, well-drained sites, especially along streams, bottoms, lower upland slopes and rich coves where it often occurs in pure stands. Yellow-poplar is very intolerant of shade and requires almost full light for successful reproduction and rapid early growth.

ECONOMIC, ORNAMENTAL AND OTHER USES: Yellow-poplar is one of our most economically important hardwoods. Large volumes of timber are harvested annually for veneer and manufacture of furniture. The wood is soft and is easily worked. It is also used widely as a shade and park tree because of its rapid growth, beautiful form, attractive foliage and its tulip-like, greenish yellow flowers and its brilliant, yellow, autumn coloration. In general, the tree is free of serious pests. It should be planted where plenty of space is available for growth because of the massive size it attains with age. On dry, upland sites it grows slowly and has a less attractive form.

Magnolia–Magnolias

SUMMER KEY TO SPECIES OF *MAGNOLIA*

1. Leaves evergreen or semi-evergreen
    2. Leaves thick and leathery, 5–8" long, densely bronze-hairy below . . . . *M. grandiflora*
    2. Leaves not thick and leathery, 4–6" long, densely silver-hairy below. . . . . *M. virginiana*
1. Leaves deciduous 3
    3. Leaves auriculate at base 4
        4. Leaves 20–30" long; silvery-hairy on lower surface; stipules, buds and fruit pubescent. . . . . *M. macrophylla*
        4. Leaves 18" long or less; not silvery-hairy on lower surface; buds and fruit glabrous 5
            5. Leaves 5–8" long; flowers 3–4" across when fully expanded . . . . *M. pyramidata*
            5. Leaves 10–18" long; flowers 8–10" across when fully expanded. . . . . *M. fraseri*
    3. Leaves not auriculate at base 6
        6. Leaves 10–20" long, crowded terminally on twig; flowers 8–10" across . . . . *M. tripetala*
        6. Leaves 6–10" long, spaced along the twig; flowers 2–4" across. . . . . *M. acuminata*

Magnolia acuminata L.

Cucumbertree

DESCRIPTION: This is a medium-sized tree, often 60–80' tall and is one of the largest of the Magnolias. It is often large enough to harvest for timber. It occurs in the northern tier of counties, most abundantly in the Blue Ridge and occasionally in the Piedmont.

Leaves – deciduous, simple, alternate; blades obovate, widely elliptic, base rounded to acute, tip acute to acuminate, 6–10" long; upper surfaces glabrous; lower surfaces pubescent. Figure 191.

Twigs – stout, brittle; buds with long silky hairs, terminal buds ½–¾", covered with a single scale; leaf scars narrow, elevated; stipular scars encircling twig.

Bark – gray-brown, furrowed into narrow, scaly ridges. Figure 192.

Flowers – perfect; yellow-green, petals 2–4" long; numerous stamens and pistils, spirally arranged; appearing April–May. Figure 193, the yellow flower of the local variety *subcordata* (Spach.) Dandy.

Fruit – cone-like aggregate of follicles, dark red, ovoid or oblong, 2½–3" long, seeds ½" long, red, suspended from ovary wall by a slender filament; maturing in July–August. Figure 194.

RECOGNITION DIFFICULTIES WITH OTHER TAXA: Cucumbertree can be distinguished from several Magnolias since its leaves do not have an auriculate or cordate base. However, it may resemble and occur in the same area as Umbrella Magnolia (*M. tripetala*), which has leaves clustered terminally on the twigs. The silky bud and pubescent twigs also distinguish the species from *M. tripetala*. A local variety, *subcordata* (Spach) Dandy, (*M. cordata* Michaux), commonly known as Yellow Flowered Magnolia, has yellow-orange flowers and hairy twigs and is found infrequently in the Piedmont region.

HABITAT: This tree occurs on moist, fertile slopes of the mountains and the Piedmont.

ECONOMIC, ORNAMENTAL AND OTHER USES: The wood of Cucumbertree is soft, but is utilized in paneling and crates. It grows rapidly and is commonly planted as an ornamental throughout its range due to its hardiness and adaptability to various sites. The seeds are consumed by many species of birds and rodents.

Magnolia fraseri Walter

Fraser Magnolia

DESCRIPTION: This is a small to medium-sized tree, seldom over 60' tall, often with multiple stems, and is restricted primarily to the Blue Ridge Mountains.

Leaves – deciduous, simple, alternate; blades obovate to spatulate, conspicuously auriculate at the base, 10–18" long, 5–8" wide; glabrous. Figure 195.

Twigs – stout, brittle branches; terminal bud purple, glabrous, 1½" long; otherwise similar to other species of magnolia.

Bark – thin, smooth, grayish brown, becoming slightly scaly.

Flowers – perfect; petals cream colored, 8–10" across; sweet scented; appearing late April–May. Figure 196.

Fruit – cone-like aggregate of follicles, bright red when mature, glabrous, oblong, 3–4½" long; seeds bright red; maturing July–August. Figure 197.

RECOGNITION DIFFICULTIES WITH OTHER TAXA: Fraser Magnolia somewhat resembles *M. macrophylla* in leaf shape; however, *M. macrophylla* has pubescent leaves which are 20–30" long. Fraser Magnolia is closely related to *M. pyramidata* which is sometimes considered as a variety. *Magnolia pyramidata* is generally smaller in leaf length, 5½–8½" long, with flowers only 3½–4" across when fully expanded. In Georgia, *M. pyramidata* is known from the lower Piedmont and Coastal Plain in scattered localities. In winter condition the large, glabrous, purplish buds of *M. fraseri* and *M. tripetala* appear similar. To distinguish, fallen leaves should be observed at the base of the tree.

HABITAT: Fraser Magnolia occurs on moist slopes and along creek and stream valleys in rich woodlands of the mountains.

ECONOMIC, ORNAMENTAL AND OTHER USES: This species is of little economic importance because of its size and form. It is occasionally used as an ornamental tree because of its large flowers and interesting leaf shape.

Magnolia grandiflora L.

Southern Magnolia, Bull Bay

DESCRIPTION: Southern Magnolia is a large beautiful, spreading evergreen tree, native to the Coastal Plain, but planted extensively throughout the State.

Leaves – evergreen, persistent 2 years, simple, alternate; blades elliptic, tip bluntly acute, 6–12" long, leathery; upper surfaces dark green and lustrous; lower surfaces rusty woolly or greenish. Figure 198.

Twigs – covered with rust colored hairs when young; buds 1–1½" long, rusty pubescent.

Bark – gray to brown, smooth at first becoming lightly furrowed into scaly, flat plates.

Flowers – perfect; petals creamy-white, 6–12, 7–8" across; on stout hairy stalks; very fragrant; appearing in late spring and early summer. Figure 199.

Fruit – cone-like aggregate of follicles, rose-red at maturity, becoming brown when older, ovoid to cylindrical, 3–4" long, pubescent; seeds bright red, suspended from follicle by slender, elastic thread; mature in October–November. Figure 200.

RECOGNITION DIFFICULTIES WITH OTHER TAXA: The only other evergreen Magnolia is Sweetbay, *M. virginiana*. *Magnolia grandiflora* is easily distinguished by its thick, larger, leathery leaves which are lustrous dark green above, and mostly rusty-brown pubescent below.

HABITAT: It occurs in swamp forests, alluvial floodplains, maritime forests and low woods of the Coastal Plain. This species is commonly planted as an ornamental and has occasionally become naturalized in the Piedmont.

ECONOMIC, ORNAMENTAL AND OTHER USES: Southern Magnolia is widely planted as a specimen tree for its showy, fragrant flowers and large shiny evergreen leaves. It is fast growing and hardy throughout most of the Southeast. The wood is used for furniture, paneling, veneer and cabinet work. The seeds are consumed by numerous species of birds and small mammals.

Magnolia macrophylla Michaux
Bigleaf Magnolia

DESCRIPTION: Bigleaf Magnolia is noted as having the largest simple leaves and flower of any dicotyledonous tree in North America. It seldom attains heights of over 50' and diameters of 8–10" in Georgia. It is rather short-lived, often reproducing by stump sprouts. The species is uncommon, and is only documented from a few localities in the upper Piedmont and southwestern counties of the Coastal Plain.

Leaves – deciduous, simple, alternate; blades cordate or lobed at the base, 20–30" long; upper surfaces glabrous, dark green; lower surfaces glaucous, pubescent. Figure 201.

Twigs – stout, brittle, densely tomentose when young; terminal winter buds bluntly pointed, flattened, covered with white hairs, 1¾–2" long; a large pith.

Bark – thin, gray, smooth, forming small inconspicuous plates on older trees.

Flowers – perfect; creamy white, petals frequently with conspicuous purplish blotches near the base inside, 10–12" in diameter; appearing April–May. Figure 202.

Fruit – cone-like aggregate of follicles, ovoid to nearly globose, densely pubescent, 2½–3" long; maturing in July–August. Figure 203.

RECOGNITION DIFFICULTIES WITH OTHER TAXA: See *M. fraseri*.

HABITAT: Bigleaf Magnolia occurs in rich wooded ravines in isolated populations in the Piedmont and upper Coastal Plain of western Georgia.

ECONOMIC, ORNAMENTAL AND OTHER USES: The species makes an attractive ornamental. However, its large leaves and brittle branches make it susceptible to wind or ice storms. Its relatively low numbers have been attributed to removal by garden collectors, but cone production, seed set and seed viability are often poor as well. The wood is not used commercially.

Magnolia pyramidata Bartram
Pyramid Magnolia

DESCRIPTION: *Magnolia pyramidata* is closely related to *M. fraseri* and is considered by some authors to be a variety of *M. fraseri*. *Magnolia pyramidata* is generally smaller in leaf length and size of flower than *M. fraseri*. See description of *M. fraseri*. In Georgia, *M. pyramidata* is known from the lower Piedmont and Coastal Plain in scattered localities.

Magnolia tripetala L.
Umbrella Magnolia

DESCRIPTION: This is a small tree, up to 40' tall and is often multi-stemmed. It occurs occasionally in the Piedmont and lower mountains in Georgia.

    Leaves – deciduous, simple, alternate, clustered terminally on the twig; blades obovate-lanceolate, narrowed at the ends, apex acute or bluntly pointed, 18–20" long; upper surfaces glabrous; lower surfaces pubescent. Figure 204.

    Twigs – stout, reddish when young, becoming brown-gray; terminal buds purple, glaucous, glabrous, usually about 1" long; otherwise, similar to other Magnolia species.

    Bark – thin, gray, smooth, shallowly furrowed with age.

    Flowers – perfect; petals white, usually 6–10" long; filaments bright purple; disagreeable odor; appearing late April–May. Figure 205, upright flower just before petals unfold.

    Fruits – cone-like aggregate of follicles, rose-red, conical-cylindrical, glabrous, 2–3" long, maturing July–September.

RECOGNITION DIFFICULTIES WITH OTHER TAXA: Umbrella Magnolia can be easily distinguished from *Magnolia acuminata* by its glabrous terminal bud and by the leaves which are clustered terminally rather than spaced along the stem. In winter condition, the buds closely resemble and cannot be distinguished from *M. fraseri*.

HABITAT: It occurs in moist, rich woods in the upper Piedmont and mountains at lower elevations.

ECONOMIC, ORNAMENTAL AND OTHER USES: This species is occasionally used as an ornamental, but has no economic value.

Magnolia virginiana L.

Sweetbay

DESCRIPTION: Sweetbay is a medium-sized tree, up to 60' tall, but frequently a large shrub. Its form is shrubbier and more decidedly deciduous in northern parts of its range. In Georgia, it is most common in the Coastal Plain and lower Piedmont.

Leaves – persisting until winter or until new leaves appear in spring, simple, alternate; blades thin leathery, oval to elliptic, narrowing toward both ends; 4–6½" long, 1–2" wide; upper surfaces dull-green; lower surfaces silvery-pubescent; aromatic, spicy odor. Figure 206.

Twigs – slender, green, hairy at first, but becoming red-brown and smooth; terminal bud about ¾" long, covered with fine, silky hairs; aromatic.

Bark – thin, grayish, smooth to irregularly furrowed and superficially scaly, fragrant when crushed.

Flowers – perfect; creamy white, 2–3" in diameter; very fragrant; appearing April–July. Figure 206.

Fruits – cone-like aggregate of follicles, dark red, ellipsoid, about 2" long; maturing July–October.

RECOGNITION DIFFICULTIES WITH OTHER TAXA: Sweetbay may occur in the same habitat with Loblolly Bay, *Gordonia lasianthus.* The two can easily be distinguished since the leaves of Sweetbay are entire with silvery pubescence underneath, while those of Loblolly Bay are shallowly toothed and glabrous beneath.

HABITAT: Characteristically, Sweetbay occurs in wet, sandy or acidic soils in low wet woodlands, river floodplains, and shrub swamps primarily in the Coastal Plain and the lower Piedmont regions of the State. It has, however, been documented in the Ridge and Valley region of Northwest Georgia in sag ponds.

ECONOMIC, ORNAMENTAL AND OTHER USES: Sweetbay is used as a landscape accent for its open form and fragrant, white flowers in the spring. It is of little economic importance for timber products because of its size, but when large enough to harvest, it is used for the same purposes as other Magnolias.

ILLICIACEAE–ANISE-TREE FAMILY

The Illiciaceae contains the monotypic genus *Illicium*. This genus has been considered in many previous treatments as a member of the Magnoliaceae. Most species of *Illicium* occur in southeastern Asia and only a few species are native to North America. Two species are native to the southeastern United States, and only *Illicium floridanum* occurs in Georgia. Several of the Asian, as well as the North American species, are cultivated because of their evergreen leaves and unusual reddish flowers.

Illicium–Anise-tree

Illicium floridanum Ellis

Anise-tree

DESCRIPTION: Anise-tree is a small rare tree, or multi-stemmed shrub, up to 20–25′ in height and usually with a crooked trunk. All parts of the plant have a spicy, rank odor when crushed. It is rare in Georgia, recorded only in the southwestern Coastal Plain in Decatur County. It is more common in the Florida Panhandle.

Leaves – evergreen, simple, alternate, often crowded on the ends of twigs; blades fleshy, leathery, elliptical, 3–6″ long, margins entire, lateral veins not distinct; upper surface dark green, glabrous; lower surface paler, glandular dotted, spicy aromatic when crushed. Figure 207.

Twigs – slender, green when young, becoming gray with age; winter buds naked.

Bark – dark brown, smooth but becoming shallowly fissured with age.

Flowers – perfect; star shaped; petals and sepals indistinguishable, deep red to purple, numerous; stamens and pistils numerous; borne singly in leaf axils on stalks about 1–1½″ long; appearing April–June. Figure 207.

Fruit – follicle, arranged in whorls that are somewhat star-shaped, dry, brownish. Figure 208.

RECOGNITION DIFFICULTIES WITH OTHER TAXA: This species is unique in its numerous dark red flowers, fruits arranged in a whorl and all plant parts with spicy odor.

HABITAT: Anise-tree grows in low, moist or wet areas along streams, ravines and bayheads.

ECONOMIC, ORNAMENTAL AND OTHER USES: The Anise-tree is only of economic value as an ornamental. It is hardy through the Piedmont of Georgia and grows best in partially sunny, moist areas. The foliage and fruit are poisonous to cattle.

ANNONACEAE–CUSTARD APPLE FAMILY

The Annonaceae is a large family of trees and shrubs, widely distributed in tropical and warm temperate regions. Many species among this group produce aromatic compounds used in medicinal preparations and perfumes. Others produce spices used in foods and flavorings. Several species produce large palatable fruits and many taxa are grown ornamentally because of large showy flowers. Two genera possessing small to medium-sized trees occur in North America, *Asimina* (pawpaws) and *Annona* (pond apples). In Georgia, only one species of pawpaw reaches tree size, *Asimina triloba* (L.) Dunal, while another species, *Asimina parviflora* (Michaux) Dunal, usually has a lower, more shrubby form, and seldom attains heights of 10–15'.

Asimina–Pawpaw

Asimina triloba (L.) Dunal

Pawpaw

DESCRIPTION: Pawpaw is a small, distinctive tree which rarely exceeds 25' in height. In many localities it occurs only as a large shrub with drooping branches. It often reproduces by root sprouts to form clumps of single stems. It is found predominantly in the mountains and the Piedmont.

Leaves – deciduous, simple, alternate; blades obovate, bases tapering, 6–12" long; upper surfaces sparsely pubescent; lower surfaces densely reddish hairy when young, becoming glabrous with age; petiole short; fetid odor when crushed. Figure 209.

Twigs – slender, light brown, new growth covered with rusty red pubescence; terminal bud flat, naked, ½" long, loosely covered with small leaves; lateral bud triangular, rusty pubescent scales; leaf scars crescent to horseshoe-shaped; bundle scars 5, arranged in a V; flower buds globose, conspicuous, reddish brown, pubescent, superposed; pith diaphragmed; aromatic when cut.

Bark – dark brown, often with small, vertical gray superficial fissures accompanied with larger gray blotches, smooth except for raised warty areas.

Flowers – perfect; maroon, ¾–2" across, petals 6, the outer row of 3 twice the length of the inner 3, sepals 3; stamens in a compact spiral; 3–7 pistils; pedicels greater than ½" long, dark brown hairy; appearing March–April in leaf axils of previous year's twig prior to or during emergence of present year's leaves. Figure 210.

Fruit – berry, green with dark gray spots in summer, yellow to dark brown-black when mature, oblong to cylindric, fleshy, 3–5" long; edible; seeds shiny, bean-shaped; maturing late summer. Figure 211.

RECOGNITION DIFFICULTIES WITH OTHER TAXA: *Asimina triloba* is very similar to the more commonly shrubby, Small-flowered Pawpaw, *A. parviflora*. However, the flowers of *A. triloba* are ¾–2" across and the flower stalks are greater than ½", while the flowers of *A. parviflora* are ⅓–½" across with stalks less than ½" in length. Likewise, the leaves of *A. triloba* are generally larger than *A. parviflora*. In winter condition, we are not able to distinguish the two species. Leaf form and arrangement may resemble understory species of *Nyssa* or *Magnolia*, but the rusty brown pubescent twigs, the naked, flattened terminal buds covered with rusty red hairs, and fetid odor of crushed leaves are distinctive.

HABITAT: Pawpaw is usually found on moist sites, especially along floodplains in the Piedmont and upper Coastal Plain. It is occasional in the understory of rich hardwood forests in the mountains.

ECONOMIC, ORNAMENTAL AND OTHER USES: The fruits were once widely eaten by Indians and early settlers and often harvested for local markets. Ornamentally, the species is an attractive plant that should be utilized for naturalizing along streams or on moist, fertile sites. The fruit is a source of food for birds and small mammals.

LAURACEAE–LAUREL FAMILY

The Laurel family contains a large number of mostly evergreen, tropical or warm temperate trees and shrubs. Worldwide, the family is economically important because of the many aromatic substances extracted from leaves, bark, fruits, and roots of several species. The genus *Cinnamomum* provides both cinnamon and camphor. The Avocado, *Persea americana* Miller, is cultivated in many tropical countries, and oil of sassafras is obtained from *Sassafras*. The leaves of *Laurus nobilis* L., Bay Laurel, are used for flavoring and in ancient Greece were placed as a garland of honor on heads of victorious athletes, war heros, and successful politicians. Several genera in this family are valuable timber trees. The Asiatic species, *Cinnamomum camphora* (L.) Nees & Eberm., is naturalized in the State.

Two native genera with arborescent species are found in Georgia, *Persea* and *Sassafras*. Diagnostic features of these taxa include simple, alternate, aromatic leaves.

Persea–Red Bay

Persea borbonia (L.) A. Sprengel
Red Bay

DESCRIPTION: Red Bay is a small to medium-sized tree, occasionally 60–70' tall and 2' in diameter, restricted to the Coastal Plain in Georgia.

Leaves – persistent, simple, alternate; blades leathery, elliptic to oblong, tapering at both ends, 2–8" long, entire, margins often misshapen due to fungal growth; dark green and glabrous above; whitish bloom below; leafstalks sparsely pubescent or smooth; aromatic. Figure 212.

Twigs – light brown, smooth to slightly hairy; terminal winter buds naked, densely hairy, ¼" long; leaf scars linear to elliptical; bundle scars single, linear.

Bark – dark-reddish brown, divided by deep, irregular fissures into flat scaly ridges on older trees. Figure 213.

Flower – perfect; yellow, small, about ¼" long; few–many flowered in axillary panicles; appearing May–June. Figure 212.

Fruit – drupes, dark blue, oblong, lustrous, up to ½" long; subtended by persistent calyx; peduncles yellow-orange, about ½–1" long; maturing September–October. Figure 214.

RECOGNITION DIFFICULTIES WITH OTHER TAXA: Swamp Bay, *P. borbonia* var. *pubescens* (Pursh) Little, is a similar taxon recognized by some authors as a variety of Red Bay. Others consider Swamp Bay a legitimate species, *P. palustris* (Raf.) Sarg. Swamp Bay differs from var. *borbonia* by its densely hairy young twigs and leafstalks. Its leaves are sparsely to densely hairy beneath, not as conspicuously glaucous, and its principal veins are rusty colored. See description of habitat differences. Swamp Bay seldom reaches heights of over 25–30'.

HABITAT: Red Bay occurs in mesic to xeric woodlands or dunes in the Coastal Plain, while Swamp Bay is found in low wet areas such as swamps, banks along marshes, and wet pine flatwoods.

ECONOMIC, ORNAMENTAL AND OTHER USES: The aromatic, spicy

leaves of Red Bay have been used as a substitute for those of the Bay Laurel for flavoring in soups and meat dishes. Red Bay is occasionally used ornamentally because of the evergreen leaves and showy fruit. The red-colored wood is used for interior finishing, cabinets and furniture. The fruit is eaten by song birds, turkey and quail.

Sassafras–Sassafras

Sassafras albidum (Nutt.) Nees

Sassafras

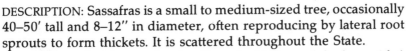

DESCRIPTION: Sassafras is a small to medium-sized tree, occasionally 40–50' tall and 8–12" in diameter, often reproducing by lateral root sprouts to form thickets. It is scattered throughout the State.

Leaves – deciduous, simple, alternate; blades unlobed, or with 1 or 3 lobes, 3–6" long, bases acute, margins entire; pubescent beneath when young; aromatic when crushed. Figure 215.

Twigs – slender, greenish with glaucous bloom; terminal buds about ½" long with 3 to 5 keeled scales; leaf scars half round; single bundle scar; spicy aromatic.

Bark – dark green on young stems, with narrow reddish-brown ridges; on older trees gray to reddish brown, moderately fissured into flat narrow ridges; bark aromatic. Figure 216.

Flowers – dioecious; yellow-green, about ½" long; sepals and petals similar; clustered at end of twigs; pistillate flowers with rudimentary stamens; appearing March–April before leaves. Figure 217.

Fruit – drupes, dark blue, ½" long; red stalk; maturing June–July. Figure 218.

RECOGNITION DIFFICULTIES WITH OTHER TAXA: Sassafras is easily recognized by its variably lobed leaves on the same plant, distinctive aromatic odor, and dark green twigs on young branches with reddish brown corky ridges. Occasionally trees are found with unlobed leaves.

HABITAT: Sassafras is an early successional species frequently occurring along fence rows, woodland margins and old fields. It is shade intolerant and is seldom found as an understory tree in a closed canopy forest.

ECONOMIC, ORNAMENTAL AND OTHER USES: Oil of sassafras, distilled from bark, twigs, and roots was formerly used in large quantities in flavoring extracts, scented soaps and pharmaceuticals. A sassafras tea was brewed by boiling roots. Fruit production is often sparse, but provides a food source for birds and mammals.

HAMAMELIDACEAE–WITCH-HAZEL FAMILY

Over 100 species of trees and shrubs in the Hamamelidaceae occur in subtropical and warm, temperate forested regions around the world. Several trees in this family produce large quantities of lumber, veneer and other valuable forest products for the world's markets.

Two species in this group attain tree size in North America, *Liquidambar styraciflua* L. and *Hamamelis virginiana* L., both of which are native to Georgia.

Hamamelis–Witch-hazel

Hamamelis virginiana L.

Witch-hazel

DESCRIPTION: Witch-hazel is a small tree, often a large shrub, which may reach heights of 30–35'. It usually possesses an irregular and somewhat flattened, spreading crown. Witch-hazel occurs throughout the State, but it is most prevalent in the upper Coastal Plain, Piedmont and mountains.

Leaves – deciduous, simple, alternate; blades obovate and asymmetrical, bases unequal, mostly 3–5" long, margins wavy to crenate; upper surfaces dark green; paler, lower surfaces with scattered stellate hairs; slightly aromatic. Figures 219, 220.

Twigs – slender, zigzag, red-brown, young twigs scurfy, becoming smooth; terminal buds stalked, curved, naked, hairy, ¼–½" long; leaf scars half-round to 3-lobed; bundle scars 3.

Bark – light brown, inner bark purplish, thin, smooth to slightly scaly.

Flowers – perfect; petals yellow, thread-like, twisted, 4, about 1" long; flower buds appearing in the spring several months before opening in the autumn. Figure 219.

Fruit – capsule, woody, elliptical, 2-beaked, ½" long, dehiscing along 2 sutures to produce 4 sharply curved points; forcibly ejecting shiny black seeds; maturing October–November of the year following flowering. Figure 220.

RECOGNITION DIFFICULTIES WITH OTHER TAXA: The leaves and stalked buds of Witch-hazel somewhat resemble those of *Alnus serrulata* (Aiton) Willd., Hazel Alder, and the shrub, *Fothergilla gardenii* Murray, Witch-alder, in the same family. Hazel Alder is easily recognized by its persistent, woody, cone-like fruits and leaves with finely toothed margins between the wavy serrations. The shrub, *Corylus americana* Walter, American Hazelnut, has leaves that resemble Witch-hazel, except that they are doubly serrate and cordate at the base.

HABITAT: Witch-hazel occurs along streams and margins of swamps and as an understory tree on moist, upland sites in mixed hardwood stands.

ECONOMIC, ORNAMENTAL AND OTHER USES: Witch-hazel is occasionally used in naturalized areas for shrub borders in partial shade on moist sites. Its unique, yellow, fragrant flowers occur in fall from October–December and are most attractive following leaf fall. It is relatively free of disease and insect pests. The aromatic extract from leaves, twigs and bark has long been used in shaving lotions and toilet water as a mild astringent. Witch-hazel is prized by "water diviners" to locate sources of water.

Liquidambar–Sweetgum

Liquidambar styraciflua L.

Sweetgum

DESCRIPTION: Sweetgum is a large tree, commonly 80' to over 100' in height, and 2–4' in diameter with a long cylindrical bole and oblong, conical crown. It is common throughout the State, but less frequent in the mountains. The common name refers to the gummy exudate which has been used as a poor substitute for chewing gum.

Leaves – deciduous, simple, alternate; blades palmately lobed, 3–6" long, margins toothed; petioles 4–5" long; turning yellow to crimson or maroon in autumn; pleasant resinous fragrance when bruised. Figure 221.

Twigs – frequently developing corky ridges, green to brown, lenticels raised, dark; terminal buds ovoid, pointed, with glossy, fringed overlapping scales; leaf scars raised; bundle scars 3, light with dark center.

Bark – gray, furrowed, forming narrow, rounded, scaly ridges. Figure 222.

Flowers – monoecious; petals absent, staminate greenish yellow, in clusters on a terminal spike; pistillate pale green, in globose clusters, pendulous in leaf axils; appearing in April with emerging leaves. Figure 223.

Fruit – spiny ball of many capsules, persistent, woody, 1–1½" in diameter; maturing late summer. Figure 224.

RECOGNITION DIFFICULTIES WITH OTHER TAXA: The deeply lobed, somewhat star-shaped leaves of Sweetgum should not pose any recognition problem in the field. In winter habit, the persistent fruit heads, presence of numerous incurved short shoots along the main branches, large terminal buds and usual presence of corky wings along the twigs make it easy to identify or separate from other hardwoods. Winged Elm also has winged twigs; however, this species lacks a terminal winter bud.

HABITAT: Sweetgum is ubiquitous in Georgia, but it attains its largest size on moist, rich alluvial soils. It is a prolific seeder and quickly invades cut-over hardwood stands and pine plantations on upland sites. It also sprouts profusely from stumps and lateral roots forming new stands.

ECONOMIC, ORNAMENTAL AND OTHER USES: Sweetgum is one of the most valuable commercial hardwoods in the Southeast with regard to the volume of timber produced. It is widely used for veneer, interior trim, furniture and pulp. It is also planted as a shade tree because of its rapid early growth on a variety of sites; however, it requires adequate space for extensive root development. Autumn coloration varies from shades of red to purple on the same tree. Disadvantages of sweetgum as a lawn or shade tree are the frequent heavy crops of persistent fruit heads which fall during winter and early spring, and the production of root sprouts from lateral roots.

PLATANACEAE–SYCAMORE FAMILY

The Sycamore family contains the single genus, *Platanus*. Three species in this genus are native to the United States. *Platanus occidentalis* L. is a common large tree in the eastern and southern states and is the only species occurring in Georgia. The other two species are found in the Southwest and California. Several species of the genus are cultivated domestically as shade or ornamental trees, and our native Sycamore is a valuable timber tree.

Platanus–Sycamore

Platanus occidentalis L.

Sycamore, Planetree

DESCRIPTION: Sycamore is a large tree, occasionally reaching 100' in height and 3–5' in diameter. Under forest conditions it forms a well-pruned cylindrical bole terminating in a broad open crown. It is found throughout the State, but is sparse in the higher mountains.

Leaves – deciduous, simple, alternate; blades broadly ovate, with 3–5 coarsely toothed lobes, 4–8" long and wide, palmately veined; upper surfaces medium green; lower surfaces pale; downy pubescent when young, becoming smooth with age except along the lower veins; base of petiole enclosing lateral bud; prominent, leaf-like stipules encircle the twig. The pubescence on Sycamore leaves is composed of myriads of microscopic stellate hairs which are freely released into the air when the leaves are disturbed mechanically. Breathing these hairs into the nostrils and throat can become very irritating and uncomfortable. Figure 225.

Twigs – slender, zigzag, greenish gray; terminal buds absent; lateral buds large, with single cap-like scale formed in petiole base and usually not visible on the twig until leaf fall; leaf scars ring-like, encircling bud; bundle scars 5–9, large, distinct; stipular scars encircle twig.

Bark – red-brown, older trees becoming light greenish gray to almost white on upper bole, scaly near base, exfoliating outer layers on upper trunk result in a multicolored red-brown and gray-white mottled appearance. Figure 226.

Flowers – monoecious; male and female in separate round, drooping heads with numerous, minute individual flowers; female heads rusty to dark red, male heads yellowish green; appearing in April–May. Figure 227.

Fruit – a multiple of achenes, each achene encircled by a ring of erect hairs; forming a globose, brown fruiting head, about 1" in diameter; suspended on a 3–6" stalk. Figure 228.

RECOGNITION DIFFICULTIES WITH OTHER TAXA: This species is distinctive mainly by the exfoliating bark, large lobed leaves and fruit heads.

HABITAT: Sycamore occurs abundantly along stream banks and on moist bottomlands, but is also tolerant of drier upland sites. It cannot withstand flooding for prolonged periods, hence it is not found in swampy habitats.

ECONOMIC, ORNAMENTAL AND OTHER USES: Sycamore is one of the largest American hardwoods. Early foresters report stem diameters in excess of 13' at breast height. The wood is hard and difficult to split because of interlocking fibers, hence it was used for implement handles, boxes, meat cutting blocks, crates, and woodenware. Presently it is used mostly for veneer, particle board and pulp. Sycamore is often planted as an ornamental or shade tree due to its resistance to pests and pollution, rapid growth and adaptability to various sites.

ROSACEAE–ROSE FAMILY

The Rosaceae comprises a large group of both herbaceous and woody species. It is important economically for many tree species such as Apples, Peaches, Pears, Plums, Almonds, and shrubs such as Raspberries and Blackberries. Numerous horticultural ornamentals that also occur in this family, include Roses, Spireas, and Cotoneaster.

Five genera of native trees in the Rosaceae occur in Georgia: *Amelanchier*, *Crataegus*, *Malus*, *Prunus*, and *Sorbus*. As a group, these species are characterized by showy, simple, bisexual flowers with numerous stamens. The leaves are usually simple and deciduous, although there are species with evergreen or compound leaves. Branch thorns and spur shoots occur in *Crataegus*, *Prunus*, and *Malus*. The fruit of the Rosaceae represented here are pomes and drupes.

Amelanchier–Serviceberry

Amelanchier arborea (Michaux f.) Fern.

Downy Serviceberry, Shadbush

DESCRIPTION: Downy Serviceberry is a small tree, up to 40' tall, often with an irregularly shaped crown and showy flowers. It occurs primarily in the mountains and Piedmont.

Leaves – deciduous, simple, alternate; blades widest at or above the middle, bases rounded to subcordate, apex abruptly tapered, 2–3 ½" long, up to 1½" wide, margins finely serrate; lower surfaces pubescent. Figure 229.

Twigs – slender, flexible, brownish, glabrous to slightly pubescent; terminal bud elongated, pointed, ½" long or longer; bud scales green-red, lateral buds slightly curved toward twig; leaf scar narrowly crescent to V-shaped; bundle scars 3.

Bark – ashy gray, sometimes streaked, smooth but becoming furrowed with age into narrow ridges.

Flowers – perfect; white, about 1" in diameter, petals linear, many stamens; borne in showy erect or drooping racemes near the end of the twig; appearing in early spring before the leaves. Figure 230.

Fruit – pome, reddish purple, nearly round, ⅓" long, fleshy, calyx persistent; matures in early summer. Figure 229.

RECOGNITION DIFFICULTIES WITH OTHER TAXA: In flower or fruit,

Downy Serviceberry is distinctive. Its leaves resemble some species of *Prunus*, although its smooth gray bark is characteristic.

HABITAT: Downy Serviceberry occurs as an understory tree in mesic forests, rocky slopes, and pine stands throughout the State.

ECONOMIC, ORNAMENTAL AND OTHER USES: Downy Serviceberry is very showy when in bloom. It flowers earlier than most other trees, prior to leaf emergence. It is adaptable to a wide range of site conditions including partial shade or full sun and is available as a horticultural specimen by many nurseries.

Crataegus–Hawthorns

DESCRIPTION: *Crataegus* is a large genus of woody plants and one of the most difficult taxonomically. Much controversy exists as to the number and rank of the taxa, apparently due to widespread hybridization and apomixis. They are small trees or shrubs with simple, deciduous, alternately arranged leaves. Leaf margins serrate, dentate or lobed. Branchlets rigid, often zigzag and usually armed with stout unbranched thorns. Flowers produced early in the season, borne singly or in clusters on short shoots. Flowers bisexual, radially symmetrial, pinkish to white with 5 petals and 5 sepals. Stamens numerous, 5–25, styles 1–5 and separate. The fruits are small, apple-like pomes, containing 1–5 one-seeded nutlets. The winter terminal buds are rounded and dark. Because of the complexity of this group and the difficulty in distinguishing the numerous species, we do not include a key to species, but include photographs which indicate a diversity of leaf shapes found in the genus. Members of this genus are found in many habitats, from swamps to upland slopes, to fence rows and other disturbed sites. Many taxa have ornamental potential for their flowers or fruits and their twisted, scraggly form or reddish flaking bark, but all are subject to rust diseases. The fleshy fruits are eaten by many songbirds and rodents. Figures 231, 232, 233.

Malus–Apples

SUMMER KEY TO SPECIES OF *MALUS*

1. Some leaves with crenate margins, apex blunt to acute . . . .
. . . . *M. angustifolia*
1. All leaves serrate, apex usually acuminate . . . . *M. coronaria*

Malus angustifolia (Aiton) Michaux
Southern Crab Apple

DESCRIPTION: This is a small tree or thicket forming shrub, occasionally 30′ tall with a short trunk and spreading, open crown. It occurs throughout the State, but less abundantly in the Coastal Plain.

Leaves – deciduous, simple, alternate; blades ovate to elliptical, base tapered (those of fertile shoots often basally lobed), apex blunt to broadly tapered, up to 2″ long and ½″ wide, margins of some leaves crenate, others serrate or nearly entire. Figure 234.

Twigs – stiff, brown; hairy when young, becoming glabrous; terminal bud blunt, small, ⅛″ long, bud scales chestnut-brown; vegetative shoots long, straight, reproductive shoots short, often stout and spiny, bearing leaves or leaf scars.

Bark – reddish brown, thin, scaly.

Flowers – perfect; pink, petals 5, about 1″ wide; fragrant; produced in clusters on spur shoots; appearing as leaves unfurl in early spring. Figure 235.

Fruit – pome, yellowish green, about 1½″ in diameter, usually broader than long, very sour to taste; maturing in late summer or autumn. Figure 236.

RECOGNITION DIFFICULTIES WITH OTHER TAXA: Southern Crab Apple somewhat resembles Sweet Crab Apple. However, the leaf base of Sweet Crab Apple is rounded, the leaf tip is acuminate, and the blade is 2 times (or less) as long as wide.

HABITAT: Southern Crab Apple is found on moist soils along streams and slopes, along fence rows and in old fields. It often forms thickets.

ECONOMIC, ORNAMENTAL AND OTHER USES: The tart fruit is used to make jellies. The wood is commercially unimportant, but is very hard and has been used for knife and implement handles. Southern Crab Apple is frequently planted as an ornamental because of its exceptionally fragrant flowers. The fruits are consumed by deer, foxes, raccoons, squirrels, and turkeys.

Malus coronaria L.
Sweet Crab Apple

DESCRIPTION: This is a small, slow-growing, short-lived tree which occurs infrequently in Georgia mostly in the Blue Ridge Mountains.

Leaves – deciduous, simple, alternate; blades ovate, base rounded, apex acuminate, up to 3½" long, margins serrate or doubly serrate; pubescent when young, becoming glabrous.

Twigs – stout, reddish brown, hairy; terminal bud blunt, ⅛" long, scales reddish; sharp pointed spur shoots bearing leaves or distinct leaf scars.

Bark – reddish brown, lightly fissured and scaly.

Flower – perfect; about 1½" in diameter, white or pink, petals 5; borne on long stalk in clusters on short shoots; appearing in late spring when the leaves have unfurled.

Fruit – pome, yellow-green, 1¼" across; long stalked; maturing in late summer.

RECOGNITION DIFFICULTIES WITH OTHER TAXA: See description of *M. angustifolia.*

HABITAT: This species occurs on moist soils of upland forests, particularly at higher elevations in the mountains of Georgia.

ECONOMIC, ORNAMENTAL AND OTHER USES: In its more northern range, the wood is utilized for tools and as firewood. Sweet Crab Apple is often planted as an ornamental for its showy blossoms. The fruits are eaten by numerous species of birds, and are used for jellies and cider.

Prunus–Cherries

SUMMER KEY TO SPECIES OF *PRUNUS*
(Note: When flowers are present and developing leaves are not, *P. angustifolia* and *P. umbellata* cannot be reliably separated.)
1. Leaves evergreen . . . . *P. caroliniana*
1. Leaves deciduous 2
   2. Plant in flower 3
      3. Flowers in racemes; branches lacking spur shoots . . . *P. serotina*
      3. Flowers in umbels; branches with spur shoots 4

4. Terminal bud present................... *P. pensylvanica*
4. Terminal bud absent.............................. 5
   5. Flowers appearing as leaves emerge; flowers 1" in diameter; bark scaly....................... *P. americana*
   5. Flowers appearing prior to leaf emergence; flowers about ½" in diameter; bark not scaly.... *P. angustifolia* or ....*P. umbellata*
2. Plant not in flower....................................... 6
  6. Terminal bud present; fruits less than ½" in diameter 7
    7. Leaf apex long acuminate, bases rounded; fruits bright red, borne in umbels...................... *P. pensylvanica*
    7. Leaf apex acute, base tapered; fruits blackish, in racemes ... .*P. serotina*
  6. Terminal bud lacking; fruits ½" or more in diameter 8
    8. Petioles with round glands near the base of blade; teeth gland tipped.......................... *P. angustifolia*
    8. Leaves not as above 9
      9. Leaves abruptly acuminate, usually doubly serrate... ....*P. americana*
      9. Leaves acute or gradually acuminate, finely serrate..... ....*P. umbellata*

Prunus americana Marshall

American Plum

DESCRIPTION: American Plum is a small tree, generally not exceeding 30' in height, often forming thickets. In Georgia, this species occurs sporadically in the Blue Ridge mountains, Piedmont, and Ridge and Valley. In the Coastal Plain it is restricted to counties in the southwestern corner of the State.

Leaves – deciduous, simple, alternate; blades elliptical, tips abruptly acuminate, bases tapered or rounded, up to 4" long and 2" wide, margins finely serrate, usually doubly serrate. Figure 237.

Twigs – rigid, reddish brown, glossy; terminal bud absent; lateral buds about ¼" long, pointed; bud scales brownish; with spur shoots bearing flowers, spiny at tips.

Bark – reddish brown, thin, smooth but breaking into shaggy dark brown plates.

Flowers – perfect; about 1" in diameter; white, petals 5, fragrant; 2–5 flowers borne in umbels; appearing before or with the leaves. Figure 237.

Fruit – drupes, tough, red skin, nearly globose, about 1" in diameter; juicy and edible, but sour; maturing in summer.

RECOGNITION DIFFICULTIES WITH OTHER TAXA: American Plum can usually be distinguished from Chickasaw Plum and Flatwoods Plum by its larger, deeper serrate leaves. The flowers of American Plum are larger than those of the other two species. The leaves have acuminate tips rather than acute. In winter condition, American Plum cannot be easily separated from the other plum species.

HABITAT: This species occurs on rocky or sandy soils along forest edges, fence rows, and in old fields.

ECONOMIC, ORNAMENTAL AND OTHER USES: American Plum has been cultivated as an orchard tree and also as an ornamental for its showy flowers. The wood is commercially unimportant. The fruit is valuable as a food source for wildlife and often used for jellies or preserves. Several cultivars, which have improved fruit, have been developed for home use.

Prunus angustifolia Marshall
Chickasaw Plum

DESCRIPTION: Chickasaw Plum is a small tree, or more often a thicket forming shrub, commonly with thorny stems. This species is fast growing and short-lived, and is scattered throughout the State.

Leaves – deciduous, simple, alternate; blades with acute tips, up to 3" long, and 1" wide, but can be much smaller, often the edges curling upward, margins finely serrate, each tooth with a tiny red gland on tip; upper surfaces glabrous; lower surfaces glabrous or sparsely pubescent; petioles with glands at the base of the leaf. Figure 238.

Twigs – slender, red when young, becoming dull with age; glossy; terminal buds false.

Bark – dark reddish brown, slightly furrowed, scaly.

Flowers – perfect; ⅓–½" in diameter, white, petals 5; 2–4 borne in umbels; appearing before the leaves emerge in early spring. Figure 239.

Fruit – drupes, yellow or red, nearly round, ½–¾" across, glaucous; edible, large stone; maturing in summer. Figure 238.

RECOGNITION DIFFICULTIES WITH OTHER TAXA: Chickasaw Plum can be distinguished from the other two native plums by its mature leaves which are glandular tipped on the marginal teeth. In flower,

Chickasaw Plum is difficult to separate from Flatwoods Plum, but it most commonly forms a thicket, whereas Flatwoods Plum is usually a single stemmed shrub or small tree.

HABITAT: Chickasaw Plum is common along fence rows, old fields, roadsides, sand dunes and other open or disturbed sites throughout the State.

ECONOMIC, ORNAMENTAL AND OTHER USES: The wood of Chicksaw Plum is of little commercial value. The species has been utilized for erosion control due to its thicket forming habit. This plum was apparently brought from the Southwest to the southeastern states by the Chickasaw Indians and cultivated for its tasty fruit long before arrival of the colonists. It is still eaten fresh and used for jellies and jams. It is eaten by deer, bears, raccoons, squirrels and birds.

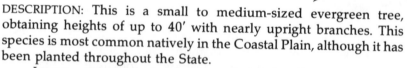

Prunus caroliniana (Miller) Aiton
Carolina Laurel Cherry

DESCRIPTION: This is a small to medium-sized evergreen tree, obtaining heights of up to 40' with nearly upright branches. This species is most common natively in the Coastal Plain, although it has been planted throughout the State.

Leaves – evergreen, simple, alternate; blades elliptical, 2–5" long and ½–1½" wide, margins nearly entire with occasional bristle tip; upper surfaces glossy, dark green; aromatic when crushed. Figures 240, 241.

Twigs – slender, greenish, becoming gray with age; terminal bud pointed, scales reddish brown; leaf scar with 3 bundle scars.

Bark – gray, thin, smooth when young, becoming darker, fissured and scaly with age.

Flowers – perfect; small, white, petals 5; borne in racemes in axils of leaves; appearing early spring. Figure 240.

Fruit – drupe, shiny black, about ½" long, oval, tip rounded to pointed; dry; maturing in fall, often persistent until following growing season. Figure 241.

RECOGNITION DIFFICULTIES WITH OTHER TAXA: Carolina Laurel Cherry is distinctive by its evergreen, shiny elliptical leaves, black, dry, persistent fruit and gray bark with horizontal lenticels.

HABITAT: This species is common in thickets, low woods, old fields and maritime forests, predominantly in the Coastal Plain. It often naturalizes from ornamental plantings.

ECONOMIC, ORNAMENTAL AND OTHER USES: *Prunus caroliniana* is a handsome, hardy tree which is a popular ornamental. Dwarfed cultivars are used in low plantings. Injured and wilted leaves contain hydrocyanic acid, which can be fatal if ingested by humans or most mammals. Young leaves are browsed by deer with no problems. The fruits can be poisonous to children.

Prunus pensylvanica L. f.

Pin Cherry, Fire Cherry

DESCRIPTION: Pin Cherry is a small tree, rarely exceeding 40' in height. It is at the southern limit of its range in Georgia where it is restricted to higher elevations of the Blue Ridge Mountains.

Leaves – deciduous, simple, alternate; blades lance-shaped to scythe-shaped, apex long acuminate, base rounded, margins finely serrate; upper surfaces shiny; both surfaces glabrous. Figure 242.

Twigs – slender, red, shiny, with spur shoots, lenticels orange, conspicuous; terminal bud ovate, pointed, red-brown scales, ciliate on margin; buds clustered near end of twig; leaf scar with 3 bundle scars.

Bark – gray to dark reddish brown, with distinct horizontal lenticels, smooth, but fissuring and scaling into broad plates that are easy to peel off. Figure 243.

Flowers – perfect; white, petals 5, less than ½" in diameter; borne in umbels of 4–5 flowers; appearing in spring as leaves expand. Figure 242.

Fruit – drupe, bright red, nearly round, about ¼" in diameter; sour; maturing in late summer to early autumn. Figure 244.

RECOGNITION DIFFICULTIES WITH OTHER TAXA: Pin Cherry most closely resembles Black Cherry, *Prunus serotina*, the leaves of which are highly variable, particularly in the mountains. However, the leaves of Black Cherry have a pubescent midrib on the lower surface while those of Pin Cherry are glabrous. The twigs of Pin Cherry are bright red, with buds clustered at the tips. The flowers are borne in umbels whereas, those of Black Cherry are borne in racemes. The bark of each is distinctly different.

HABITAT: Pin Cherry is restricted in Georgia to a few northeastern mountainous counties. It occurs on moist, open or burned areas at higher elevations in the Southeast. It is frequent below the summit of Brasstown Bald in Union County.

ECONOMIC, ORNAMENTAL AND OTHER USES: Pin Cherry is harvested for fuel wood where abundant. The fruits are consumed by wildlife and birds.

Prunus serotina Ehrh.

Black Cherry

DESCRIPTION: Black Cherry is a medium-sized to large, rapidly growing tree with ascending branches, reaching 80–90' tall and up to 3' in diameter. Black Cherry occurs throughout the State.

Leaves – deciduous, simple, alternate; blades variable, elliptical to lance-shaped, base rounded, apex short-acuminate, 2–6" long, 1–1 ½" wide, margins finely toothed, the tip of each tooth reddish; upper surfaces shiny and glabrous; lower surfaces with dense hairs along the midrib; glands on the petioles near the leaf base. Figures 245, 247.

Twigs – slender, turning reddish brown, smooth; terminal buds blunt or pointed, bud scales chestnut colored; leaf scar with 3 bundle scars.

Bark – reddish brown, thin, smooth, lenticels horizontal and conspicuous when young, becoming fissured with thin, scaly plates, dark reddish black; inner bark reddish brown, aromatic and bitter. Figure 246.

Flowers – perfect; white, small; borne in racemes, 3–6" long, terminally or in leaf axils of new shoots; appearing as the leaves are developing in early spring. Figure 245.

Fruit – drupes, dark purple to black, oval, about ⅓" in diameter; bitter tasting; maturing throughout the summer and into autumn. Figure 247.

RECOGNITION DIFFICULTIES WITH OTHER TAXA: See discussion of *P. pensylvanica*. A variety of Black Cherry, *P. serotina* var. *alabamensis* (C. Mohr) Little, has leaves that are pubescent over the lower blade, blunt tips, and pubescent flowering stalks. It occurs predominantly in the western part of Georgia, but occasionally in the central portion of the Coastal Plain. It is considered by some authorities as a separate species because it leafs out about 2 weeks later than Black Cherry and holds its leaves much longer. Figure 248, leaves of *P. serotina* var. *alabamensis* C. Mohr.

HABITAT: Black Cherry is found on a wide array of sites along roadsides, fence rows and deciduous forests throughout the State. Large trees are mostly restricted to rich moist hardwood forests.

ECONOMIC, ORNAMENTAL AND OTHER USES: The wood of Black Cherry is very valuable for furniture manufacturing because of its rich color and close-grained structure. It is of much commercial importance in more northern parts of its range. The fruit, although bitter, is edible and it is often used in wine making, flavoring for liqueurs and brandies, jellies or preserves. It is also consumed in large quantities by wildlife and birds. Wild Cherry cough syrup is made from extracts of the inner bark. The wilted leaves and twigs contain hydrocyanic acid which is harmful or fatal if ingested in large amounts by livestock or animals. Deer and other mammals browse freely on the foliage.

Prunus umbellata Elliott
Flatwoods Plum, Hog Plum

DESCRIPTION: *Prunus umbellata* is a small tree, often with a crooked trunk. It seldom attains heights greater than 20'. The flowers and leaves are similar to *P. angustifolia*; however, the leaves of *P. umbellata* lack small red glands on the marginal teeth. The fruit is small, about ¼" across, red-dark purple or black with thick sour pulp, maturing late summer. *Prunus umbellata* usually occurs as single scattered trees whereas, *P. angustifolia* often forms thickets. It occurs throughout the Piedmont and Coastal Plain. Figure 249, leaves, fruit; Figure 250, flower.

Sorbus–Mountain-Ash

Sorbus americana Marshall
[*Pyrus americana* (Marshall) DC.]
American Mountain-Ash

DESCRIPTION: American Mountain-Ash is a small tree, up to 30' tall with a straight trunk, up to 8–10" in diameter. In Georgia, this species is found only at higher elevations in the Blue Ridge Mountains.

Leaves – deciduous, pinnately compound, alternate; blade 6–10" long; leaflets 9–17, opposite, 1½–3½" long, over 3 times as long as broad, margins toothed; upper surfaces glabrous, dark green; lower surfaces pubescent or glabrous, whitish; petiole nearly 3" long, grooved, reddish; stipules quite small and appressed to the petiole. Figure 251.

Twigs – stout, reddish brown, pubescent when young, becoming smooth, lenticels elongated, conspicuous; terminal bud often curved at the tip, about ¾" long, bud scales reddish, resinous, inner scales densely hairy; lateral buds about ¼" long; leaf scars crescent to U-shaped, distinctly elevated; bundle scars usually 5; pith large.

Bark – gray, thin, gradually becoming scaly, aromatic if bruised.

Flowers – perfect; small, less than ⅛" in diameter, white, petals 5, stamen numerous; borne in dense, compound corymbs 3–5" across; appearing June–July. Figure 252.

Fruit – pome, orange-red, round or oval, about ¼" in diameter; persistent through winter; maturing late summer through autumn. Figure 253.

RECOGNITION DIFFICULTIES WITH OTHER TAXA: *Sorbus americana* should be very distinctive due to its showy, persistent fruits, pinnately compound leaves with red petioles and restricted habitat at high elevations.

HABITAT: American Mountain-Ash is restricted to rocky slopes at high elevations, in Union, Towns, and Rabun counties at the southern limit of its range. Northward, it occurs more abundantly.

ECONOMIC, ORNAMENTAL AND OTHER USES: This species is one of the most striking ornamental trees in our native flora and is often planted for its brightly colored fruit and handsome foliage. The fruit is consumed by many birds, especially grouse, grosbeaks and Cedar Waxwings.

LEGUMINOSAE (FABACEAE)–LEGUME FAMILY

The Leguminosae is one of the three largest families of Angiosperms in the world, comprising some 550 genera and over 13,000 species. There are three subfamilies, sometimes recognized as separate families, including Mimosidae (Mimosaceae) Caesalpinioideae (Caesalpiniaceae), and Papilionoideae (Papilionaceae). These subfamilies are separated by flower morphology. Worldwide, it is one of the most economically important plant families, providing many food crops, fodder, gums, resins, oils and dyes. In addition, members of over 140 genera are cultivated for ornamental purposes. Of the many legume genera found in North America, only four reach tree size in Georgia: *Cercis, Cladrastis, Gleditsia,* and *Robinia.* The leaves of *Cercis* are simple, those of the other genera are pinnately compound. There are several woody species of *Robinia,* but only one reaches tree size. *Cladrastis* and *Cercis* are monotypic, and *Gleditsia* has only two species.

Cercis–Redbud

Cercis canadensis L.

Redbud, Judas Tree

DESCRIPTION: Redbud is a small tree, seldom over 35–40' tall, having a short trunk and numerous upright spreading branches. It occurs throughout the State, but it is more prevalent in the Piedmont and mountains than in the Coastal Plain.

Leaves – deciduous, simple, alternate; blades broad-ovate, base cordate, apex acute, 3–5" in diameter, margins entire, palmately veined; upper surfaces glabrous; lower surfaces pubescent to glabrous; petioles conspicuously swollen at base of leaf and at the node; stipules small, papery. Figure 254.

Twigs – zigzag, slender, light brown to reddish, lenticels small, horizontal; terminal bud absent; lateral buds often superposed, ⅛" or less long, ovoid, 2 scales; leaf scars triangular, fringed at top; bundle scars 2, large.

Bark – dark gray to brown, becoming slightly furrowed and breaking into thin, scaly plates.

Flowers – perfect; petals purplish pink, ½" long; pedicels ⅓–½" long with 4–8 per fascicle; produced on the twig of previous year; appearing in early spring before the leaves. Figure 255.

Fruit – legumes, flat, oblong, 3–4" long; stalked; dark brown; often persistent into winter. Figure 256.

RECOGNITION DIFFICULTIES WITH OTHER TAXA: Redbud is unlike any other species with which it occurs and is easily recognized by the palmately veined, cordate leaves with conspicuous swollen petioles. The purplish pink flowers borne on the leafless twigs are diagnostic. The zigzag twigs with triangular, raised leaf scars fringed at the top, small leaf buds, and persistent flat legumes aid in identification.

HABITAT: Redbud occurs on a wide range of sites, along streams and fertile, moist bottomlands to drier slopes and ridges as an understory species throughout most areas of the State. This species is appreciably abundant in areas with calcareous soils.

ECONOMIC, ORNAMENTAL AND OTHER USES: Redbud is often planted ornamentally for its showy purplish pink flowers which bloom early before the leaves. It grows well in partial shade or sun and is relatively free of serious insects and diseases. Although a legume, the species does not have nitrogen fixing root nodules.

Cladrastis–Yellowwood

Cladrastis kentukea (Dum.-Cours.) Rudd

[*Cladrastis lutea* (Michaux f.) K. Koch]

Yellowwood

DESCRIPTION: This is a medium-sized tree occasionally reaching 50' in height. Yellowwood occurs rarely in the State, only in the Blue Ridge mountains and the Ridge and Valley Province.

Leaves – deciduous, pinnately compound, alternate; 8–12" long; leaflets 7–11, subopposite, elliptic to ovate, 3–4" long, 1½–2" wide, entire; petioles enlarged at base and summit, enclosing bud. Figure 257.

Twigs – slender, zigzag, glabrous; terminal bud absent; lateral buds naked and enclosed in the hollow base of the petiole; bundle scars 3–9.

Bark – light brown to gray; smooth, somewhat resembling the bark of American beech, *Fagus grandifolia* Ehrh.

Flowers – perfect; white, showy, 1–1¼" long, fragrant; inflorescence 4–12" long, drooping; appearing April–May; heavy flowering in alternate years. Figure 258.

Fruit – legumes, thin, flattened, brown, oblong, 3–4" long, similar to that of *Cercis canadensis*; maturing July–August.

RECOGNITION DIFFICULTIES WITH OTHER TAXA: The compound leaves and the smooth bark are distinctive characteristics of Yellowwood. In summer, the compound leaves might be mistaken for *Fraxinus* spp.; however, Yellowwood leaves are alternate and ash leaves are opposite. The smooth bark, in winter could possibly be confused with *Fagus grandifolia*, although *Fagus* has very distinctive elongated winter buds. Terminal buds are lacking in Yellowwood, and the lateral buds are small, naked, and superposed.

HABITAT: Yellowwood occurs on rich, moist sites along streams or in coves, especially on calcareous soil. It is rare in Georgia.

ECONOMIC, ORNAMENTAL AND OTHER USES: The heartwood of *Cladrastris kentukea* is yellow and has been used as a dye. Yellowwood makes an excellent ornamental tree for yard or landscape planting because of its attractive flowers and foliage. Although the species is usually found on calcareous soils, it also grows well on more acid soils in open sun or partial shade. Few serious insect or disease problems have been observed and the tree should receive more attention for ornamental use in the upper Piedmont and mountain regions. Yellowwood is a nitrogen fixing legume.

Gleditsia–Honeylocusts

SUMMER KEY TO SPECIES OF *GLEDITSIA*
Note: Where the ranges of these two species overlap in the Coastal Plain, neither can be easily distinguished in summer or winter condition unless fruit is available.
1. Fruit 8–24" long, elongate, with fleshy pulp between the seeds. . .
   . . . . *G. triacanthos*
1. Fruit 1–2" long, ovate-elliptic, without pulp between the seeds. . .
   . . . . *G. aquatica*

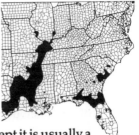

Gleditsia aquatica Marshall

Waterlocust

   Waterlocust closely resembles Honeylocust, except it is usually a smaller tree (see *G. triacanthos*) and can be distinguished by the strikingly different fruit which is a short, obliquely oval legume 1–2" long. In Georgia, this species is confined to wet areas along flood-plains and swamps in the Coastal Plain. Figure 259.

Gleditsia triacanthos L.

Honeylocust

DESCRIPTION: Honeylocust is a medium-sized to large tree, 50–80' tall, 2–3' in diameter, usually with a short, thorny trunk which branches early to form several stout ascending branches and an open, flattened crown. Individual branches of older trees possess irregular contorted shapes and form. Honeylocust is found scattered throughout the State, an extension of its natural range.

Leaves – deciduous, pinnately or bipinnately compound or both, alternate; leaflets about 1″ long and ½″ broad. Figure 260.

Twigs – stout, zigzag, shiny brown, usually with branched, heavy thorns; terminal bud absent; lateral buds minute, often hidden by leaf scar; leaf scar U-shaped with 3 bundle scars.

Bark – gray to black, generally smooth on young trees, becoming fissured to form longitudinal, scaly plates with curved edges on older trees; trunk frequently with numerous clusters of branched, stout, persistent woody thorns. Figure 261.

Flowers – perfect or imperfect, usually male and female on separate twigs; greenish yellow, small, ¼″; clustered in compact racemes; appearing in April–May. Figure 262.

Fruit – legumes, large, heavy, elongate, 8–24″ long; with drying, it forms corkscrew twists; dark brown-black when mature; sweet, pulpy tissue between the seeds, maturing late fall. Figure 263.

RECOGNITION DIFFICULTIES WITH OTHER TAXA: Honeylocust and the closely related Waterlocust can be distinguished best by the fruit. The fruit of Honeylocust is linear-oblong, whereas the fruit of Waterlocust is oval, about 1½″ in diameter and lacks pulp. The Waterlocust is found in moist bottomlands and river swamps of the Coastal Plain. Honeylocust can be distinguished from Black Locust by the once to twice pinnately compound leaves and branched thorns, whereas Black Locust has only once pinnately compound leaves and short, unbranched stipular spines. In winter conditions, Honeylocust can be distinguished by bark differences. Honeylocust has relatively smooth bark broken into long, narrow plates with roughened edges and branched thorns, whereas Black Locust has bark with deeply furrowed prominent, lacy ridges and stipular spines on the twigs.

HABITAT: Honeylocust has become naturalized throughout the State, typically along floodplains and stream banks, but also on drier slopes, in old fields, along roadsides, and in open waste places.

ECONOMIC, ORNAMENTAL AND OTHER USES: The wood of *Gleditsia triacanthos* is hard, strong and durable, hence, it was formerly used for fence posts and railway ties. Today, Honeylocust is planted for windbreaks and hedges. The fruit is also used in making a locust beer. The long, twisted fruits make it an attractive tree, but the stout thorns along the branches and bole are dangerous and undesirable in an ornamental yard or lawn tree. A thornless form, *G. triacanthos* f. *inermis* Schneid, has been described and many thornless cultivars have been developed for ornamental use. These cultivars are often plagued with insect and disease problems. Cultivars have also been genetically selected for heavy pod production for cattle feed. Honeylocust is not a nitrogen fixing legume.

Robinia–Locust

Robinia pseudoacacia L.

Black Locust

DESCRIPTION: This is a medium-sized, short-lived tree, frequently only 40–60' tall, but occasionally reaching over 90' in height, often with forked, twisted or crooked trunks forming a broad, irregular open crown. Originally, Black Locust was confined to the mountainous section of the State, but it has been widely planted and has become naturalized throughout much of the Piedmont.

Leaves – deciduous, pinnately compound, alternate; 8–14" long; 7–21 leaflets, ½–2" long, elliptic or oval, entire; tip blunt or notched, sometimes with short bristle; glabrous; bases of the petiole and bases of the leaflet stalks swollen. Figure 264.

Twigs – zigzag, with stout paired stipular spines at each node, dark brown; terminal bud absent; lateral buds hidden beneath leaf scar.

Bark – gray-brown to almost black, thick, deeply furrowed into prominent lacy or reticulate, ridges. Figure 265.

Flowers – white, showy; dangling in racemes 4–6" long; fragrant; appearing after the leaves in April–May. Figure 266.

Fruit – legumes, brown, 2–4" long, flat; maturing July–November. Figure 267.

RECOGNITION DIFFICULTIES WITH OTHER TAXA: Black Locust might be confused with Honeylocust (See description of *Gleditsia triacanthos*). A shrub species, *Robinia hispida* L., has pink flowers and bristly twigs.

HABITAT: Black Locust is adapted to many habitats from moist mountain slopes to drier, rocky soils. Although native to the mountains, it is widely planted and naturalized throughout the Piedmont. Black Locust is fast growing and usually establishes in early successional areas such as clearcuts and burned areas, and abandoned pastures. Following such disturbances to a site, the tree prolifically root sprouts.

ECONOMIC, ORNAMENTAL AND OTHER USES: Black Locust is a nitrogen fixer and can grow on nutrient poor sites. For this reason, it is often used on reclamation sites for soil improvement and erosion control. The heartwood is very resistant to rot and is frequently used for fence posts and railroad ties. The tree is susceptible to damage and death by the locust borer which mine throughout the twigs, branches and bole. It is not generally recommended for use as an ornamental tree. The fragrant flowers provide excellent bee forage for honey production.

RUTACEAE–RUE FAMILY

Most tree species of the Rutaceae are found in the warmer subtropical or tropical regions of the world. The family is of great horticultural value because of the genus *Citrus*. In Georgia, only three small trees occur naturally; two in the genus *Zanthoxylum* and one in the genus *Ptelea*. Trifoliate Orange, *Poncirus trifoliata* (L.) Raf., an introduced species from China, has escaped from cultivation and become naturalized. In these genera, the leaves are deciduous, alternate and pinnately or trifoliately compound.

Ptelea–Hoptree

Ptelea trifoliata L.
Common Hoptree, Wafer Ash

DESCRIPTION: This is a small tree, sometimes 20–25′ tall, with a slender trunk and broad crown, occurring in scattered localities throughout the State.

Leaves – deciduous, trifoliately compound, (rarely 5-foliate), alternate; 4–7″ long; leaflets sessile, ovate-elliptical, margin wavy-toothed to entire; upper surface of leaflets dark green, glabrous; lower surface pale, glabrous or pubescent; petioles greater than 3″ long; aromatic when crushed; glandular dotted. Figure 268.

Twigs – slender, red-brown, slightly warty, lenticels large, brown, conspicuous; winter terminal buds absent; lateral buds minute, sunken and often covered by petiole or leaf scar; leaf scar U-shaped to shield-shaped; 3 bundle scars; pith white; rank odor when bruised.

Bark – brownish gray, thin, smooth with few thin scales and warty outgrowths.

Flowers – polygamous; greenish-yellow; ¼″ wide; appearing in early spring in terminal clusters.

Fruit – samaras, circular, flattened, winged, almost 1″ wide; in conspicuous pendent clusters; maturing in early autumn and persisting into winter. Figure 269.

RECOGNITION DIFFICULTIES WITH OTHER TAXA: *Ptelea trifoliata* is easily recognized by the aromatic trifoliate leaves and round winged fruit in pendant clusters. The Hoptree is known to occur in the same localities as Bladdernut, *Staphylea trifolia* L., which also has 3 leaflets. Hoptree has alternate leaves and the end leaflet is short stalked, whereas, Bladdernut has opposite leaves, and the end leaflet long stalked. Young seedlings of Hoptree might be mistaken for Poison Ivy, *Toxicodendron radicans* (L.) Kuntze, or Fragrant Sumac, *Rhus aromatica* Aiton. Poison Ivy is distinctive by its visible hairy buds, and a long stalked terminal leaflet. Although Fragrant Sumac has a short stalked terminal leaflet and hidden buds, it can be distinguished from Hoptree seedlings by the shallow round toothed leaflets, the circular bundle scars, and pleasantly aromatic leaves when crushed. The twigs of the exotic Trifoliate Orange have stout thorns, the fruit is an orange-like, sour berry, and it is usually a shrub.

HABITAT: Hoptree usually occurs on dry, rocky uplands and slopes around margins of woods or as a small understory tree. It is infrequent, but widely scattered throughout the State.

ECONOMIC, ORNAMENTAL AND OTHER USES: Hoptree is occasionally used as an ornamental because of its interesting appearance and site adaptability, but it has found more popularity in England among land-scape gardeners than at home. The bitter, aromatic fruit has reportedly been used as a substitute for hops in brewing beer, and the bark has been brewed to make bitters in the home preparation of tonics.

Zanthoxylum–Prickly-ashes

SUMMER KEY TO SPECIES OF *ZANTHOXYLUM*
1. Leaflets pubescent; flowers in small axillary clusters; bark lacking conical knobs and spines .... *Z. americanum*
1. Leaflets glabrous; flowers in terminal clusters; bark with conical knobs and spines .... *Z. clava-herculis*

Zanthoxylum americanum Miller
Prickly-ash, Toothache-tree

DESCRIPTION: Prickly-ash is seldom more than a large shrub, but it occasionally reaches 20–25′ in height. More often, it forms much branched, dense thickets in the understory. This species is recorded from only a few counties in Georgia in the Piedmont and upper Coastal Plain.

Leaves – deciduous, once-pinnately compound, alternate; 5–10" long, rachis usually spiny; leaflets 7–13, elliptical; tips acute or acuminate, finely and shallowly toothed, 1–2" long; pubescent on both sides. Figure 270.

Twigs – grayish brown, armed with spines, usually two per node; terminal and lateral buds reddish brown, hairy, superposed; leaf scars triangular to rounded with three bundle scars; bruised twigs with citrus odor.

Bark – gray to brown, thin, smooth; aromatic, with weak lemon odor.

Flowers – dioecious; petals yellow-green, less than ¼" wide; in small axillary clusters; appearing in spring before leaves.

Fruit – follicles, small, reddish brown, less than ¼", maturing in late summer and splitting open; seeds lustrous black.

RECOGNITION DIFFICULTIES WITH OTHER TAXA: Prickly-ash flowers occur in small axillary clusters while those of Hercules' Club are in large terminal clusters. The leaflets are pubescent rather than glabrous, and the buds are reddish-brown and hairy rather than black to dark brown and smooth as in the latter. Devil's-walkingstick, *Aralia spinosa*, has 2–3 pinnately compound leaves and the stem is armed with prickles.

HABITAT: Prickly-ash occurs in dry, open, upland deciduous woods.

ECONOMIC, ORNAMENTAL AND OTHER USES: Similar to its close relative, *Z. clava-herculis*, Prickly-ash contains the alkaloid, xantholin. Both species were formerly used medicinally to numb the mouth, either with an extract from the fruit or by chewing the inner bark.

Zanthoxylum clava-herculis L.

Hercules'-club, Toothache-tree

DESCRIPTION: This species is a small tree, or occasionally, a shrub 20–30' tall, 8–10" in diameter. It is restricted to coastal counties and a few counties in the southwestern part of the State near the Florida boundary.

Leaves – tardily deciduous, once-pinnately compound, alternate; rachis spiny, leaflets leathery, 5–19, narrowly ovate, pointed at tip, 1½–2½" long, shallowly toothed with glands inset from the notches of the teeth; upper surface shiny, lower surface essentially glabrous, glandular dotted; citrus odor when crushed. Figure 271.

Twigs – brown, armed with scattered, stout spines; terminal and lateral buds small, globose, smooth, dark brown-black; leaf scars rounded or triangular; bundle scars 3; citrus odor when broken.

Bark – light to medium gray, thin, with conspicuous corky, dome-like outgrowths terminating in a sharp prickle that eventually sloughs, the corky outgrowth continuing to widen at base as tree increases in girth. Figure 272.

Flowers – dioecious or polygamous; petals small, greenish yellow, about ¼" wide; in terminal clusters; appearing early spring.

Fruit – follicles, reddish brown, ¼" long; seeds black, lustrous, suspended by a thread; appearing in early summer. Figure 273.

RECOGNITION DIFFICULTIES WITH OTHER TAXA: Hercules'-club is rather distinct because of the pronounced corky outgrowths and stout spines along the trunk, and by the presence of flowers in large terminal panicles. Also, the leaflets in Hercules'-club are glabrous, and shiny green above; whereas those in *Z. americanum* are pubescent on both surfaces and dark, dull green above. *Aralia spinosa* L., another armed, small tree, has exceptionally large, bipinnately compound leaves up to 4' long and 3' wide, which will distinguish it from either of the species of *Zanthoxylum*.

HABITAT: *Zanthoxylum clava-herculis* occurs on sand dunes and maritime forests of the Coastal Plain and sandy bluffs along streams and rivers.

ECONOMIC, ORNAMENTAL AND OTHER USES: The wood of this species has no commercial value. Both species of *Zanthoxylum* are referred to as Toothache-tree due to alkaloids which have a numbing effect when parts of the plant is chewed. Twigs from these plants were reportedly used medicinally by early settlers for relief from toothaches.

ANACARDIACEAE–CASHEW FAMILY

The Anacardiaceae is a large family of trees, shrubs and vines found mainly in warmer regions of the world, but extending into the north temperate zones. Many drugs, dyes, waxes and tannins are obtained from juices or resinous sap contained in the stem and bark. Depending on the species, the cut stems exude either a white milky sap or a clear fluid which quickly turns black upon exposure to air. In some species, the sap is highly toxic and irritating to the skin as in Poison Sumac, *Toxicodendron vernix* (L.) Kuntze, or Poison Ivy, *T. radicans* L. Both these species are widespread throughout Georgia and eastern North America. Chinese lacquer is obtained from the poisonous sap of *Rhus verniciflua* Stokes. Pistachio nuts come from plants in the genus *Pistacia*. Cashew nuts are from the tropical American species, *Anacardium occidentale* L. The tropical Mango fruit is produced by *Mangifera indica* L. A few species in this family are prized for their heavy and colorful wood, including Quebracho wood, *Schinopsis quebracho-colorado* (Schldl.) F. Barkley & T. Meyer, from South America. This species also yields large amounts of tannin. *Schinus molle* L., Peppertree, introduced into Florida, has now become a pest.

In Georgia, only five native arborescent species occur, three in the genus *Rhus*, one in the genus *Toxicodendron*, and one in the genus *Cotinus*, none of which are of economic importance today. *Toxicodendron vernix* should be avoided because of its highly toxic sap which can cause quite serious skin irritation that may require medical attention.

Cotinus–Smoketree

Cotinus obovatus Raf.

Smoketree

DESCRIPTION: This is a small tree or large shrub occasionally 25–30' tall, usually with a short trunk dividing into several wide-spreading branches. The hairy, filamentous fruit stalks give the plant a smokey appearance. It is a rare tree in Georgia, known from a single locality on Pigeon Mountain in the northwestern part of the State.

Leaves – deciduous, simple, alternate; blades obovate, blunt-tipped or notched, 2–6" long, up to 3½" wide, entire or slightly wavy margins; dark green above; pubescent beneath.

Twigs – slender, purplish when young, grayish with age, prominent corky lenticels; terminal and lateral buds small, pointed, hairy, reddish scales; leaf scars with minute folds; fruity-aromatic sap when crushed.

Bark – grayish brown, thin, broken into oblong scales.

Flowers – plants usually dioecious, often sterile; small, greenish-yellow; occurring in large open terminal clusters 5–6" long, on long stalks covered with short purplish or brown hairs; appearing in early spring.

Fruit – drupes, small, ¼" long, rounded to elongate flattened, dry; stalks feathery, showy, slender; maturing late summer.

RECOGNITION DIFFICULTIES WITH OTHER TAXA: Smoketree is distinctive with its wide, blunt-tipped leaves, yellow odorous twigs, and feathery sprays of fruits.

HABITAT: Smoketree is restricted to limestone soils in ravines or rocky uplands. It is recorded in Georgia only on Pigeon Mountain.

ECONOMIC, ORNAMENTAL AND OTHER USES: The wood of Smoketree is durable, but is not utilized because of its scarcity. A European relative, *C. coggygria* Scop., is often planted as an ornamental because of its showy orange-scarlet foliage in autumn and the smokey appearing fruit stalks.

Rhus–Sumacs

SUMMER KEY TO SPECIES OF *RHUS*
1. Leaf rachis winged.................................. *R. copallina*
1. Leaf rachis not winged 2
    2. Twigs and petioles velvety pubescent .... *R. typhina*
    2. Twigs and petioles glabrous and glaucous........... *R. glabra*

Rhus copallina L.

Winged Sumac, Dwarf Sumac,
Shining Sumac

DESCRIPTION: Winged Sumac becomes a small tree 20–25' tall, with a short trunk and slender spreading branches. It frequently sprouts from lateral roots to form dense clumps of compact trees. It occurs throughout the State.

    Leaves – deciduous, pinnately compound, alternate; 8–12" long; rachis with green marginal wings between the leaflets; leaflets oblong-lanceolate, 1–2" long, margins entire; upper surfaces dark green, shiny; lower surfaces pale, pubescent; bright red color in autumn. Figures 274, 276.

    Twigs – slender to moderate, green to reddish brown, pubescent, lenticels conspicuous, elongated, reddish; terminal bud absent; winter lateral buds globose, hairy, naked; leaf scars broadly crescent-shaped; sap watery.

    Bark – reddish brown, thin, conspicuous, horizontally elongated lenticels, becoming warty with age and dividing into thin scaly plates. Figure 275.

    Flowers – Dioecious or polygamous; greenish white, small; in terminal, pubescent panicles; appearing early summer. Plants functionally dioecious since pistils of polygamous flowers abort. The panicles of staminate plants are more open than panicles of pistillate plants. Figure 274, pistillate flowers.

Fruit – drupes, reddish brown, ovoid, ⅛" in diameter; in compact erect or drooping panicles; maturing in fall and often persisting through winter. Figure 276.

RECOGNITION DIFFICULTIES WITH OTHER TAXA: *Rhus copallina* resembles *R. glabra*, but can easily be distinguished by its winged leaf rachis and dark green shining leaflets. In winter, the slender twigs and broad crescent-shaped leaf scars of *R. copallina* distinguish it from *R. glabra*, which has stouter twigs and horseshoe-shaped leaf scars.

HABITAT: Winged Sumac often occurs in dense thickets in old fields, around borders of woods, roadsides, powerlines, or other open areas, on well-drained soils throughout the State. It is shade intolerant, persisting in the understory only until crown closure.

ECONOMIC, ORNAMENTAL AND OTHER USES: *Rhus copallina* possesses much potential as an ornamental individual specimen tree on many upland dry sites throughout the State. The dark green, shining foliage, winged rachis of the leaves, brilliant red autumn coloration, and its open, irregular branching habit make it an attractive landscape plant. The fresh drupes have a lemony taste and can be used to make a pinkish lemonade-type beverage. The bark and leaves have been used as a local source of tannin for tanning leather.

Rhus glabra L.
Smooth Sumac

DESCRIPTION: Smooth Sumac is usually a large shrub, but occasionally it reaches tree size, up to 20' tall. It commonly reproduces from shallow horizontal roots and forms dense thickets. It is common in the mountains and Piedmont of Georgia and infrequently occurs in the Coastal Plain.

Leaves – deciduous, pinnately compound, alternate; 12–24" long; leaflets serrate, 2–4" long and numerous; upper surfaces dark green; lower surfaces with waxy white bloom; base of petiole encloses an axillary bud. Figure 277.

Twigs – stout, glabrous, covered with white bloom, somewhat flattened; terminal bud absent; lateral buds silvery to tan pubescent; leaf scars horseshoe-shaped, nearly encircling bud; pith large, orange-brown; sap milky, sticky.

Bark – brown, thin, smooth with conspicuous horizontally elongated lenticels, becoming slightly scaly with age.

Flowers – similar to *R. copallina*, except the panicles are usually larger; staminate and perfect panicles more open, often 8–12" long, pistillate panicles compact and up to 12" in length.

Fruit – drupes, dark to brilliant red, about ⅛" in diameter; covered with short, sticky red hairs; numerous in compact clusters, 8–12" long; maturing in late summer, persistent during winter. Figure 278.

RECOGNITION DIFFICULTIES WITH OTHER TAXA: See *R. copallina* for comparison. *Rhus glabra* has glaucous twigs, whereas *R. typhina* has velvety pubescent twigs. Also, the fruit of *R. glabra* forms a broader panicle than does *R. typhina*.

HABITAT: Smooth Sumac quickly invades old fields or openings in the forest after disturbances such as timber harvests or fire. The species occurs throughout the mountains and Piedmont on a wide diversity of well-drained, drier sites. It is shade intolerant and seldom occurs in the understory of closed forest canopies.

ECONOMIC, ORNAMENTAL AND OTHER USES: Smooth Sumac has little value as an ornamental plant. It has a short life span and is susceptible to storm damage because of its large leaves and brittle branches. However, this species is often kept in natural openings as an ornamental because of its brilliant autumn coloration of foliage and fruit. The fruit is eaten by game and song birds. It is browsed by deer and the bark is often eaten by small mammals during winter.

Rhus typhina L.

Staghorn Sumac

DESCRIPTION: Staghorn Sumac is a tall shrub or small tree, documented in Georgia from only one location near the crest of Yonah Mountain in White County.

Leaves – deciduous, pinnately compound, alternate; 12–24" long; leaflet margins serrate; rachis pubescent; upper surfaces dark green; lower surfaces with whitish bloom; turning bright orange to purple in autumn. Figure 279.

Twigs – very stout, densely, velvety hairy; terminal bud absent; lateral buds small, conical, covered with matted woolly hairs; buds nearly surrounded by broad U-shaped leaf scar; sap milky.

Bark – dark brown, thin, smooth with numerous horizontally elongated lenticels, becoming slightly scaly on the lower, older portion of the trunk.

Flowers – similar to other *Rhus* species.

Fruit – drupes, dark red, about 3/16" in diameter; dark red woolly pubescent; occurring in upright clusters, up to 12" long; maturing in late summer and autumn, persistent during winter.

RECOGNITION DIFFICULTIES WITH OTHER TAXA: Staghorn Sumac is easily separated from *R. copallina* and *R. glabra* by its deep reddish brown twigs densely covered with long russet-colored hairs.

HABITAT: This species is recorded from open, dry, rocky soils only at one locality in Georgia, Yonah Mountain in White County.

ECONOMIC, ORNAMENTAL AND OTHER USES: Staghorn Sumac is sometimes used as an ornamental for its brilliant, orange-red foliage in autumn and its interesting, coarse branching habit in winter. The stout, woolly twigs somewhat resemble deer antlers in their "velvet stage," hence the common name, Staghorn Sumac. Its use as an ornamental in Georgia should probably be restricted to the upper Piedmont and mountainous sections.

Toxicodendron–Poison Sumac

Toxicodendron vernix (L.) Kuntze

(*Rhus vernix* L.)

Poison Sumac, Thunderwood

DESCRIPTION: Poison Sumac is a shrub or small tree 25–30' in height and is found in scattered localities throughout the State.

Leaves – deciduous, pinnately compound, alternate, 8–13" long; leaflets opposite, 7–15, elliptic or ovate, margins entire; turning orange to bright red in autumn. Figure 280.

Twigs – stout, smooth, reddish; terminal winter bud present with 2 purple scales; leaf scars heart-shaped to triangular, not surrounding the buds; clear sap which turns black upon exposure to air.

Bark – gray to brown, smooth to slightly fissured, prominent raised lenticels similar to those of *Rhus glabra* and *R. copallina*; occasionally streaked with black where colorless, toxic sap has exuded from wounds or fissures and oxidized upon exposure to air. Figure 281, note black sap exudates.

Flowers – dioecious or polygamous; petals greenish yellow, small, ⅛" long; in drooping panicles from leaf axils, 8–10" long; appearing early summer.

Fruit – drupes, whitish, ¼" in diameter, smooth; in drooping branched clusters, often persisting into winter. Figure 282, drupes turn creamy white in late fall.

RECOGNITION DIFFICULTIES WITH OTHER TAXA: The pinnately compound leaves of Poison Sumac are most often mistaken for those of young *Fraxinus* species. However, the leaves (*not* leaflets) are alternately arranged along the twig, not opposite as in the ashes. The drooping clusters of green, berry-like drupes in summer turn a whitish color in fall. *Note*: If the plant has pinnately compound, *alternate* leaves, and *opposite* leaflets with smooth margins—avoid it!

HABITAT: This species is frequent in swamps and low woods of the Coastal Plain and occasional in wet, poorly drained bogs or hillside seepages in the Piedmont. It occurs less frequently in the mountains.

ECONOMIC, ORNAMENTAL AND OTHER USES: Poison Sumac is one of the most toxic plants in North America. The clear sap causes severe skin inflammation. Lesions appear one or two days following contact. Although the crushed fruit is highly toxic to most persons, it is apparently nontoxic to birds and small mammals. *Note*: The smoke should be avoided from burning leaves or twigs of this species because the volatile oil from the sap during combustion is highly toxic to the skin.

CYRILLACEAE–CYRILLA FAMILY

The Cyrillaceae is an American family consisting of three genera of deciduous or evergreen shrubs or small trees. Two of these genera, *Cliftonia* and *Cyrilla*, are monotypic and are indigenous to the southeastern United States. The family is of little economic importance; however, both of our native species are frequently cultivated as ornamental specimens.

Cliftonia–Cliftonia

Cliftonia monophylla (Lam.) Britton ex Sarg.

Titi, Buckwheat-tree

DESCRIPTION: This is a small evergreen tree or thicket-forming shrub with short, often crooked trunks producing many branches. It is widely distributed on moist to wet sites throughout the lower Coastal Plain in Georgia.

Leaves – evergreen, simple, alternate; blades leathery, elliptic to oblanceolate, tips blunt, 1–2" long, ½–¾" wide, margins entire, lateral veins pronounced; upper surfaces dark green and shiny; lower surfaces whitish, glabrous, glandular dotted; nearly sessile. Figures 283, 284.

Twigs – slender, numerous, remotely 3-angled, reddish brown occasionally with a grayish bloom; terminal buds ½" long; lateral buds ovoid, smaller, appressed; leaf scars shield-shaped; single bundle scar.

Bark – dark reddish brown, thin, weakly fissured to form small, persistent, somewhat elongated scales.

Flowers – perfect; ¼" wide; white or light pink, 5–8 petals, fragrant; sepals unequal; in terminal racemes; appearing early spring. Figure 283.

Fruit – nut-like drupe, winged, shiny yellow, ¼" long, elliptical, borne in showy clusters 1½–2½" long; maturing in late summer, turning brown and persisting through winter. Figure 284.

RECOGNITION DIFFICULTIES WITH OTHER TAXA: The leathery, evergreen leaves with pronounced marginal veins and the persistent fruit are distinctive characteristics of Titi which should not be confused with other species.

HABITAT: Titi is common in many wet areas, along frequently inundated flood plains, bayheads, and edges of swamps.

ECONOMIC, ORNAMENTAL AND OTHER USES: Titi is of no economic importance, but it is occasionally cultivated as a rather showy and fragrant ornamental plant with interesting, persistent fruit clusters and dense evergreen foliage.

Cyrilla–Cyrilla

Cyrilla racemiflora L.
Swamp Cyrilla, Red Titi

DESCRIPTION: Swamp Cyrilla is often a shrub, occasionally reaching tree stature with short, frequently crooked stems that divide into numerous wide-spreading branches. It often forms nearly impenetrable thickets along the margins of swamps, wet roadside depressions, and other wet areas in the Coastal Plain.

Leaves – tardily deciduous, simple, alternate; blades leathery, narrowly obovate to oblanceolate, 2–4" long, ½–1" wide, entire; both surfaces glabrous. Figures 285, 286.

Twigs – slender, often 3-angled, smooth, lustrous brown; terminal buds ovoid, ¼" long or less, with chestnut-brown scales; leaf scars shield-shaped, fringed; single bundle scar.

Bark – reddish brown, thin, lustrous at first, then dividing into thin shreddy scales, becomes thicker and spongy when growing in water.

Flowers – perfect; petals white, tiny; produced in stiff racemes up to 6" long, near the end of the previous year's twig, just below the new growth; appearing May–July. Figure 285.

Fruit – drupe, brown, dry, ovoid, ⅛" long, unwinged; in upright clusters 4–6" long, appearing late summer, persistent into winter. Figure 286.

RECOGNITION DIFFICULTIES WITH OTHER TAXA: A similar taxon, *Cyrilla racemiflora* var. *parvifolia* Sarg., is considered a separate species by some botanists. This variety differs from var. *racemiflora* by its smaller leaves (less that 2" long), globular fruits and inflorescences less than 4" long. *Cyrilla*, with its racemes clustered at the end of the previous year's twig, can easily be distinguished from *Cliftonia*, which has terminal racemes on the current year twigs.

HABITAT: Swamp Cyrilla is common in shallow swamps, around the margins of ponds and roadside depressions throughout the Coastal Plain.

ECONOMIC, ORNAMENTAL AND OTHER USES: Swamp Cyrilla is of no economic importance. Occasionally, it is used locally as an ornamental plant because of its fragrant flowers and shrubby growth habit. Leaf coloration in late autumn and winter can be showy, ranging from brilliant shades of orange to scarlet.

AQUIFOLIACEAE–THE HOLLY FAMILY

The Aquifoliaceae has three genera, the largest of which is *Ilex*, with nearly 400 species in temperate and tropical regions. Two other small genera, *Nemopanthus* and *Phelline*, are restricted to northeastern North America and New Caledonia, respectively.

The white wood of *Ilex* is important economically for carving and inlay work. The evergreen species of holly, particularly *I. opaca* Aiton, are used for Christmas decorations. Several species are cultivated as ornamentals.

Both evergreen and deciduous species of *Ilex* are native to the Southeast. They are dioecious, the pistillate and staminate flowers are both tiny and white. The berries are red or black. The deciduous hollies present identification difficulties, particularly with male or sterile specimens.

Ilex–Hollies

SUMMER KEY TO SPECIES OF *ILEX*

1. Leaves evergreen 2
  2. Margins of the leaves with sharp, coarse teeth; teeth with a stiff, sharp spine . . . . *I. opaca*
  2. Margins of the leaves entire, or with rounded or fine teeth; teeth lacking a stiff, sharp spine 3
    3. Leaves crenate along entire leaf margin . . . . *I. vomitoria*
    3. Leaves not as above 4
      4. Leaves less than 1½″ long and less than ¼″ wide; linear to linear-oblong . . . . *I. myrtifolia*
      4. Leaves usually exceeding 1½″ in length and ¼″ wide; not linear 5
        5. Leaves entire, or with bristly teeth above the middle of the blade, blades usually less than 2 × as long as broad; fruit black. . . . . *I. coriacea*
        5. Leaves entire, or with a few, small teeth near the apex, blades usually greater than 2 × as long as broad; fruit red or orange. . . . . *I. cassine*
1. Leaves deciduous 6
  6. Plant in fruit. 7
    7. One or more sepals of fruit usually deciduous; fruits dull; most leaf blade bases rounded. *I. amelanchier*
    7. All sepals of fruit present; fruits shiny; most leaf bases tapered 8
      8. Sepals six or seven; seeds usually six, smooth, not striped or ribbed. . . . . *I. verticillata*
      8. Sepals four or five; seeds usually three to five, ribbed or striped 9
        9. Pedicels more than ½″. . . . . *I. longipes*
        9. Pedicels less than ½″ 10
          10. Sepals without marginal hairs. . . . . *I. decidua*
          10. Sepals with marginal hairs 11
            11. Largest leaves over 4″, most leaf tips long tapered; growing in medium to wet soils, rich in humus. . . . . *I. montana*
            11. Largest leaves under 4″, leaves not long tapered; growing in medium to dry, sandy soils. . . . . *I. ambigua*
  6. Plant not in fruit. 12
    12. Most lateral buds rounded (bud scales often mucronate in *I. amelanchier*); net veins of leaf visible on underside of leaves. 13
      13. Leaves rounded at base. . . . . *I. amelanchier*
      13. Leaves tapering at base . . . . *I. verticillata*
    12. Most lateral buds pointed, scales acuminate; net veins not visible on underside of leaves. 14

14. Largest leaf blades over 4″, most leaf tips long acuminate.................................. *I. montana*

14. Largest leaf blades under 4″, short acuminate or shallowly notched, rarely obtuse, never long acuminate... 15

    15. Leaf blade margins rarely flat, at least some margins strongly to moderately undulate, often strongly involute at base......................... *I. decidua*

    15. Most leaf blade margins flat or only slightly as above..................................... 16

        16. Secondary veins on lower leaf surface lighter than the rest of lower leaf surface...... *I. ambigua*

        16. Secondary veins on lower leaf surface the same shade or darker than the rest of the lower leaf surface .... *I. longipes*

Ilex ambigua (Michaux) Torrey
Carolina Holly

DESCRIPTION: *Ilex ambigua* is a small tree, rarely exceeding 20′, most often a shrub. It occurs commonly in the Coastal Plain, occasionally in the mountains and rarely in the Piedmont.

Leaves – deciduous, simple, alternate; blades oblanceolate, lanceolate, elliptic or ovate, apices usually obtuse to acuminate, bases usually tapered, up to 4″ long, margins finely serrate; secondary veins on lower leaf surface lighter than the rest of leaf. Figure 287.

Twigs – slender, gray; buds pointed, scales keeled, acuminate.

Bark – grayish, smooth, thin.

Flowers – dioecious; about ¼″ in diameter; petals and sepals usually 4, sometimes 5, sepals with marginal hairs; in axillary clusters; appearing May–June.

Fruit – drupe, globose, shiny, red, about ⅓″ in diameter; sepals persisting; seeds 3–5, seeds ribbed or striped; maturing in autumn, not persisting into winter. Figure 287.

RECOGNITION DIFFICULTIES WITH OTHER TAXA: *Ilex ambigua* resembles *I. montana* and much confusion exists about the identity of these two taxa. According to Krakow (1989), these taxa warrant recognition as separate species. The most useful field characteristic used to separate the two is the leaf length and leaf tip. *Ilex ambigua* is less than 4″ long and not long tapered. The two species occupy different habitats.

HABITAT: *Ilex ambigua* occurs throughout the State, but is restricted to dry, sandy soils.

ECONOMIC, ORNAMENTAL AND OTHER USES: The fruits of *Ilex ambigua* are eaten by birds.

Ilex amelanchier M. A. Curtis
Sarvis Holly

DESCRIPTION: Sarvis Holly is a large shrub which rarely reaches tree stature. It is rare throughout its range in the Southeast, and is documented in Georgia in a few Coastal Plain counties. The leaves are simple, deciduous, and lance-shaped with rounded bases and entire or finely toothed margins. The upper surfaces of the leaves are dull green and glabrous, while the lower surfaces are finely pubescent. The plants are dioecious: the staminate flowers are produced in clusters in the leaf axils, the pistillate are solitary and also occur in leaf axils or leafless nodes. The fruit is a dull red, nearly globose drupe, less than ½" in diameter, with one to all sepals falling off. The lateral buds are rounded and bud scales often have a bristle tip. It occurs along streams and margins of wet areas in the Coastal Plain. Figure 288, leaves.

Ilex cassine L.
Dahoon

DESCRIPTION: Dahoon is a small to medium-sized tree, rarely exceeding 25' in height. This species is restricted to the Coastal Plain in Georgia.

Leaves – evergreen, simple, alternate; blades elliptical to lance-shaped or broadest above the middle, variable in length from 1¼ to 4" long or longer, up to 1½" wide, entire or one or more teeth near the apex, sometimes revolute, bristle-tipped; glabrous except along the midrib of lower surface. Figure 289.

Twigs – slender, gray, minutely hairy, smooth with numerous inconspicuous lenticels; terminal buds tiny, less than ⅛" long, rounded; leaf scars half-round to crescent-shaped; single bundle scar.

Bark – similar to other hollies.

Flowers – dioecious; similar to other hollies; staminate in axillary clusters; pistillate solitary or in clusters of 3 or 4 in leaf axils; appearing May–June.

Fruit – drupe, globose, red, orange, or sometimes yellow, about ¼" in diameter; maturing in late autumn and persisting through the winter. Figure 289.

RECOGNITION DIFFICULTIES WITH OTHER TAXA: The evergreen leaves and color of fruit of *I. cassine* may resemble those of *I. opaca*; however, the leaves of *I. opaca* are stiffer and usually have sharp, spiny-toothed margins. *Ilex opaca* would not occupy the poorly drained habitat of *I. cassine*.

HABITAT: Dahoon occurs in non-alluvial swamps, cypress ponds, and streambanks of the lower Coastal Plain.

ECONOMIC, ORNAMENTAL AND OTHER USES: The wood of Dahoon is not of commercial value. It is often grown as an ornamental for its evergreen foliage and red berries. It is usually pruned for a shrubby growth form. Small mammals and birds feed on the fruits.

Ilex coriacea (Pursh) Chapman
Large Gallberry

DESCRIPTION: This is usually a shrub, but occasionally a small tree, no more than 20' in height. It is scattered throughout the Coastal Plain and occurs occasionally in the Piedmont.

Leaves – evergreen, simple, alternate; blades elliptic to widest above the middle, apex acute, 1½–3" long, ¾–1¾" wide, margins entire with irregular, small, bristle-tipped teeth near the apex; lower surfaces often with fine black dots, glabrous.

Twigs – sticky, finely hairy when young, otherwise similar to other Hollies.

Bark – similar to other hollies.

Flowers – similar to other hollies.

Fruit – drupe, subglobose, shiny black, about ⅜" in diameter, fleshy, sweet; not persisting into winter.

RECOGNITION DIFFICULTIES WITH OTHER TAXA: This species is very similar to the shrub, *Ilex glabra*, Inkberry. *I. coriacea* is characterized by leaves with acute tips, entire margins with bristly teeth above the middle and with fruits that are fleshy and sweet, whereas *I. glabra* has blunt-tipped leaves with rounded teeth above the middle and dry, bitter, persistent fruits.

HABITAT: *I. coriacea* occurs along stream borders, cypress ponds, sloughs and other low, wet areas predominantly in the Coastal Plain.

ECONOMIC, ORNAMENTAL AND OTHER USES: None.

Ilex decidua Walter

Possumhaw

DESCRIPTION: *Ilex decidua* is a small, deciduous tree or shrub which occurs throughout Georgia. It has a short trunk, branching close to the ground, and seldom reaches heights of over 20'.

Leaves – deciduous, simple, alternate; blades 1½–3" long, widest above the middle, base long tapered, short acuminate (rarely obtuse), margins undulate; lower surfaces pubescent, at least on the midrib; mostly clustered on short shoots. Figure 290.

Twigs – slender, glabrous, silvery gray, numerous spur shoots; lateral buds pointed, scales acuminate.

Bark – light brown to gray, thin, smooth, often becoming warty and roughened.

Flowers – similar to other hollies, petals and sepals usually 4, rarely 5, sepals with marginal hairs; usually clustered with leaves at tip of spur shoots.

Fruit – drupe, small, shiny, red, nearly round, ¼" in diameter, sepals persistent; pulp bitter; 3–5 seeds; maturing in autumn and persisting until next season. Figure 290.

RECOGNITION DIFFICULTIES WITH OTHER TAXA: *I. decidua* has a distinctive leaf shape that is less variable than other species of holly. Some, individuals of *I. ambigua* may have leaf margins similar to that of *I. decidua*, however, the midribs of *I. decidua* are glabrous or minutely pubescent. If in flower or fruit, the two can be distinguished in that *I. decidua* has flower parts (petals, sepals) in 4s and *I. ambigua* has flower parts in 5s. *Ilex longipes* is very similar to *I. decidua*, but differs in length of fruit stalk.

HABITAT: Possumhaw is common on river floodplains and stream and pond borders predominantly in the Coastal Plain.

ECONOMIC, ORNAMENTAL AND OTHER USES: The leafless branches of these trees, with showy red to orange fruit, are collected at Christmas time for decorations. As a landscape plant, the tree is effective as a winter ornamental because the fruit is so conspicuous on the bare branches. The young twigs are browsed by deer. The wood is not of commercial use because the trees are so small.

Ilex longipes Chapman ex Trel.

I. decidua var. *longipes* (Chapman) Ahles

Georgia Holly

DESCRIPTION: Georgia Holly is usually a large shrub, but infrequently attains tree height. It is not common in the State, most frequently documented from the Ridge and Valley Province along rocky wooded slopes. *I. longipes* is very similar to *I. decidua* and is considered by some as a variety of the latter. *Ilex longipes* differs in that the flower and fruit stalks range from ½–¾" long while those of *I. decidua* are less than ½" in length.

Ilex montana Torrey & Gray

Mountain Winterberry

DESCRIPTION: Mountain Winterberry is a deciduous, small tree or shrub with a short trunk. It has been variously known as *I. monticola*, Gray, *I. ambigua* var. *monticola* (Gray) Wunderlin & Poppleton and *I. ambigua* var. *montana* (Torrey & Gray) Ahles. The leaves of this taxon are usually greater than 4" in length. The blades are elliptical or ovate, with acuminate tips and sharply toothed margins. The drupes are about ½" in diameter, red, and persist into winter. The lateral buds are pointed. In general, the larger leaves with conspicuous teeth and larger fruit distinguish this species. It occurs in mesic forests of the mountains. Figure 291, leaves.

Ilex myrtifolia Walter

Myrtle-leaved Holly

DESCRIPTION: This is a small, evergreen tree or more commonly a shrub, most frequently occurring in the Coastal Plain.

Leaves – evergreen, simple, alternate; blades linear or narrowly elliptic, bristle-tipped, margins entire and revolute, ½–1¼" long and ⅛–¼" wide. Figure 292.

Twigs – slender, stiff, brown; buds similar to other hollies; branches rigid, crooked.

Bark – whitish gray, usually warty and rough.

Flowers – similar to other hollies; appearing May–June.

Fruit – drupe, red, nearly globose, about ¼" in diameter; maturing in autumn and persisting into winter. Figure 292.

RECOGNITION DIFFICULTIES WITH OTHER TAXA: This species is distinctive by its linear, evergreen leaves and should not be confused with any other native trees or shrubs.

HABITAT: Myrtle-leaved Holly occurs on poor sandy soils along depressions in pine flatwoods or cypress ponds throughout the Coastal Plain. It is rarely reported in the Piedmont.

ECONOMIC, ORNAMENTAL AND OTHER USES: This species is available in the horticultural trade and makes an unusual shrub for landscaping with its crooked, rigid form and narrow evergreen leaves.

Ilex opaca Aiton

American Holly

DESCRIPTION: This is a medium-sized evergreen tree, attaining heights of 70' and diameters of up to 2', although usually smaller. Its growth form is conical with branching at nearly right angles. It is common throughout the State.

Leaves – evergreen, simple, alternate; blade stiff, leathery, broadly elliptical, margins wavy to dentate, spiny-toothed (rarely entire); upper surface shiny dark green; lower surface yellowish green; both surfaces glabrous. Figure 293.

Twigs – stout, gray, with rust colored hairs when young, becoming glabrous with age; buds similar to other hollies.

Bark – gray, thin, smooth, or sometimes roughened and warty. Figure 294.

Flowers – similar to other hollies; appearing in late spring.

Fruit – drupe, red or orange, nearly globose, ¼–⅜" in diameter; maturing in autumn and persisting until flowering period of next season. Figure 293.

RECOGNITION DIFFICULTIES WITH OTHER TAXA: None.

HABITAT: This species occurs in mesic deciduous forests throughout the State as an understory species.

ECONOMIC, ORNAMENTAL AND OTHER USES: American Holly is one of the most familiar trees of eastern North America. It is the Christmas Holly which is harvested for its evergreen leaves and persistent red berries. It is a well known ornamental with numerous cultivars available. It is a very hardy tree for many landscape uses and is generally pest-free. The white wood is valued for use in decorative inlays in the manufacture of fine furniture.

Ilex verticillata (L.) Gray
Common Winterberry

DESCRIPTION: Common Winterberry is rarely a small tree, up to 25' tall and is more commonly a large shrub. It is documented primarily in the State in the Piedmont and Blue Ridge Mountains. The leaves are extremely variable in shape. The base of the leaf is usually tapered, the tip pointed, margins sharply toothed and the venation conspicuous. Flowers have six or seven sepals and petals. The fruits are red, about ¼" in diameter and usually contain six seeds. This species shows resemblances to *I. montana*, however, the leaves of *I. verticillata* are firm in texture and the veins prominently impressed on the lower surface, whereas those of *I. montana* are thin and lack the conspicuous venation. Figure 295, leaves and fruit.

Ilex vomitoria Aiton
Yaupon

DESCRIPTION: Yaupon is an evergreen shrub or small tree, occasionally 25' tall, which often forms thickets from root sprouts. It is common in the outer Coastal Plain and rare in the Piedmont.

Leaves – evergreen, simple, alternate; blades leathery, oval or oblong, leaf tips blunt, ½–1½" long, ¼–½" wide, margins with rounded teeth along entire blade; dark green, shiny. Figure 296.

Twigs – stiff, grayish, finely hairy when young; buds similar to other hollies.

Bark – reddish brown, thin.

Flowers – similar to other hollies; appearing early spring.

Fruit – drupe, rounded, about ¼" in diameter, red; numerous on short shoots; maturing October–November. Figure 296.

RECOGNITION DIFFICULTIES WITH OTHER TAXA: This species is distinctive from other evergreen hollies with the small, blunt-tipped leaves and round toothed leaf margins around the entire blade.

HABITAT: Yaupon is common along coastal dunes and coastal forests and is occasional in sand hills.

ECONOMIC, ORNAMENTAL AND OTHER USES: This species is often used for hedges, due to its rapid growth, handsome dark green foliage and strikingly contrasted red berries produced in profusion. It grows well on dry sites and is cold hardy throughout the State. The leaves were used by Indians to prepare a ceremonial tea to induce vomiting, thus the derivation of the scientific name.

CELASTRACEAE–SPINDLE TREE FAMILY

The Celastraceae is a large family of 55 genera and 850 species. Most of the members of this family occur in tropical regions, but there are numerous species in North America, Europe and Asia. Only six genera occur in North America, with *Euonymus* being the only one native to Georgia. The genus has little economic importance, although a widely cultivated species is *Euonymus alatus* (Thunb.) Siebold, a shrub with distinctive corky winged branches and brilliant red autumn foliage.

Euonymus–Burningbush

Euonymus atropurpureus Jacq.

Eastern Wahoo, Burningbush

DESCRIPTION: This species is a shrub or small tree, up to 25' tall. It is infrequent in Georgia, occurring in a few scattered counties in several physiographic regions.

Leaves – deciduous, simple, opposite; blades elliptic to ovate, 2–5" long, 1–2" wide, margins finely toothed; upper surfaces glabrous, lower surfaces sparsely pubescent; petioles up to ½" long. Figure 297.

Twigs – often 4-angled when young, green; buds less than ⅛" long, pointed.

Bark – ashy gray, thin, smooth.

Flowers – perfect; petals 4, maroon or dark purple with a transparent margin; small; in axillary cymes; appearing in May.

Fruit – capsule, splitting when mature, but not conspicuously exposing the seeds; pinkish, about ½" in diameter, smooth, unequally 4-lobed; maturing October and often persisting into winter. Figure 297.

RECOGNITION DIFFICULTIES WITH OTHER TAXA: *Euonymus atropurpureus* resembles the more common shrub, *E. americanus* L. The latter has flowers with 5 petals, bright red fruits, with warty protuberances on the surface that split and reflex when mature, exposing the seeds.

HABITAT: Eastern Wahoo occurs along stream banks and rich woods particularly in calcareous soils.

ECONOMIC, ORNAMENTAL AND OTHER USES: This species is sometimes planted as an ornamental because of the autumn coloration and persistent fruit. The leaves and twigs are a preferred food for white tail deer and the seeds are eaten by birds.

STAPHYLEACEAE–BLADDERNUT FAMILY

The Staphyleaceae comprises six genera and approximately 24 species occurring in north temperate regions. Two of the seven species of *Staphylea* are native to the United States, one of which is native to Georgia. The family is of little economic importance, although a few species are cultivated as ornamental shrubs and trees.

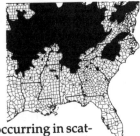

Staphylea–Bladdernut

Staphylea trifolia L.

Bladdernut

DESCRIPTION: This species is a small tree 20–25' tall, occurring in scattered localities in the Piedmont, Cumberland Plateau, and the Ridge and Valley Provinces and less frequently in the Coastal Plain where it is restricted to counties along the Chattahoochee River in southwestern Georgia.

Leaves – deciduous, trifoliately compound, opposite; 6–9" long; leaflets 2–4" long, finely serrated, pubescent; terminal leaflet with long stalk; lateral leaflets subsessile. Figure 298.

Twigs – green to brown, often striped; terminal bud usually absent, axillary buds ovoid, small, 4 blunt scales; leaf scars opposite, half-round, 3 bundle scars (sometimes 5–7).

Bark – greenish gray, smooth, becoming dark and slightly fissured with age.

Flowers – perfect; greenish white, bell-shaped, 5 petals, ½" long; flower stalks about ¾" long and subtended by a white bract; in drooping clusters 3½–4" long at the tip of new branchlets; appearing in late April before the leaves are fully expanded. Figure 299.

Fruit – capsules, 3-lobed at apex, inflated, papery, resembling a Japanese lantern, green to brown, 1½–2" long; conspicuous all summer, maturing late summer. Figure 300.

RECOGNITION DIFFICULTIES WITH OTHER TAXA: Bladdernut has opposite, trifoliate leaves. *Ptelea trifoliata*, another trifoliate-leaved species, has alternate leaves. Boxelder, *Acer negundo* L., has opposite leaves of 3–5 leaflets, and when young, might be confused with Bladdernut. But, unlike Bladdernut, Boxelder has narrow leaf scars which meet at points on opposite sides of the twig.

HABITAT: This species occurs in moist, rich deciduous woods.

ECONOMIC, ORNAMENTAL AND OTHER USES: Bladdernut is of no economic importance. It is used locally as an ornamental because of its rather showy clusters of yellow flowers and its interesting bladder-like fruits which persist from summer to late fall.

ACERACEAE–MAPLE FAMILY

The Aceraceae is represented in North America by *Acer*, with nine species in Georgia. These are small to large deciduous trees. Characteristically, maples have opposite leaves and opposite branching patterns. The fruits are distinctive, consisting of a pair of winged samaras joined together at the base. The leaves are variable in shape, from simple or compound, entire or deeply toothed, unlobed to deeply lobed. Species have bisexual and unisexual flowers and may be dioecious or monoecious or polygamous. Several species are used ornamentally for their attractive form and for their colorful autumn foliage. The wood of a few species is of considerable economic importance.

Acer–Maples

SUMMER KEY TO SPECIES OF *ACER*

1. Leaves pinnately compound .... *A. negundo*
1. Leaves simple 2
   2. Leaves serrated; sinuses between lobes V-shaped 3
      3. Flowers appearing before the leaves, fruits maturing in spring; buds sessile, with several visible overlapping scales 4
         4. Leaves deeply 5-lobed, the terminal lobe with inwardly sloping sides toward base; crushed twigs with strong fetid odor.................................. *A. saccharinum*
         4. Leaves 3–5 lobed, the sides of the terminal lobe sloping outwardly toward base or parallel; crushed twigs without strong fetid odor.......................... *A. rubrum*
      3. Flowers appearing with or after leaf emergence; fruits maturing in late summer; buds stalked, with 2 visible scales 5
         5. Leaves with finely serrated margins, bark greenish with white longitudinal stripes .... *A. pensylvanicum*
         5. Leaves with coarsely serrated margins, bark reddish brown without white stripes..................... *A. spicatum*
   2. Leaves with wavy margins or entire; sinuses rounded 6
      6. Leaves 1½–3½″ across............................... 7
         7. Leaves whitish beneath, terminal lobes of some leaves broader toward apex than toward base, tips of lobes acute to rounded. .... *A. barbatum*
         7. Leaves greenish-yellow beneath, terminal lobe narrower toward apex than base, tips of lobes pointed, often acuminate and drooping..................... *A. leucoderme*
      6. Leaves 3–6″ across 8
         8. Leaves glabrous or sparingly pubescent beneath, margins flattened, lobe tips not drooping; buds light brown; bark gray, fissured into flattened longitudinal plates........ .... *A. saccharum*
         8. Leaves pubescent beneath, margins wavy, turned downward, lobe tips drooping; buds dark brown; bark brown to almost black, deeply fissured with prominent rough ridges..................................... *A. nigrum*

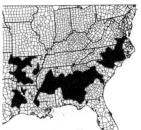

Acer barbatum Michaux

[*A. floridanum* (Chapman) Pax.]

Florida Maple, Southern Sugar Maple

DESCRIPTION: This is a medium-sized tree, 40–60′ tall, occasionally up to 2′ in diameter. It is closely related to and resembles the more northern Sugar Maple, *A. saccharum*. It occurs occasionally in the Piedmont, the northwestern portion of the Coastal Plain and the Ridge and Valley Province.

Leaves – deciduous, simple, opposite; lobes 3–5, tips acute to rounded, terminal lobes of some leaves broader toward apex than toward base, often as wide as long, sinuses rounded, up to 3½" long, margins wavy or entire; upper surfaces dark green; lower surfaces whitish, hairy. Figure 301.

Twigs – slender, reddish brown; buds about ⅛" long; otherwise, similar to *A. saccharum*.

Bark – light gray and smooth on younger trees, usually indistinguishable from other young maples such as *A. leucoderme* or *A. rubrum*, but on older trees becoming dark gray-brown with shallow furrows producing long, irregular plates, resembling that of *A. saccharum*. Figure 302.

Flowers – usually dioecious, but also with perfect and unisexual flowers; bell-shaped, small, ⅛" long; on slender stalks; in drooping clusters; appearing in early spring. Figure 303 shows mostly female flowers, some perfect.

Fruit – samara, paired, brown, ¾–1" long; maturing in autumn. Figure 304.

RECOGNITION DIFFICULTIES WITH OTHER TAXA: *Acer barbatum* is closely related to Sugar Maple. It is considered by some authorities as a variety of this species, but is a smaller tree with smaller leaves. Another similar taxon, Chalk Maple (*A. leucoderme*), is distinguished by leaves that are yellowish green and pubescent beneath and by its light-gray, almost chalky smooth bark on much of the trunk which becomes deeply furrowed and dark brown to almost black 2–3' above the ground on older trees.

HABITAT: Florida Maple occurs along streams and moist sites throughout much of the Piedmont and southwestern portion of the Coastal Plain. It is occasional in the upper tier of Northwest Georgia counties where it overlaps with *A. saccharum*. The species is a slow growing understory tree.

ECONOMIC, ORNAMENTAL AND OTHER USES: Florida Maple is harvested as a timber tree in areas where it attains commercial size, but sap is not tapped for the production of maple syrup. The tree is occasionally planted as a small shade or lawn tree because of its attractive bright yellow to red autumn foliage and rounded dense crown when grown in the open. It is relatively free of insect and disease problems and grows well on moist sites in partial shade or open areas.

Acer leucoderme Small
Chalk Maple

DESCRIPTION: Chalk Maple is a small tree often with multiple stems, occasionally reaching 40' in height and 8–10" in diameter. It is closely related to Sugar Maple, but the leaves are smaller, 2–3½" across, usually pale yellow-green with varying degrees of pubescence underneath. The bark is smooth and light gray to chalky-white on the upper trunk, but becomes furrowed and turns dark brown to almost black near the ground on older trees. Young trees up to a few inches in diameter remain light gray and smooth and are difficult to separate from other maples. This species is difficult to separate from *A. barbatum* on leaf traits alone, but the latter usually has a whitish, soft pubescence on the underside of its leaves and acute to blunt or rounded lobe tips, whereas the leaves of Chalk Maple, although pubescent underneath, have more pointed, often acuminate, lobe tips, with the lobes narrower at the apex than at the base. Chalk Maple occurs in moist ravines and along slopes mostly restricted to the Piedmont and mountainous regions of the State. It is of little economic importance; however, it is gaining acceptance as a desirable landscape plant. It can be an attractive multi-stemmed lawn tree with an open spreading crown and interesting bark features. It is essentially free of pests and disease and can tolerate sun as well as heavy shade. The autumn coloration varies from shades of yellowish brown to red. Figure 305, leaves; Figure 306, bark of older tree, becoming black at the base.

Acer negundo L.
Boxelder

DESCRIPTION: Boxelder is a small to medium-sized, short-lived tree, usually less than 50' tall, but may reach 75–80' and over 2' in diameter in moist, fertile floodplains. It commonly possesses a short trunk with numerous epicormic branches. Boxelder occurs most prevalently in the Piedmont.

Leaves – deciduous, pinnately compound, opposite; leaflets 3–5, occasionally 7, 2–4" long, 1½–2½" wide, coarsely toothed or slightly lobed on margins; lower surfaces with varying degrees of pubescence. Figure 307.

Twigs – greenish to purple with a white bloom, usually glabrous; terminal buds pointed, ⅛–¼" long, reddish, woolly, slightly stalked; lateral buds nearly globose, enclosed by petiole base; the tips of opposing V-shaped leaf scars meet.

Bark – gray-brown and smooth on young trees, developing shallow fissures with narrow, often rounded ridges with age; newly formed epicormic shoots along the trunk are usually bright to dark green in color. Figure 308.

Flowers – dioecious; small, about ¼" long; staminate in long-stalked clusters; pistillate in long-stalked pendulous racemes; appearing in early spring before the leaves.

Fruit – samara, paired, wings 1–2" long; numerous in pendulous racemes; maturing through the summer.

RECOGNITION DIFFICULTIES WITH OTHER TAXA: Boxelder should present little difficulty in field recognition with its opposite, compound leaves and green twigs. Boxelder might be mistaken for an ash, especially Green Ash, which also has green stems and opposite compound leaves. However, the leaf scars that meet in raised points, and lateral buds enclosed by the petiole bases are distinctive for Boxelder. The bark of ashes is deeply furrowed with wavy to corky ridges, whereas, that of Boxelder is shallowly furrowed. The leaves of young seedlings closely resemble the leaves of Poison Ivy, *Toxicodendron radicans* (L). Kuntze. However, leaf arrangement differs, that of Poison Ivy is alternate rather than opposite.

HABITAT: Boxelder occurs along streams, floodplains, edges of swamps and other moist sites. Although shade tolerant, it tends to reproduce prolifically in open disturbed areas.

ECONOMIC, ORNAMENTAL AND OTHER USES: Boxelder has few economic uses today other than for hardwood pulp in the paper industry. The wood has been used for fuel and cheap crate material. Because of its rapid juvenile growth and adaptability to a wide range of soil types, it is planted for quick shade and for shelterbelt or windbreaks. It has the disadvantage of being a short-lived tree and is highly susceptible to wind or storm damage because of its weak wood. Autumn color is not particularly attractive, ranging from greenish yellow to brown.

Acer nigrum Michaux f.
Black Maple

DESCRIPTION: Black Maple is closely related to Sugar Maple (*A. saccharum*) and has been considered as a variety of this species. It is a medium-sized tree, up to 80' tall and up to 2–3' in diameter. The leaves of Black Maple, although similar to Sugar Maple, often have two stipules at the base of the petiole, the margins are more wavy and the leaf hangs more droopily from the twig. The characteristic bark is black and more deeply furrowed than Sugar Maple. It has been documented in the State in Dade County and reported from Walker County. It is much more common in adjacent Alabama and Tennessee. The wood of Black Maple is hard and is interchanged with that of Sugar Maple for numerous uses, especially in the manufacture of furniture. The species is also tapped for sap to make maple syrup in more northern parts of its range. It is widely used as an ornamental for lawns, parks, and city streets due to its spectacular autumn foliage which turns yellow to brilliant red. Figure 309, leaves.

Acer pensylvanicum L.
Striped Maple

DESCRIPTION: This is a small tree, often a shrub, rarely 30–40' tall, with a short trunk, seldom reaching 8" in diameter. It occurs in the Blue Ridge mountains at higher elevations.

    Leaves – deciduous, simple, opposite; blades broadly 3-lobed, sinuses V-shaped, tips of lobes long pointed, base rounded to heart-shaped, 5–6" long, margins finely doubly serrate; yellowish green; turning pale yellow in autumn. Figure 310.

    Twigs – stout, older twigs and younger bark striped or green, glabrous; terminal buds ½" long, bright red, short-stalked, bud scales 2; lateral buds long-stalked, bud scales keeled, single pair visible; leaf scars crescent-shaped.

    Bark – young stems green to brown and distinctively marked with white longitudinal streaks; older bark reddish-brown with pale, longitudinal streaks, somewhat roughened and warty at maturity. Figure 311.

Flowers – monoecious; yellow, bell-shaped, petals 5, ⅜" wide; in pendulous clusters up to 6" long; appearing late spring with or after leaf emergence. Figure 310, female flowers.

Fruit – samara, paired, widely divergent wings less than 1" long; in clusters; maturing in late summer and autumn.

RECOGNITION DIFFICULTIES WITH OTHER TAXA: *Acer spicatum* has somewhat similar foliage, but can be distinguished from Striped Maple by its brown, unstriped bark and hairy, slender twigs. Striped Maple should be distinctive at all times of the year.

HABITAT: Striped Maple is common on moist upland soils as an understory species at higher elevations of the Blue Ridge Mountains in Georgia.

ECONOMIC, ORNAMENTAL AND OTHER USES: Striped Maple is occasionally used as an ornamental plant because of its interesting and distinctive bark features. It probably has restricted use in Georgia because of site limitations requiring moist soils and cooler temperature in summer. Small trees are frequently browsed by deer and the thin bark eaten by rodents during the winter months.

Acer rubrum L.

Red Maple

DESCRIPTION: Red Maple is a medium to large-sized tree, 60–90' in height, and 2–3' in diameter. It is ubiquitous in Georgia.

Leaves – deciduous, simple, opposite; blades variable in shape from 3–5 distinct lobes to almost no lobes, sinuses V-shaped, variable in size, irregularly serrate; variable in pubescence, but lower surfaces usually whitish; petioles red; scarlet, orange or yellow in autumn. Figure 312.

Twigs – reddish; terminal bud blunt, reddish, sessile, with several visible overlapping scales; lateral buds not stalked; leaf scars crescent-shaped; globose lateral accessory flower buds, on each side of axillary bud.

Bark – light gray, thin, smooth on young trees, similar in appearance to other maples; older trees dark gray and forming long, narrow scaly plates with shallow fissures. Figure 313.

Flowers – monoecious, dioecious or polygamous; red, small, but conspicuous since they appear before the leaves in axillary clusters in early spring. Figure 314, female flowers.

Fruit – samara, usually scarlet or brownish, conspicuous, paired, wings about ¾" long; maturing in spring. Figure 315.

RECOGNITION DIFFICULTIES WITH OTHER TAXA: Both Red and Silver Maple leaves are whitish or silvery beneath, but Red Maple has shallow sinuses between the terminal lobes. The terminal lobe is less than ½ the length of the blade, in contrast to the long terminal lobe of Silver Maple. The bruised twig of Silver Maple has a rank odor which is not found in Red Maple, a trait that can be used to separate the two in winter condition.

HABITAT: Red Maple occurs throughout the State in low wet areas, along streams, floodplains, in rich deciduous woods or on drier upland sites. It frequently occurs on open, disturbed sites in almost pure stands.

ECONOMIC, ORNAMENTAL AND OTHER USES: The wood of Red Maple is of poorer quality than Sugar Maple or other hard maples, but large trees are frequently used for veneer and lower grades of furniture. Smaller trees are most often harvested for pulpwood and fuelwood. The species is a favorite ornamental shade tree because of rapid growth on varied sites. Appealing traits include bright flowers and fruit in early spring before the leaves appear. Fall color is variable from brilliant red to dark red. The tree is relatively free of insects and disease with the exception of small fungal spots on the leaves in late summer.

Acer saccharinum L.

Silver Maple

DESCRIPTION: Silver Maple is a medium-sized tree, ranging from 50–80' tall and up to 3' in diameter. It usually has a short trunk which divides into several large upright branches at an early age. It occurs infrequently in scattered localities in the State.

Leaves – deciduous, simple, opposite; blades deeply 5-lobed, the sides of the terminal lobes sloped inward, sinuses V-shaped, margins irregularly doubly toothed; lower surfaces whitish or silvery; petioles red. Figure 316.

Twigs – slender, dark red, shiny; terminal bud similar to Red Maple, also has lateral accessory globose flower buds; broken twigs with distinct, disagreeable fetid odor.

Bark – smooth and light gray on young stems; lightly fissured and scaly on older trunks.

Flowers – monoecious or dioecious; greenish yellow, small; male and female in many-flowered fascicles; appearing before the leaves develop.

Fruit – samara, yellowish brown, paired, wings widely divergent, 2–3" long; maturing early spring; one samara usually aborting.

RECOGNITION DIFFICULTIES WITH OTHER TAXA: Silver Maple should present few recognition difficulties because of its deeply dissected, 5-lobed and long pointed, coarsely serrated leaves which are silvery-white beneath. Unlike other maples, the twigs have a strong, pungent disagreeable odor that is quite distinct.

HABITAT: Silver Maple occurs along streambanks, river levees, and floodplains, but it is not abundant or common anywhere in the State. It is found sporadically in the Coastal Plain, Piedmont and Cumberland Plateau.

ECONOMIC, ORNAMENTAL AND OTHER USES: Silver Maple is of little or no commercial importance. The wood is relatively soft and brittle and used only for wood pulp. Its rapid, early growth and adaptability to a wide range of sites have made this species a popular shade tree in many localities and several cultivars have been developed. However, because of brittle wood, it is subject to damage from wind or ice storms. Individual trees often sprout profusely at the base from root suckers and form numerous epicormic branches along the trunk. The species is also severely attacked by numerous pests and diseases.

Acer saccharum Marsh.

Sugar Maple

DESCRIPTION: This is a long-lived, medium to large-sized tree, commonly 60–80' in height and 2–3' in diameter. It occurs in the Ridge and Valley, Blue Ridge Mountains and upper Piedmont of Georgia.

Leaves – deciduous, simple, opposite; blades palmately 5-lobed (occasionally 3-lobed), sinuses rounded, 3–5" long, lobe margins entire or wavy; glabrous; turning bright red, orange or yellow in autumn. Figure 317.

Twigs – reddish brown; shiny; numerous pale lenticels; terminal buds narrow, conical, about ¼" long, many scaled; lateral accessory flower buds lacking.

Bark – gray and lightly fissured on young trees, becoming darker and deeply furrowed into long scaly vertical ridges or plates which are frequently free on the ends; highly variable among individual trees.

Flowers – polygamous; yellowish green; occurring in clusters; appearing with the leaves.

Fruit – samara, with nearly parallel wings, about 1" long; maturing in autumn.

RECOGNITION DIFFICULTIES WITH OTHER TAXA: In areas where Sugar Maple occurs with *A. nigrum*, *A. barbatum*, or *A. leucoderme*, recognition difficulties exist, particularly between young trees. Many of these difficulties are previously discussed under the different taxa.

HABITAT: Sugar Maple occurs on moist, well-drained soils of the mountains and occasionally in the upper Piedmont on rich, northern slopes.

ECONOMIC, ORNAMENTAL AND OTHER USES: Although Sugar Maple is of little commercial importance in Georgia because of its limited occurrence, the species is one of the most valuable hardwoods in North America. The wood is heavy, hard and durable and is utilized for furniture, flooring, veneer and numerous specialty items. Although the maple syrup industry has greatly declined over the years, it is still an important industry of New England. Sugar Maples are used extensively as an ornamental for lawn, park and street trees where space for root growth is not limiting and pollution is low. Although sensitive to pollution, it is fairly resistant to pests and disease. No other native tree matches the brilliant yellow, orange, and red coloration of Sugar Maple in autumn.

Acer spicatum L.

Mountain Maple

DESCRIPTION: This species is often a shrub, only occasionally a small tree, reaching 30′ in height with a short trunk. It seldom attains 6″ in diameter. It commonly produces several upright branches forming a bushy, drooping appearance. Mountain Maple is recorded from Towns and Union Counties at higher elevations.

Leaves – deciduous, simple, opposite; blades usually heart-shaped at base, lobes 3–5, sinuses broadly V-shaped, shallow, 3–5″ long, coarsely serrate. Figure 318.

Twigs – slender, hairy; terminal buds reddish brown with short gray hairs, ⅛–¼" long; lateral buds distinctly long-stalked, bud scales 2; leaf scars V- or U-shaped; pith brown.

Bark – reddish brown, thin and smooth, becoming slightly scaly with age.

Flowers – monoecious; petals yellowish green; staminate and pistillate in terminal, erect racemes or panicles; appearing after the leaves in early summer (June). Figure 318.

Fruit – samara, paired, with widely divergent wings, about ½" long, clustered on slender stalks; bright red to yellow in mid-summer; maturing in late summer or autumn.

RECOGNITION DIFFICULTIES WITH OTHER TAXA: See description of striped maple, *A. pensylvanicum.*

HABITAT: Mountain Maple is found on moist slopes at the higher elevations in the Blue Ridge Mountains of Union and Towns Counties.

ECONOMIC, ORNAMENTAL AND OTHER USES: This species is infrequently used in the mountains as an ornamental and is less attractive than Striped Maple. The young trees are browsed by deer and several rodents feed on the bark. Ruffed-grouse feed on the winter buds.

HIPPOCASTANACEAE–BUCKEYE FAMILY

The Hippocastanaceae is a small family of two genera (*Aesculus* and *Billia*) and comprises about 24 species of trees or shrubs, native mostly to North and South America. Six species of *Aesculus* are native to the United States and five of these occur in Georgia. Hybrids are produced frequently within the genus. The genus *Billia* contains two evergreen species ranging from Columbia north into Mexico.

The distinctive opposite, palmately compound leaves with 5–7 pinnately veined leaflets provide easy recognition of *Aesculus.* The bark, twig, and leaf differences are of little aid in species identification, consequently flowers are usually necessary. The showy staminate or perfect flowers are borne in a terminal panicle. Only the flowers near the base of the inflorescence are perfect and fertile. The fruit is a capsule with 1–3 large, lustrous, chestnut brown seeds, each with a prominent pale scar.

Economically, the family is most important for ornamental uses. Especially well-known is the Horse-chestnut tree, *Aesculus hippocastanum* L., a native of northern Greece but widely cultivated throughout many temperate parts of the world. This species resembles our native buckeyes, but differs in the shape of the leaflets, being broadest above the middle and doubly toothed along the margins. Also, the larger, white flowers of Horse-chestnut are mottled with red and yellow and are generally much showier. The young leaves and seeds of all species of *Aesculus* produce the alkaloid aesculin which is reportedly a dangerous poison to humans and livestock. Although poisonous, a common folklore still exists that a buckeye seed brings the bearer good fortune and some persons carry one with them at all times.

Aesculus–Buckeyes

SUMMER KEY TO SPECIES OF *AESCULUS*
1. Petals equal, or nearly so, in length, yellow; twigs with fetid odor when crushed; fruits spiny........................... *A. glabra*
1. Petals distinctly unequal in length, or if equal, the petals white and stamens 3–4 times the length of petals; twigs without fetid odor; fruits not spiny 2
   2. Flowers white, stamens 3–4 times the length of the petals; inflorescence narrow, 8–12" long...................... *A. parviflora*
   2. Flowers yellow or red, stamens included or barely exerted beyond the corolla; inflorescence broad, 4–10" long................ 3
      3. Calyx not glandular-hairy; fruit 1–2" long; small tree..... 4
         4. Petals hairy but not glandular on margin, yellow or tinged with red .... *A. sylvatica*
         4. Petals hairless but glandular on margin, scarlet..... *A. pavia*
      3. Calyx glandular-hairy; fruit 2–3" across; large tree..... *A. flava*

Aesculus flava Solander ex Hope

(*A. octandra* Marshall)

Yellow Buckeye

DESCRIPTION: Yellow Buckeye is a large tree, often 70–90' in height and 2–3' in diameter. In Georgia, it is found only in the upper tier of counties across the State, usually at higher elevations in the mountains, and in a few adjacent counties in the upper Piedmont.

    Leaves – deciduous, palmately compound, opposite; leaflets 5–7, obovate, acute at base and apex, 4–6" long, 1½–2½" wide, margins finely and irregularly toothed; upper surfaces dark green and glabrous; lower surfaces dull; rachis stout, 4–6" long. Figure 319.

    Twigs – stout, gray-brown, lenticels conspicuous; terminal buds acute, large, about ⅔" long, outer scales rounded on back; leaf scars large and triangular to round; bundle scars 6–7 in V-shape; pith large, white and continuous; lacks ill scent.

Bark – dark gray-brown, smooth, becoming slightly furrowed, broken into flattened plates with age. Figure 320.

Flowers – polygamous, petals yellow, upper petals often streaked with red, corolla tubular with 4 very unequal petals; calyx tomentose; stamens shorter than the petals; erect terminal panicles; flower stalks with glandular trichomes; appearing April–May. Figure 321.

Fruit – capsules, 2–3" in diameter, leathery, globose to obovate, usually containing 2 seeds; seeds shiny brown, with a conspicuous pale scar. Figure 322.

RECOGNITION DIFFICULTIES WITH OTHER TAXA: Yellow Buckeye may occur simultaneously with Ohio Buckeye (*A. glabra*) in a restricted area in Northwest Georgia, otherwise, Yellow Buckeye is the only buckeye species developing into a large tree in the Blue Ridge mountains. The fruit of Yellow Buckeye is leathery smooth, whereas that of Ohio Buckeye is spiny. The Yellow Buckeye petals are unequal in length and longer than the stamens, while the petals of Ohio Buckeye are nearly equal in length and are shorter than the stamens. The twigs of Ohio Buckeye have a fetid odor when bruised, a trait not present in Yellow Buckeye. In winter, Yellow Buckeye can be distinguished from Georgia Buckeye, *A. sylvatica*, since the terminal bud of Yellow Buckeye is slightly larger, ⅔" as compared to ½". The fruit of Yellow Buckeye is about 2–3" long, whereas the fruit of Georgia Buckeye is 2" or less. Georgia Buckeye stamens are exerted beyond the petals and the calyx and flower stalks are not glandular. *Aesculus flava* is reported to hybridize with *A. sylvatica*, *A. pavia*, and *A. glabra*. However, hybridization between *A. flava* and *A. glabra* is documented in adjacent states only. In general, *A. flava* is found in mountainous areas, *A. sylvatica* in the Piedmont and *A. pavia* on the Coastal Plain. However, there is considerable overlap in ranges.

HABITAT: Yellow Buckeye occurs as an occasional tree on rich mountain slopes or along streams and coves, in mixture with other hardwoods.

ECONOMIC, ORNAMENTAL AND OTHER USES: The wood of Yellow Buckeye is soft and creamy white. It is used occasionally for toys, boxes, and small woodenware. The species is used as an ornamental tree because of its leaf shape, showy flowers, and yellow autumn coloration. It should be planted on moist, fertile sites with adequate space for full crown development.

Aesculus glabra Willd.
Ohio Buckeye, Fetid Buckeye

DESCRIPTION: Ohio Buckeye is a medium to large-sized tree which has only recently been documented in Georgia, occurring in a single locality in Walker County. It is much more common in the East-Central United States. Ohio Buckeye differs from Yellow Buckeye by several characteristics, the most conspicuous being the spiny fruit. The flower petals are almost equal in length, while those of Yellow Buckeye are unequal. One common name often used, Fetid Buckeye, refers to the offensive odor of the leaves, twigs and flowers when crushed, a fairly reliable distinguishing feature. Generally, the winter bud scales are conspicuously keeled, although this trait is variable. Figure 323.

Aesculus parviflora Walter
Bottlebrush Buckeye

DESCRIPTION: Bottlebrush Buckeye may attain heights of 15–20', but generally it occurs as a many stemmed shrub. It occurs infrequently in Georgia, in the southwestern part of the State in counties along the Chattahoochee River.

Leaves – deciduous, palmately compound, opposite; leaflets 5–7, lanceolate to obovate, 3–6" long, 1½–2½" wide; lower surfaces commonly tomentose.

Twigs – stout, brown to gray, lenticels raised, light brown; terminal bud smaller than other buckeyes, about ¼" long with 4 exposed scales; lateral buds minute, gray-brown and glaucous.

Bark – grayish brown, thin, smooth to lightly fissured.

Flowers – perfect; petals white, 4–5, the fifth petal small or absent; 5 sepals; stamens exerted, 3–4 times the length of the petals; in long, slender showy panicles 8–12" long, 2–4" wide; appearing July–August. Figure 324.

Fruit – capsules, globose, 1–1½" in diameter; borne on long drooping stalks; smooth; maturing October–November. Figure 325.

RECOGNITION DIFFICULTIES WITH OTHER TAXA: The common name,

Bottlebrush Buckeye, refers to the distinctive flowers with long stamens. In winter condition, one can distinguish it from *A. pavia* by the small terminal buds, usually with 4 weakly imbricate, slightly pubescent scales, and the persistent elongated fruit stalks.

HABITAT: *Aesculus parviflora* is restricted to moist, well-drained soils in open woodlands as an understory plant.

ECONOMIC, ORNAMENTAL AND OTHER USES: Bottlebrush Buckeye is an excellent and attractive specimen plant for lawns, borders and massing in showy clumps. It grows well in sun or partial shade on moist, acid or basic soils, and should be utilized more frequently in landscapes, where appropriate.

Aesculus pavia L.
Red Buckeye

DESCRIPTION: Red Buckeye is a small tree, seldom over 20–25' tall and 4–6" in diameter. It occurs commonly throughout the Coastal Plain and in scattered localities in the western Piedmont and northward to the Ridge and Valley.

Leaves – deciduous, palmately compound, opposite; leaflets 5–7, lanceolate to obovate, 2½–6" long, 1½–2½" wide; upper surfaces dark green, usually with sunken veins; lower surfaces dull green, pubescent.

Twigs – stout, reddish brown, lenticels raised, light brown; terminal bud ¼–½" long; lateral buds much smaller; leaf scars triangular to round; bundle scars 6–7, in V-shape.

Bark – gray to brown, thin, smooth to weakly fissured.

Flowers – perfect; petals deep red to reddish yellow, 4–5, flowers about 1–1½" long; calyx tubular, glandular-hairy, 4–5 lobed; stamens unequal, usually 7 and slightly exerted beyond the corolla; in large terminal panicles, 6–10" long, 4–6" wide; appearing April–May with developing leaves. Figure 326.

Fruit – capsules, similar to other buckeyes, except usually slightly smaller, about 1–2" in diameter; maturing September–October.

RECOGNITION DIFFICULTIES WITH OTHER TAXA: Red Buckeye overlaps geographically and hybridizes with Georgia Buckeye. The flowers of Red Buckeye are red and the stamens are longer than the lateral petals, whereas the flowers of Georgia Buckeye are yellow and the stamens are usually shorter than the lateral petals. In the absence of flowers, the two are difficult to separate.

HABITAT: Red Buckeye is an understory tree in rich, moist soil of deciduous forests and along streambanks throughout the Coastal Plain and lower Piedmont.

ECONOMIC, ORNAMENTAL AND OTHER USES: This species is often used as an ornamental due to its short stature and showy red spring flowers. A cultivar developed from a hybrid cross between Red Buckeye and the European Horse-chestnut is a popular horticultural tree form with slightly prickly fruits and red flowers.

Aesculus sylvatica Bartram

Painted Buckeye, Georgia Buckeye

DESCRIPTION: This species is usually a small tree seldom over 20–25' tall, although trees up to 60' in height have been documented along the Oconee River. It is usually restricted to the Piedmont occurring in a variety of sites, but most often on well-drained, open wooded slopes. It is distinguished by its yellow-green flowers tinged with red, stamens shorter than the lateral petals, and by the lack of glands on the calyx and pedicel. It is known to hybridize with *A. pavia* resulting in plants with reddish flowers. Georgia Buckeye is not as showy in flower as either *A. pavia* or *A. parviflora*, but it is a handsome small tree, adapted to a wide range of sites and should be used more frequently in residential landscapes. Figure 327, flower; Figure 328, fruit and seed.

SAPINDACEAE–SOAPBERRY FAMILY

The Sapindaceae is a large family of over 1500 species of trees, shrubs, and woody vines, mostly restricted to tropical and subtropical regions. A single arborescent species occurs in the State, *Sapindus marginatus* Willd.

Sapindus–Soapberry

Sapindus marginatus Willd.
Florida Soapberry

DESCRIPTION: This is a small tree, occasionally 25' in height and 10" in diameter, forming an open, rounded crown.

Leaves – tardily deciduous, pinnately compound, alternate; up to 15" long; leaflets 7–13, leathery, elliptic to lance-shaped, falcate, apex acuminate, base unequal, up to 7" long, margins entire; upper surfaces glabrous, dark green, lustrous; lower surfaces pale green. Figure 329.

Twigs – fluted, greenish yellow, lenticels pale; terminal buds absent; lateral buds globose, usually superposed with upper bud larger; leaf scars large, 3-lobed.

Bark – grayish brown, smooth at first, but becoming warty in appearance with both oblong and horizontal ridges, later separating by vertical splits, exposing darker inner layers of bark.

Flowers – perfect, also unisexual and polygamous; yellow-green, small; in many flowered terminal and axillary, pubescent panicles; appearing late April–May after full foliage. Figure 329.

Fruit – berry, distinctly lopsided, keeled on back side, ¾" in diameter, thin yellow flesh, becoming yellowish brown to black, wrinkled and hard when fully mature; seed dark brown, obovoid, ½" in diameter. Figure 330.

RECOGNITION DIFFICULTIES WITH OTHER TAXA: The leaves of Florida Soapberry, at first glance, might be mistaken for young Water Hickory or Pecan because of the pinnately compound, falcate leaflets. However, the leaflets occur alternately to subopposite along an unwinged rachis and have entire margins.

HABITAT: This species is rare and locally sparse on St. Catherines, Hurricane, and Colonel's Islands, Liberty County, Georgia.

ECONOMIC, ORNAMENTAL AND OTHER USES: Florida Soapberry is

planted ornamentally as a lawn tree around homes because it is rather showy with masses of yellow flowers throughout the crown. The fruit clusters are also of interest, but can become a nuisance when they mature and drop because they produce a fetid odor. The fruits contain the poisonous substance, saponin, which produces a soapy lather when mixed with water.

RHAMNACEAE–BUCKTHORN FAMILY

The Rhamnaceae is a large family of temperate and tropical trees, shrubs and woody vines. In Georgia, a single tree species occurs, *Rhamnus caroliniana* Walter. Members of this family generally do not produce timber of economic importance. Several genera are used ornamentally and a number of taxa provide medicinal products, e.g., the purgative, known as *cascara sagrada*, is obtained from the California *Rhamnus purshiana* DC.

Rhamnus–Buckthorn

Rhamnus caroliniana Walter

Carolina Buckthorn

DESCRIPTION: Carolina Buckthorn is a small tree that reaches heights of 30–40' and a diameter of 6–8". It is an attractive tree with slender branches and open crown, and is scattered throughout the State, but is more prevalent in the Piedmont and Ridge and Valley than in the Coastal Plain.

Leaves – deciduous, simple, alternate; blades elliptic to oblong, 4–6" long, parallel veins from midrib prominent; margins finely toothed. Figure 331.

Twigs – slender, reddish brown, becoming gray; terminal bud naked, densely hairy, ¼" long; leaf scars crescent to elliptical, bundle scars 3; fetid odor when crushed.

Bark – gray, often marked with dark blotches, thin, nearly smooth with narrow, shallow fissures near base.

Flowers – perfect; 5 white petals, small, corolla less than ¼" wide, inconspicuous; in few-flowered clusters in leaf axils; appearing in early summer. Figure 331.

Fruit – drupes, red in summer, becoming black at maturity, globose, about ⅓" in diameter; maturing in autumn. Figure 332.

RECOGNITION DIFFICULTIES WITH OTHER TAXA: *Rhamnus caroliniana* might be confused with some deciduous hollies during early fruit development. However, the leaves are very distinctive with the parallel lateral veins and the fruits are black at maturity, while those of the deciduous hollies are red.

HABITAT: Carolina Buckthorn is scattered locally in rich, deciduous forests throughout the State. This species is frequently associated with soils of limestone origin.

ECONOMIC, ORNAMENTAL AND OTHER USES: Carolina Buckthorn has been planted sparingly as an ornamental for its attractive pale green foliage and fruit clusters. Numerous birds consume the fruit.

TILIACEAE–**BASSWOOD FAMILY**

The Tiliaceae is a family of mostly woody plants containing 41 genera and over 400 species. Most species are confined to the tropics but a few extend into temperate regions. *Tilia,* the only genus of the family that contains trees in North America, includes several polymorphic taxa which cause widely differing opinions as to the number of species. The characters used to separate these taxa are based largely on leaf pubescence, color, and size, all of which intergrade considerably, even on the same tree. Kurz and Godfrey (1962) give an excellent account of these problems. We follow their suggestion and treat this polymorphic complex as a single, inclusive taxon, *Tilia americana* Miller.

Tilia–Basswood

Tilia americana Miller

Basswood, Linden

DESCRIPTION: Basswood is a medium to large tree, ranging from 60–100' tall and 2–3' in diameter. It occurs throughout the State but is more prevalent in the Piedmont and mountains than in the Coastal Plain.

    Leaves – deciduous, simple, alternate; 2-ranked; blades firm textured, widely ovate to heart-shaped, base unequally heart-shaped or nearly straight across, margins serrate; glabrous to tomentose, often with stellate pubescence. Figure 333.

    Twigs – slender, zigzag, yellowish brown; terminal bud absent; lateral buds asymmetrical, ovoid, dark red to green, 2–4 bud scales;

leaf scars half-round to crescent-shaped; bundle scars three or more; stipular scars prominent.

Bark – dark gray to brown, deeply furrowed into narrow scaly ridges on older trees.

Flowers – perfect or bisexual; yellowish or green, about ½" wide, 5 petals; occurring in small clusters on a slender stalk with a pendant leaf-like narrow bract; bract 4–5" long; appearing early summer. Figure 334.

Fruit – nuts, globose, about ⅓" in diameter; on a stalk attached to a leaf-like bract; appearing late summer to autumn, often persisting into winter. Figure 335.

RECOGNITION DIFFICULTIES WITH OTHER TAXA: The leaves of Basswood and unlobed leaves of Mulberry are similar. However, Basswood twigs lack the milky sap found in Mulberry. The lateral buds of *Tilia* are usually twisted and have only 2–3 large bud scales, whereas, those of Mulberry are sharp-pointed, straight and possess 4–8 tightly overlapping scales. The unique bracted fruit clusters of Basswood are a distinctive feature.

HABITAT: Basswood occurs on moist, fertile, well-drained slopes and stream bottoms in mixture with numerous hardwoods.

ECONOMIC, ORNAMENTAL AND OTHER USES: Basswood has long been prized as a valuable timber tree because of its soft, light, non-scented wood. It was formerly in much demand for food boxes, toys, picture frames, and excelsior. Today the wood is used mostly in the veneer and furniture industry and for soft hardwood pulp and paper. Basswood flowers are visited by bees and basswood honey is a favored product. The inner bark of Basswood contains long, very strong fibers which were utilized by the Indians in making rope and mats. The species is often used for shade and lawn trees but because of its ultimate size it is probably best suited for parks and golf courses and other open areas. Native species of Basswood are also subject to numerous disease and insect pests, hence several smaller, more resistant European species or cultivars are now used for ornamental plantings.

THEACEAE–TEA FAMILY

The Theaceae includes three genera found in North America and native to Georgia: *Gordonia*, *Stewartia*, and a monotypic genus, *Franklinia*, which is now extinct in the wild. This family is familiar to southern gardeners because of the Asiatic group of Camellias. Characteristic of the Theaceae are large showy flowers with 5 petals and numerous stamens. The leaves are alternate and deciduous in *Stewartia* and *Franklinia*, but evergreen in the single species of *Gordonia*.

Franklinia–Franklinia

Franklinia alatamaha Bartram ex Marshall

Franklinia, Franklin-tree

DESCRIPTION: Franklinia is a small tree of historical significance because it has been extinct in the wild for nearly 200 years. It is known today only as a cultivated plant. The species is grown ornamentally for its attractive flowers which appear in late summer and its showy red-orange autumn foliage. Although endemic to the Coastal Plain of Georgia, Franklinia is hardy as far north as Boston.

The tree was first discovered in 1765 by John and William Bartram along the banks of the Altamaha River (then spelled Alatamaha) near Fort Barrington, McIntosh County, Georgia. William Bartram reportedly returned to the site in 1773 and again in 1778 to obtain seed and plants which were propagated in Philadelphia. Moses Marshall apparently relocated the population in 1790, the last time Franklinia was observed growing in its native habitat. It has been speculated that the species was exterminated by collectors for shipment to London nurseries. William Bartram named the species for Benjamin Franklin and the Altamaha River. Later, it was placed in the closely related genus *Gordonia* [*Gordonia alatamaha* (Bartram) Sarg.]. Thus, for several decades the extinct species was commonly referred to as the "Lost Gordonia".

Franklinia may be distinguished from *Gordonia lasianthus*, Loblolly-bay, by its deciduous leaves, globular fruit capsules and nearly sessile flowers. The tree is also of much smaller stature than Loblolly-bay and the bark is smooth and thin, rather than thick and deeply furrowed as in the latter. Figure 336, flower and leaves of *Franklinia*.

Note: For readers who desire more historical information about *Franklinia*, refer to Jenkins, C. F. 1943, Franklin's Tree. Natl. Hort. Mag. 22:119–127, or to Harper, F. and A. N. Leeds, 1937, A supplementary chapter on *Franklinia Alatamaha*, Bartonia 19:1–13.

Gordonia–Gordonia

Gordonia lasianthus (L.) Ellis
Loblolly-bay, Gordonia

DESCRIPTION: This species is a small to medium-sized evergreen tree, up to 75' tall on rich sites, and shrubby on poorer, drier soils. It occurs in Georgia throughout the Coastal Plain.

Leaves – evergreen, simple, alternate; blades leathery, elliptical, tips acute or obtuse, 3–6" long, 1½–2" wide, margins with shallow serrations; upper surfaces glabrous, dark green; lower surfaces glabrous, pale. Figure 337.

Twigs – stout, reddish, smooth; terminal and lateral winter buds naked, globular, ¼–⅓" long, with silky hairs.

Bark – dark gray to reddish brown, smooth or lightly fissured on young trees, becoming thick and deeply fissured into narrow flat ridges on older trees. Figure 338.

Flowers – perfect; showy, white, 3" across, petals 5, fringed; stamens numerous, yellow, filaments united; borne singly on long reddish stalks in axillary clusters, usually only one flower opening at a time; fragrant; blooming throughout the summer. Figure 337.

Fruit – capsules, ovoid, ½" in diameter, splitting along 5 sutures; with silky hairs; seeds winged; maturing in autumn. Figure 339.

RECOGNITION DIFFICULTIES WITH OTHER TAXA: Loblolly-bay may occur in the same habitat with Sweetbay, *Magnolia virginiana* L. The two can easily be distinguished since the leaves of Loblolly-bay are shallowly toothed and glabrous beneath rather than entire margins with silvery pubescence beneath.

HABITAT: This species occurs on low, wet soils of bays and edges of swamps throughout the Coastal Plain, up to the sand hills of the fall line.

ECONOMIC, ORNAMENTAL AND OTHER USES: Loblolly-bay is a tree of minor commercial importance, however, its bark has been used locally for tanning leather. Because of its dark-green foliage and showy flowers it should become more widely used as an ornamental tree on moist sites.

Stewartia–Stewartias

SUMMER KEY TO SPECIES OF *STEWARTIA*

1. Flowers with yellow stamens;. 5 distinct styles; fruits 5-angled and beaked at the summit; mountains or Piedmont . . . . *S. ovata*
1. Flowers with purple stamens; styles fused; fruits not angled or beaked at the summit; Coastal Plain or lower Piedmont . . . . . *S. malacodendron*

Stewartia malacodendron L.

Virginia Stewartia, Silky Camellia

DESCRIPTION: This is a deciduous shrub or small tree, seldom over 20' in height or 4" in diameter. It is uncommon, in scattered localities of the lower Piedmont and Coastal Plain.

Leaves – deciduous, simple, alternate; blades ovate-elliptical, with acute or acuminate tips, 2–4" long, margins serrate and finely ciliate; upper surfaces glabrous, dark green, lower surfaces light green, finely pubescent. Figure 340.

Twigs – slender, gray; young twigs pubescent; winter buds silky pubescent, minute, 2 outer hairy scales; single raised bundle scar; pith spongy.

Bark – brown, smooth, flaking in irregular strips when older.

Flowers – perfect; showy, white, 2½–3" across, petals 5; stamens numerous, filaments purple; styles 5, united; appearing May–June.

Fruit – capsules, woody, pubescent, subglobose, about ½" wide or wider, splitting into 4 or 5 parts at maturity in autumn. Figure 340.

HABITAT: Virginia Stewartia occurs as an understory tree or shrub in rich, moist forests of the lower Piedmont and Coastal Plain in scattered localities.

RECOGNITION DIFFICULTIES WITH OTHER TAXA: In flower, Virginia Stewartia is conspicuous and unmistakable; however, with only foliage present, it is somewhat inconspicuous with its alternate, thin-textured leaves. The leaves might be confused with *Styrax*, although *Stewartia* has ciliated leaf margins and lacks the branched hairs beneath. The twig bark of *Stewartia* is shreddy, the winter buds are spindle-shaped, the two bud scales are silky pubescent, and the fruits are often persistent; whereas the twigs of *Styrax* have branched hairs, the buds are naked and the fruit does not persist into winter.

ECONOMIC, ORNAMENTAL AND OTHER USES: The flowers of this

species resemble the cultivated Camellias and it is occasionally used as an ornamental.

Stewartia ovata (Cav.) Weatherby

Mountain Stewartia, Mountain-Camellia

DESCRIPTION: Mountain Stewartia is a small understory tree which is scattered in much of the State with the exception of the Coastal Plain.

Leaves – similar to those of Virginia Stewartia, but up to 6" long. Figure 341.

Twigs – slender and glabrous, gray; winter buds about ¼" long with one pubescent scale enclosing the developing leaves.

Bark – grayish brown, slightly furrowed and shreddy.

Flowers – perfect; showy, white, petals 5, wavy margins; stamens numerous, anthers yellow; styles 5, separate; appearing in late June–July. Figure 341.

Fruit – capsules, woody, pubescent, ¾" in diameter, apically dehiscent, strongly 5 angled and beaked; seeds angled or winged with dull surfaces; maturing August–September.

HABITAT: This species occurs in scattered localities in the mountains of the Blue Ridge, the Ridge and Valley and the Piedmont in moist woods, along streams and ravines.

RECOGNITION DIFFICULTIES WITH OTHER TAXA: Mountain Stewartia and Virginia Stewartia do not occur in the same habitats in Georgia. Mountain Stewartia is found in the mountains and Piedmont and Virginia Stewartia is found only in the Coastal Plain or lower Piedmont.

ECONOMIC, ORNAMENTAL AND OTHER USES: *Stewartia ovata* is used occasionally as an ornamental, but is not often available in the horticultural trade because of propagation difficulties.

ARALIACEAE–GINSENG FAMILY

The Araliaceae is mostly tropical in distribution, with only one tree native to the United States and Georgia, *Aralia spinosa*. Economically, this family is of little domestic importance. Many cultivars of the English Ivy, *Hedera helix* L., a vine indigenous to Europe, are grown ornamentally as ground cover. The medicinal Ginseng roots are obtained in the Appalachian Mountains from the herb, *Panax quinquefolium* L. Several species of *Schefflera* are grown as house plants.

Aralia–Aralia

Aralia spinosa L.
Devil's-walkingstick

DESCRIPTION: This species is usually a large shrub, but it often develops into a small, vigorous tree reaching heights of 25–30'. The exceptionally stout, spiny branches and very large pinnately compound leaves produce an open, spreading crown with a grotesque appearance. It is common throughout the State.

Leaves – deciduous, 2–3 pinnately compound, alternate; petiole and rachis spiny, large, up to 4' long, 2–3' wide; petiole enlarged at base; leaflets ovate, 1–4" long, margins finely serrate, nearly glabrous. Figure 342.

Twigs – very stout, light brown, armed with sharp prickles, orange lenticels; terminal bud ½–¾" long, bud scales several; lateral buds about ¼" long, triangular, flattened; leaf scar U-shaped, often with a row of prickles surrounding the scar; bundle scars many in a single row; pith very large, white, homogeneous.

Bark – brown, thin, very spiny with shallow flattened interwoven ridges; inner bark yellow.

Flowers – perfect or staminate; greenish white, regular; small, in many-flowered terminal panicles 3–4' long; appearing late summer. Figure 343.

Fruit – globose berry-like drupes with 5 seeds, black, juicy, about ⅜" in diameter; style persistent; in large panicle; maturing late summer to early autumn. Figure 344.

RECOGNITION DIFFICULTIES WITH OTHER TAXA: *Zanthoxylum americanum* has armed stems, but the spines are usually 2 per node; the leaves are once-pinnately compound.

HABITAT: This species frequently occurs on moist sites along streams and bottomlands as an understory species, and occasionally on drier upland slopes throughout the State.

NYSSACEAE–TUPELO FAMILY

This is a relatively small family of trees or shrubs, containing three genera and eight species in eastern North America and Asia. *Nyssa* is the only genus indigenous to the United States, and some authors still retain this genus in the Cornaceae. Three species of *Nyssa* occur in Georgia. Some taxonomists recognize four species, maintaining specific rank of *Nyssa biflora* Walter rather than a variety of *N. sylvatica* Marshall, as presented here. The family is of considerable economic importance because of various timber products and the ornamental use of several species.

Nyssa–Tupelos

SUMMER KEY TO SPECIES OF *NYSSA*
1. Fruits (or pistillate flowers) solitary on a stalk, fruit 1" or more long; usually some leaves 6" or longer 2
    2. Mature fruits red; the stones with papery wings; leaves blunt with a mucronate tip; often multi-trunked .... *N. ogeche*
    2. Mature fruits blue-black; stones ribbed; leaf tips acute to acuminate; single, erect trunk........................ *N. aquatica*
1. Fruits (or pistillate flowers) 2 or 3–5 to a stalk, fruits less than 1" long; leaves less than 6" in length 3
    3. Bases of trunks not swollen; leaves thin; fruits 3 or 4 per cluster; stone not ribbed .... *N. sylvatica* var. *sylvatica*
    3. Bases of trunks swollen; leaves thick; fruits usually 2 per cluster; stone ribbed........................ *N. sylvatica* var. *biflora*

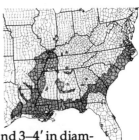

Nyssa aquatica L.

Water Tupelo

DESCRIPTION: This is a large tree, often over 100' tall and 3–4' in diameter, with large swollen buttresses. It is a common wetland species of the Coastal Plain.

Leaves – deciduous, simple, alternate; blades ovate to oblong-ovate, bases cuneate to subcordate, tips acute to acuminate, 5–7" long, margins entire or with one or more irregularly spaced teeth; upper surfaces dark green, glabrous; lower surfaces pale, downy; petiole 1–2" long. Figure 345.

Twigs – moderately stout, reddish brown, nearly glabrous; pith diaphragmed; terminal buds globose, yellowish, about ⅛" long, glabrous; lateral buds minute and inconspicuous; leaf scars with 3 bundle scars.

Bark – grayish brown to brown, moderately furrowed into rather narrow longitudinal scaly ridges. Figure 346.

Flowers – green, small, inconspicuous, about ¼" long; staminate in dense clusters at end of peduncle; pistillate solitary on peduncle; appearing April–May. Figure 347, staminate flowers.

Fruit – drupes, dark blue or purple at maturity, oblong, about 1" long; stalk longer than fruit; stone with longitudinal ridges; maturing in summer. Figure 348.

RECOGNITION DIFFICULTIES WITH OTHER TAXA: Water Tupelo can be distinguished from Ogeechee Tupelo by its acuminate leaf tips, glabrous twigs, and petioles 1–2" long. Ogeechee Tupelo has blunt leaf tips, velvety pubescent twigs, and petioles less than 1" long. The bluish purple fruit of Water Tupelo is borne on a stalk longer than the length of the fruit. The red fruit of Ogeechee Tupelo are borne on stalks that do not exceed the length of the fruit and the stone possesses numerous papery, well-defined, wing-like membranes.

HABITAT: *Nyssa aquatica* is common in river swamps of the Coastal Plain, where it is often inundated for long periods of time in winter and spring. Frequently, Water Tupelo occurs in pure stands or mixed with Bald Cypress and wetland hardwoods. It occurs occasionally in river swamps in the lower Piedmont.

ECONOMIC, ORNAMENTAL AND OTHER USES: Water Tupelo is an important timber tree for plywood and veneer stock, and a source of hardwood pulp. The root wood and buttresses near the base are light and somewhat spongy because of large intercellular air spaces and has been used locally for fishing floats and corks. Tupelo honey is a prized commodity in many localities.

Nyssa ogeche Bartram ex Marshall

Ogeechee Tupelo, Ogeechee-lime

DESCRIPTION: This is a small to medium-sized tree usually less than

40' tall, typically with swollen buttresses and multiple, crooked stems. It has a rather restricted distribution along the rivers of the lower Coastal Plain.

Leaves – similar to *N. aquatica*, 4–6" long; leaf tips rounded to blunt, often with a mucronate tip petiole less than 1" long. Figure 349.

Twigs – slender, light reddish brown, rusty pubescent; winter buds globose, inner scale bright red, glabrous; terminal and lateral buds about the same size as *N. aquatica*; leaf scars with 3 bundle scars; pith diaphragmed.

Bark – dark brown; irregularly fissured into longitudinal plates similar in appearance to *N. aquatica*.

Flowers – staminate or polygamous; flowers similar to *N. aquatica*; staminate in dense, globose clusters on long peduncles; pistillate flowers solitary on short peduncle; appearing in April.

Fruit – drupes, oblong, red, 1–1½" long; pendulous on short stalks ½" long or less; stones attached by papery wings to the skin of the fruit; maturing August–October. Figure 350.

RECOGNITION DIFFICULTIES WITH OTHER TAXA: See *N. aquatica* for distinguishing characteristics.

HABITAT: Ogeechee Tupelo occurs on wet sites along streams and in swamps with long periods of inundation in winter and spring.

ECONOMIC, ORNAMENTAL AND OTHER USES: The name of this tree is derived from the Ogeechee River in Georgia where it was first discovered by William Bartram, and from the acid juice of the fruit which was used as a substitute for limes. The tree is of little commercial importance.

Nyssa sylvatica Marshall var. *sylvatica*
Blackgum, Black Tupelo

DESCRIPTION: Blackgum is a medium to large tree occasionally reaching 90–100' tall and 2–3' in diameter. It is common throughout Georgia.

Leaves – deciduous, simple, alternate; blades thin, broadly lanceolate to obovate, or elliptical, tips rounded to acute or acuminate, bases cuneate to rounded, 2–6" long, margins entire, or irregularly toothed; turns crimson in autumn. Figure 351.

Twigs – slender, grayish brown, with numerous pale lenticels; terminal buds acute, about ¼" long; lateral buds sharp pointed and divergent, about ⅛" in length, bud scales reddish brown, glabrous, overlapping; leaf scars with 3 bundle scars; pith diaphragmed.

Bark – light to dark gray or brown on young trees, with small rectangular plates, becoming deeply fissured and blocky on older trees often with "alligator hide" appearance. Figure 352.

Flowers – dioecious; greenish yellow, tiny, less than ¼" long; staminate borne in clusters at the ends of stalks; pistillate 3–5 per stalk; appearing April–May during leaf development. Figure 353.

Fruit – drupes, blue-black at maturity, ¼ to ½" long; borne 2–3 per stalk; stone indistinctly ribbed. Figure 354.

RECOGNITION DIFFICULTIES WITH OTHER TAXA: Young Blackgum trees can be confused with Persimmon on upland sites when fruit and flowers are unavailable. However, the margins of leaves on shoots of Blackgum are sometimes irregularly one to few-toothed while margins of Persimmon leaves are never toothed. Terminal buds of Blackgum are present, but are aborted in Persimmon. Blackgum has 3 bundle scars, whereas Persimmon has a single bundle scar. (See also description of *Nyssa sylvatica* var. *biflora*.)

HABITAT: Blackgum is ubiquitous in Georgia. The best formed trees occur on moist, well-drained soils along streams or flats, but they cannot survive the prolonged flooding of swamp habitats. It is also common on dry, upland sites in association with other hardwoods.

ECONOMIC, ORNAMENTAL AND OTHER USES: The common name "Blackgum" is a misnomer because the tree does not produce gum or latex of any kind. The wood possesses interlocked grain and cannot be split, even with wedges or other devices. Consequently, the wood was formerly used for mauls, implement handles, skid poles, and floors. Frayed twigs have been used as toothbrushes. Presently, the species is harvested for hardwood pulp and veneer for plywood and paneling. Blackgum is an excellent shade and ornamental tree because of its dense green foliage and brilliant red autumn coloration. The species is also prized as a "bee tree."

Nyssa sylvatica var. *biflora* (Walter) Sarg.

(*N. biflora* Walter)

Swamp Tupelo, Swamp Black Gum

DESCRIPTION: This is a medium-sized to large tree, 60–100' tall, with swollen buttresses similar to Water Tupelo, but very similar to Blackgum in leaf and crown form. It occurs in swamps throughout much of the Coastal Plain and occasionally in the Piedmont and the northwestern part of the State in wet depressions.

Leaves – smaller than those of Blackgum, 2–4" long, 1–2½" wide; oblanceolate to narrowly elliptical, tips rounded to obtuse to sub-acute; upper surfaces lustrous, lower surface paler, becoming glabrous; brilliant red in autumn. Figure 355.

Twigs – slender, grayish brown; winter buds acute, dark red-brown, inner scales pubescent; indistinguishable from Blackgum.

Bark – similar to Blackgum, but with pronounced swollen buttresses.

Flowers – similar to Blackgum, but appearing when the leaves are almost fully developed.

Fruit – similar in size and shape to that of Blackgum; 1–2 fruits per stalk; stone prominently ribbed; maturing August–October.

RECOGNITION DIFFICULTIES WITH OTHER TAXA: Swamp Tupelo closely resembles Blackgum, *N. sylvatica*, but Swamp Tupelo has 1–2 fruits per stalk and the stone of the fruit is prominently ribbed, while Blackgum has 3 or more fruits per stalk and the stone is only slightly ribbed.

HABITAT: This species is common in nonalluvial swamps, flatwoods, and shallow ponds in the Coastal Plain, and is occasional in the north-western part of the State in sag pond habitats.

ECONOMIC, ORNAMENTAL AND OTHER USES: Similar to Blackgum; however, timber form and quality are comparable to Water Tupelo.

CORNACEAE–DOGWOOD FAMILY

The Cornaceae is represented in North America by the single genus *Cornus*. The native *Cornus* species are small trees and shrubs. In Georgia, the best known species is the flowering dogwood, *Cornus florida* L.f., which has four large, showy, white bracts below the flower clusters, these appearing before the leaves. This species is used extensively in the Southeast as an ornamental. Several *Cornus* species reach tree size in the State.

The nomenclature of a number of species in this genus has been variously applied, resulting in confusion regarding identity of the taxa. Although we have chosen to follow Little (1976) for *C. stricta* Lam. and *C. drummondii* C. A. Meyer (excluding *C. asperifolia* Michaux which is a shrub), others follow Wilson (1964) and recognize *C. foemina* and *C. drummondii* (including *C. asperifolia*). Based on the presence of intermediate characteristics in some specimens, hybridization is reported to occur between several taxa.

This group is characterized by (usually) opposite leaves with several conspicuous pinnate veins which curve upwardly and run parallel with the margin. The flowers are small, perfect, and are borne in a cluster. The fruit is a drupe.

Cornus–Dogwoods

SUMMER KEY TO SPECIES OF CORNUS

1. Leaves alternate................................... C. alternifolia
1. Leaves opposite....................................... 2
    2. Four large, petal-like bracts surrounding the flowers; drupes red; twigs green or purple with small dark lenticels; mature bark breaking into square, scaly blocks .... C. florida
    2. Flower cluster not surrounded by showy bracts; drupes blue or white; twigs red with large light lenticels; mature bark thin, red-brown, becoming ridged................................ 3
        3. Leaves with stiff hairs on upper surface; drupes white.....
        ....C. drummondii
        3. Leaves smooth or sparsely pubescent; drupes blue ... C. stricta

Cornus alternifolia L. f.

Alternate-leaf Dogwood

DESCRIPTION: This species is a small tree, often a shrub, which is most prevalent in the mountains, but is localized in the upper Piedmont, and extends into several southwestern counties in the Coastal Plain.

    Leaves – deciduous, simple, alternate, clustered at ends of twigs; blades elliptic to oval, 3–5" long, margins inconspicuously toothed, lateral veins arched upward, paralleling the margin; upper surfaces glabrous, green; lower surfaces sparsely hairy, pale; petioles up to 2" long, swollen at leaf base and at node. Figure 356.

    Twigs – slender, greenish at the tips, but soon turning dark red, large, light lenticels; terminal bud with 2–3 overlapping scales; leaf scars crescent-shaped, bundle scars 3; pith white; acrid odor when bruised.

    Bark – dark reddish brown, smooth at first, becoming lightly furrowed and slightly scaly on older stems.

    Flowers – perfect, petals white, small, about ¼" wide; in flat-topped, showy clusters, 2–4" wide at end of leafy twigs; appearing May to June. Figure 356.

    Fruit – drupes, blue-black, about ¼" long; numerous, on red stalks; maturing in August–September. Figure 357.

RECOGNITION DIFFICULTIES WITH OTHER TAXA: The alternate leaf arrangement for this species is unique for dogwoods; however, when the leaves are crowded, this feature is not obvious. The long petiole, up to 2½" long, is distinctive for *C. alternifolia*.

HABITAT: The species occurs on rich, moist soils along margins of woodlands and as an understory tree in mixed hardwoods.

ECONOMIC, ORNAMENTAL AND OTHER USES: Occasionally, *C. alternifolia* is used as an ornamental plant for its numerous showy flower clusters and reddish purple leaf coloration in autumn. This species deserves more attention for use in natural areas and near buildings where horizontal features are needed to break vertical architectural lines. The fruit is consumed by numerous birds and small mammals.

Cornus drummondii C. A. Meyer
Roughleaf Dogwood

DESCRIPTION: Roughleaf Dogwood is usually a thicket-forming shrub, reproducing by root sprouts, but occasionally reaches the size of a small tree. It is rare in Georgia, recorded from only Dade County.

Leaves – deciduous, simple, opposite; blades similar in size and shape to *C. alternifolia*, densely covered with white hairs when first expanded, later becoming green and rough, with stiff hairs on the upper surface; pale and pubescent beneath.

Twigs – slender, light green and pubescent in early spring, becoming reddish brown to gray; leaf buds with 2–3 overlapping scales, terminal buds less than ¼"; lateral buds smaller; flower buds slender.

Bark – gray to reddish brown, thin, later becoming finely fissured and ridged.

Flowers – very similar to *C. alternifolia*.

Fruit – drupes, white, about ¼" in diameter; borne in loose clusters on red stalks; 1–2 seeded; maturing in late summer.

RECOGNITION DIFFICULTIES WITH OTHER TAXA: *Cornus drummondii* is doubtfully distinct from *C. asperifolia*, a shrubby taxon with rough leaves, which is reported in Georgia in Piedmont and Coastal Plain counties.

HABITAT: Outside of the State, *C. drummondii* is reported on a wide variety of sites, frequently along moist stream banks, but also on wooded bluffs, and limestone outcrops. In Georgia, this species is recorded only from the northwestern tip of the State.

ECONOMIC, ORNAMENTAL AND OTHER USES: Roughleaf Dogwood could be desirable in some landscape situations where a thick hedge or border is needed. It provides excellent ground cover for wildlife, and numerous species of birds feed on its fruit.

Cornus florida L.
Flowering Dogwood

DESCRIPTION: This species is a small tree, ubiquitous in all regions of the State in the understory of hardwoods.

Leaves – deciduous, simple, opposite; blades ovate to broadly elliptic, 3–6" long, bases rounded, veins curving to run parallel with the margin; sparsely pubescent; petiole short, about ¼–½" long; crimson in autumn. Figure 358.

Twigs – slender, green or purplish, with small dark lenticels; terminal leaf buds pointed, with 2 valvate scales; lateral buds small, enclosed by petiole; leaf scars nearly encircling twig, V-shaped; bundle scars 3; terminal flower buds set the previous season, about ¼", globular, with 4 scales.

Bark – dark brown, rough, broken into small rectangular plates at an early age; on older trees breaking into square, scaly blocks, thereby somewhat resembling Persimmon, except plates not as large, dark nor as deeply fissured. Figure 359.

Flowers – perfect; yellowish green, 4 petals, about ¼" across; in tight clusters, surrounded by 4 large, showy white, petal-like bracts, 1½–2" long, resembling a flower; appearing in early spring before the leaves. Figure 360.

Fruit – drupes; shiny red, elliptical, about ¼–½" long; calyx lobes persistent; maturing September–October. Figure 361.

RECOGNITION DIFFICULTIES WITH OTHER TAXA: This species is distinctive from our other species of dogwood in having flowers surrounded by showy white bracts. In fall and winter it is distinguished by clusters of bright red fruit, globose terminal flower buds, and blocky "alligator hide" bark.

HABITAT: Flowering Dogwood occurs as an understory tree on well-drained, upland soils and on deep, mesic soils along streams and lower slopes.

ECONOMIC, ORNAMENTAL AND OTHER USES: The wood of Flowering Dogwood is very hard and heavy and was once a major source of shuttles and spools for the textile industry. It is still used for mallets, golf club heads and other specialty products. Flowering Dogwood is one of our most showy and beautiful native trees, and it is probably the most widespread ornamental tree in North America. It is excellent as a specimen tree in all seasons and suitable for many landscape uses. Numerous cultivars have been selected for the differently colored bracts and the brilliant autumn leaf coloration.

Cornus stricta Lam.

(*Cornus foemina* Miller)

Swamp Dogwood

DESCRIPTION: This species is a large shrub which occasionally attains tree size (25' tall, 3–4" in diameter). Swamp Dogwood grows throughout most of Georgia. The leaves are opposite and similar in shape to *C. florida*, except usually smaller. The flowers are borne in showy white to yellowish clusters, similar to those of *C. alternifolia*, and the fruits are dark blue to purple globose drupes, about ¼" in diameter, borne in loose clusters. The young twigs and bark are green to reddish brown and glabrous, the older bark becoming distinctively streaked with reddish brown, thin, narrow plates. Swamp Dogwood is common along streams and in bottomlands of the Piedmont and Coastal Plain, but is infrequent to rare in the mountains. *Cornus amomum*, another shrubby species which occurs in wetlands, has pubescent maroon twigs and leaves with russet colored pubescence beneath. The latter is found chiefly in the mountains and the Piedmont. Figure 362, leaves and flowers; Figure 363, fruit.

CLETHRACEAE–PEPPERBUSH FAMILY

This family of tall shrubs or low trees consists of two genera, *Clethra* and *Schizocardia*, native to North, Central, and South America, Asia, and Pacific Islands. Only *Clethra* is represented in the United States. A few species of Asian *Clethra* are cultivated as ornamental plants in many parts of the country primarily for their fragrant summer flowers.

Clethra–Clethra

Clethra acuminata Michaux
Cinnamon Clethra, Sweet Pepperbush

DESCRIPTION: This species is most often a large, multi-stemmed shrub. It does, however, become a small tree in many of the moist, rich coves of White, Union, Towns, and Rabun Counties.

Leaves – deciduous, simple, alternate; blades elliptic, tips long acuminate, 3–6" long, margins finely serrate; essentially glabrous. Figure 364.

Twigs – densely pubescent with branched hairs; terminal bud ovoid, ¼–½" long, outer bud scales as long as bud; lateral buds minute; leaf scar triangular; single bundle scar.

Bark – red-brown on younger stems, thin, smooth, shiny, quickly exfoliating into horizontal curls and loose strips.

Flowers – perfect; white, 5 petals less than 1" long, stamens and styles exerted beyond the petals; occurring in terminal racemes; sepals and raceme rachis woolly, white, stellate pubescent; appearing July–August. Figure 365.

Fruit – capsules, about ⅛" wide, subglobose, splitting in 3 parts; densely pubescent; maturing in autumn and persisting through the winter. Figure 364.

RECOGNITION DIFFICULTIES WITH OTHER TAXA: Sweet Pepperbush is recognized by having a single bundle scar, long terminal buds, long pointed leaves, exfoliating bark, and persistent fruit in the winter. This combination of traits make this plant distinctive. *Clethra alnifolia* L. is a shrub of the Coastal Plain and does not overlap in range.

HABITAT: *Clethra acuminata* occurs in rich, moist slopes and coves in the mountains, usually above 2500' in elevation.

ECONOMIC, ORNAMENTAL AND OTHER USES: Sweet Pepperbush is frequently cultivated in gardens because of its fragrant summer blooms and colorful, exfoliating bark.

ERICACEAE–HEATH FAMILY

The Ericaceae is comprised of about 1900 species of mostly shrubs, perennial herbs and small trees, widely distributed throughout the world. The family is economically important for species of ornamental and crop value. The genus *Vaccinium* includes blueberries and cranberries. The azaleas, rhododendrons, and Mountain Laurel are particularly prized as landscape specimens and have been extensively selected for color of flower, cold hardiness, and form. The large genus, *Erica*, contains the well-known, pleasantly smelling heaths of northern Europe.

Elliottia–Elliottia

Elliottia racemosa Muhlenb. ex Elliott
Elliottia, Georgia Plume

DESCRIPTION: Elliottia is one of our rarest native trees, restricted to a few localities in eastern and southeastern Georgia. When in flower, it is particularly attractive. Usually it is a small tree, only occasionally reaching 35–40' in height and 6–8" in diameter. The species was discovered around 1800 near Waynesboro, Georgia, by Stephen Elliott, a South Carolina botanist. For many decades the fruit was unknown. Although fruit and viable seeds may be rare in several localities where the species occurs, we have obtained fruit and viable seed from plants in Tattnall County, Georgia and have subsequently observed fruit production in these plants for several years. The plant reproduces vegetatively by means of root collar sprouts when injured by fire or mechanical means.

Leaves – deciduous, simple, alternate; blades oblong, apex acute with short bristle, base tapered, about 4" long, 1–2" wide, lateral veins arch toward apex and form marginal loops; upper surfaces dark green; lower surfaces pale, pubescent; petioles about ½" long, flattened with enlarged base nearly covering axillary buds. Figure 366.

Twigs – orange-brown when young, becoming grayish brown and roughened with age; terminal winter buds acute, about ⅛" long, scales fringed with white hairs; leaf scars shield-shaped with a single bundle scar.

Bark – pale gray, thin, lightly furrowed when young; somewhat similar to Sourwood, but not as deeply furrowed on older trees.

Flowers – perfect; about ¾" long, petals 4, narrow, linear, white; in terminal erect racemes or panicles, 6–12" long; appearing late June. Figure 367.

Fruit – capsules, dark brown to blackish; 4 or 5-lobed, about ⅜" in diameter; seeds minute, light brown, flattened with thin, membranous margins; capsules persisting into winter. Figure 368.

RECOGNITION DIFFICULTIES WITH OTHER TAXA: Elliottia should be distinctive in all seasons. No other native tree possesses such elongate clusters of terminal, white, showy flowers in early summer. The fruits persist into winter, and the bark resembles young Sourwood.

HABITAT: Although Elliottia is very rare and local in distribution, it occurs on a wide range of sites from xeric sandhills, sandstone rock outcrop, moist sands of mixed hardwoods, and scattered pines in the Coastal Plain and lower Piedmont. These sites are located mostly within the drainage systems of the Altamaha-Ogeechee-Savannah Rivers. An exception is a single locality within the Alapaha River drainage.

ECONOMIC, ORNAMENTAL AND OTHER USES: Elliottia is currently a State-protected species, considered in an endangered status, although it is not listed on the Federal Endangered and Threatened Species List.

Kalmia–Kalmia

Kalmia latifolia L.
Mountain Laurel

DESCRIPTION: Mountain Laurel is usually a large, thicket-forming evergreen shrub with short crooked stems and stout branches which form a compact rounded crown. Occasionally, this species attains heights of 20–25' with a single short trunk 8–10" in diameter. It is common in the mountains but extends along streambanks into the Piedmont and Coastal Plain in localized areas.

Leaves – evergreen, simple, alternate; blades leathery, elliptical, 3–4" long, 1–1½" wide, entire, midrib terminates in an inconspicuous greenish-white swollen tip; both surfaces glabrous. Figure 369.

Twigs – green to reddish brown; flower buds produced in autumn, terminally and in axils of upper leaves, covered with glandular hairy scales; winter leaf buds formed in leaf axils below those producing flower buds; leaf scars half round and embedded in the twig.

Bark – dark reddish brown, thin, slightly scaly.

Flowers – perfect; reddish pink to white (deep pink and crinkled in bud), angular, saucer-shaped corolla with 10 pouches in which anthers are buried to spring out when insects touch the exposed filaments; in showy clusters, 4–6" across; terminal and in axils of upper leaves; appearing April–June. Figure 369.

Fruit – capsules, dry, 5-celled, about ¼" wide; maturing September–October.

RECOGNITION DIFFICULTIES WITH OTHER TAXA: Mountain Laurel is very distinctive in bloom. In the absence of flowers, it may resemble Rosebay Rhododendron, *R. maximum*, which also forms thickets in the mountains. However, the latter species usually has large drooping leaves, often greenish-yellow in color, 3–8" long with rolled edges in contrast to those of Mountain Laurel with flat dark green leaves 2–5" long. A shrubby, evergreen rhododendron, *R. minus*, which is common at lower elevations in the mountains and occasional in the Piedmont, somewhat resembles Mountain Laurel when flowers are not present. Leaves of *R. minus* are dotted with glands on the lower surface (as well as the calyx, corolla, pedicels, and twigs), whereas leaves of Mountain Laurel have stalked glands when young, but become smooth with age.

HABITAT: Mountain Laurel is common on dry slopes and ridges of the mountains and occasional along stream banks in the Piedmont. In the Coastal Plain, it is usually confined to ravines along the Savannah, Chattahoochee, and Flint Rivers.

ECONOMIC, ORNAMENTAL AND OTHER USES: Mountain Laurel is one of our most beautiful and showy native flowering plants. It is widely used as an ornamental throughout its range. It is excellent for borders and mass plantings in the mountains, however, it often does not transplant well in the Piedmont and Coastal Plain.

Lyonia–Lyonia

Lyonia ferruginea (Walter) Nutt.
Tree Lyonia, Staggerbush

DESCRIPTION: This evergreen species is usually a shrub with crooked, contorted stems forming a small, irregular, open crown. Occasionally, it reaches tree size under favorable conditions, becoming 20–25' tall and 6–8" in diameter. It occurs in Georgia along the coast and in flatwoods of the lower Coastal Plain.

Leaves – evergreen, simple, alternate; blades elliptic to obovate, 1–3" long, about 1" wide, tip bluntly mucronate; margins entire and revolute, wavy; lower surface rusty scaly. Figure 370.

Twigs – slender, gray to rusty scaly, becoming reddish brown; terminal and lateral buds minute, sharp-pointed with 2 exposed scales, appressed; leaf scars half-round with a single bundle scar.

Bark – gray to reddish brown, lightly furrowed into long, narrow scaly ridges.

Flowers – perfect; white or pink, globular, urn-shaped corolla, small, about ¼" long, in small clusters in axils of leaves; appearing April–May. Figure 370.

Fruit – capsules, dry, ovoid, about ¼" long; splitting open into 5 parts; maturing September–October, and persistent into winter.

RECOGNITION DIFFICULTIES WITH OTHER TAXA: Staggerbush leaves may resemble those of *Bumelia tenax* and *B. lanuginosa*. However, the brownish rusty lower leaf surfaces of Staggerbush is due to the presence of scales rather than hairs. The latter two species also have thorns; Staggerbush does not.

HABITAT: Staggerbush occurs occasionally in the lower Coastal Plain in sandy maritime soils and dunes and scrubby pine hardwoods.

ECONOMIC, ORNAMENTAL AND OTHER USES: *Lyonia ferruginea* has no commercial value. But, due to the pronounced crookedness of numerous, single stems, it can add an interesting diversity to the landscape.

Oxydendrum–Sourwood

Oxydendrum arboreum (L.) DC.
Sourwood

DESCRIPTION: Sourwood is a small to medium-size tree often reaching 50' tall and 10–12" in diameter. It occurs throughout the State, but is more abundant in the mountains and Piedmont than in the Coastal Plain.

Leaves – deciduous, simple, alternate; blades elliptical, up to 7" long, 1½–3½" wide, margins finely toothed; yellowish green, turning dark red in autumn; sour to taste. Figure 371.

Twigs – slender, zigzag, yellow-green, lenticels conspicuous; terminal winter bud absent; lateral buds small, partially embedded in bark; leaf scars half-round or shield-shaped and raised with a single bundle scar.

Bark – lustrous gray to brown, often with a tinge of red, deeply furrowed on older trees, with interlacing ridges which frequently divide transversely to give a blocky appearance. Figure 372.

Flowers – perfect; white, bell-shaped, about ⅓" long; in one-sided raceme from tips of branches, forming a drooping spray 5–10" long, resembling lily-of-the-valley flowers; appearing June–July. Figure 373.

Fruit – capsules, small, ⅜" long, 5-celled; maturing in autumn and often persisting through winter on drooping to upright, curved stalks.

RECOGNITION DIFFICULTIES WITH OTHER TAXA: Sourwood is easily recognized by its drooping flower clusters in early to mid-summer and the drooping fruit sprays which persist into early winter. In summer, the long, greenish yellow, elliptical, finely toothed leaves and the distinctive, deeply furrowed bark set it aside from other taxa.

HABITAT: Sourwood usually occurs as a single tree on moist slopes of mixed hardwood forests; yet it is frequently found on drier sites along ridges and around the edges of fields or roadsides.

ECONOMIC, ORNAMENTAL AND OTHER USES: Sourwood flowers provide a preferred source of nectar for honeybees and Sourwood honey is widely marketed. This species has striking ornamental potential and is generally under utilized by landscapers. In autumn, the brilliant red foliage contrasts with the showy dangling fruit clusters. It is essentially pest-free and can be grown in sun or partial shade.

Rhododendron–Rhododendron

SUMMER KEY TO SPECIES OF *RHODODENDRON*

1. Leaves 4–12" long, pointed at the tips, tapered at the base.......
   ....*R. maximum*
1. Leaves 3½–6" long, blunt at the tip, rounded at the base ....
   ....*R. catawbiense*

Rhododendron catawbiense Michaux

Purple Rhododendron

DESCRIPTION: Purple Rhododendron is an evergreen, thicket-forming shrub or small tree with large showy clusters of purplish flowers. It is found sparingly at higher elevations in the Blue Ridge Mountains in the uppermost tier of counties in Northeast Georgia and also at lower mountain elevations in several northwestern counties.

Leaves – evergreen, simple, alternate; blades leathery, widely elliptic, base rounded, blunt at tip, 3½–6" long, margins sometimes revolute; upper surfaces shiny, dark green; lower surfaces whitish. Figure 374.

Twigs – stout, green; lateral buds small; flower buds terminal, 1-1½" long with many overlapping sticky scales; leaf scars heart-shaped to linear; bundle scars one to several.

Bark – reddish brown, thin, smooth at first, becoming slightly fissured into thin, scaly ridges.

Flowers – perfect; deep pink to purple, rarely white, 5-lobed, greater than 1" in diameter; in terminal clusters; April–June. Figure 374.

Fruit – capsules, elongate, about ¾" long, sticky, glandular; maturing July–October.

RECOGNITION DIFFICULTIES WITH OTHER TAXA: *Rhododendron catawbiense* occurs with *R. maximum* at high elevations and can be distinguished by its smaller leaves which are rounded to blunt at the tip and a rounded rather than tapered leaf base.

HABITAT: Purple Rhododendron occurs along ridges, on bluffs, and as an understory species in mixed hardwood forests on moist, rocky slopes.

ECONOMIC, ORNAMENTAL AND OTHER USES: Purple Rhododendron is one of the most attractive and showy native plants in North America. It is a featured attraction for visitors and tourists each spring in the southern Appalachian Mountains. It is a prized ornamental specimen for moist, acidic, shady sites and is planted in borders or massed for effect.

Rhododendron maximum L.

Rosebay Rhododendron

DESCRIPTION: Rosebay Rhododendron is an evergreen thicket-forming shrub or small tree usually with short crooked stems and branches producing a compact crown. Occasionally, it may reach 30' in height and 8–10" in diameter. The species is common in the mountainous section of Georgia and occurs sparingly in the adjacent Piedmont.

Leaves – evergreen, simple, alternate; blades leathery, oblong, tips pointed, bases tapered, 4–12" long, 2–3" wide, margins revolute, entire; upper surfaces pale to dark green, lustrous; lower surfaces paler. Figure 375.

Twigs – stout, green to reddish brown; buds similar to *R. catawbiense*.

Bark – reddish brown, thin, broken into thin scales.

Flowers – perfect; showy, white, pink or light purple, 5-lobed, greater than 1" in diameter; in terminal clusters; appearing June–August. Figure 375.

Fruit – capsules, dark reddish brown, elongate, 5-celled, about ½" long, crowned with the remnants of the style; sticky, glandular; maturing September–October and persistent during the winter.

RECOGNITION DIFFICULTIES WITH OTHER TAXA: See *R. catawbiense*.

HABITAT: Rosebay Rhododendron occurs on moist, rocky slopes and stream banks of the mountains and upper Piedmont in local areas.

ECONOMIC, ORNAMENTAL AND OTHER USES: Rosebay Rhododendron is one of the largest and hardiest rhododendrons grown commercially. It requires moist, acidic soil and some shade protection. Several cultivars with white to purple flowers have been selected for the horticultural trade.

Vaccinium–Blueberry

Vaccinium arboreum Marshall

Sparkleberry, Huckleberry

DESCRIPTION: Sparkleberry is usually a large shrub, but frequently attains small tree size with a short trunk and many crooked, twisted branches. It is common throughout most of the State, particularly in the Coastal Plain and Piedmont.

Leaves – tardily deciduous, almost persistent in the Coastal Plain, simple, alternate; oval to elliptic, tips blunt and sometimes mucronate, bases rounded to narrowed, ½–2" long, veins prominent; dark green, glossy. Figure 376.

Twigs – slender, crooked, many-branched, reddish; terminal buds absent; lateral buds globose, small; leaf scars small, half-round; single bundle scar.

Bark – reddish brown, thin, divided into narrow, shreddy ridges.

Flowers – white, bell-shaped, about ¼"; abundant in leafy-bracted racemes 2–3" across; appearing after foliage in April–May. Figure 376.

Fruit – berry, black, about ¼" in diameter; many seeded; lustrous; maturing September to October, often persisting into winter. Figure 377.

RECOGNITION DIFFICULTIES WITH OTHER TAXA: Sparkleberry should not be difficult to separate from other species of *Vaccinium* because of its larger size, distinctive glossy foliage, gnarled stem, and branch form.

HABITAT: Sparkleberry occurs on a wide range of sites throughout the State from dry sandy and rocky uplands, granitic outcrops to moist, well-drained areas around forest margins and streams. Unlike most other blueberries, it will grow quite well on neutral to slightly alkaline soils.

ECONOMIC, ORNAMENTAL AND OTHER USES: *Vaccinium arboreum* should be used more for ornamental purposes because of its attractive glossy foliage which turns reddish-purple in autumn and its gnarled, somewhat grotesque winter silhouette; however, it grows slowly. The fruit is dry and non-palatable to humans, but it is consumed in quantity by song and game birds, deer, bear and numerous small mammals.

SAPOTACEAE–SAPODILLA FAMILY

The Sapotaceae is a moderately large family of about 600 species, occurring primarily in the tropics and subtropics. The common name of the family derives from Sapodilla, the chewing gum of the Aztecs [*Manilkara zapota* (L.) Van Royen], which produces chicle used today in chewing gum. Of six genera that occur in North America, only the genus *Bumelia* is found in Georgia. Members of the genus are trees and shrubs with spiny branches, alternate leaves, and perfect white flowers clustered in the axils of leaves. Stubby spur shoots with clustered leaves are often produced on the branches. Three species of *Bumelia* attain tree stature in the State, none of which is of economic value.

Bumelia–Buckthorns

SUMMER KEY TO SPECIES OF *BUMELIA*
1. Leaves glabrous, or nearly so...................... *B. lycioides*
1. Leaves densely hairy on lower surface...................... 2
   2. Pubescence on lower leaf surface rusty or whitish woolly.....
      .... *B. lanuginosa*
   2. Pubescence on lower leaf surface with appressed golden or coppery hairs .... *B. tenax*

Bumelia lanuginosa (Michaux) Pers.

Gum Bumelia

DESCRIPTION: Gum Bumelia is an irregularly shaped shrub or small tree occasionally 30–40' tall, which becomes thicket-forming on some sites. It occurs primarily in the Coastal Plain.

Leaves – persistent, simple, alternate; blades obovate to elliptical, tips blunt, sometimes with a short spine, 2–3" long, about 1" broad, margins entire; upper surfaces shiny, dark green; lower surfaces dull, rusty or whitish woolly pubescent; petioles pubescent. Figure 378.

Twigs – stout, often zigzag, spur shoots common, often armed with unbranched thorns; terminal buds absent; lateral buds minute, with red woolly hairs; leaf scars circular to broad V-shaped; gummy, milky sap.

Bark – gray to dark brown on larger trunks, divided into scaly ridges, separated by narrow shallow fissures.

Flowers – perfect; 5-lobed white corollas, about ⅛" wide; clustered in leaf axils; sepals and flower stalks rusty pubescent; appearing in summer. Figure 378.

Fruit – drupe-like berry with single seed, blackish, subglobose, about ½" long; maturing in autumn.

RECOGNITION DIFFICULTIES WITH OTHER TAXA: Gum Bumelia is similar to *B. tenax*, except that the latter has lustrous, coppery or golden pubescence which is more appressed.

HABITAT: Gum Bumelia grows in dry, sandy woods of open forests or thickets, primarily in the Coastal Plain with occasional occurrence in the Piedmont.

ECONOMIC, ORNAMENTAL OR OTHER USES: Gum Bumelia apparently derives its common name from the gum which will exude when cuts are made into the inner bark. The wood has been used locally for tool handles and cabinets. Today, a few specialized nurseries produce seedlings of Gum Bumelia and the closely related *B. tenax* as specialty plants for naturalizing on dry, severe sites.

Bumelia lycioides (L.) Pers.

Buckthorn Bumelia

DESCRIPTION: This small tree or shrub is seldom over 20' tall, often with short, twisted stems. It occurs throughout much of the Piedmont and Ridge and Valley Provinces, but is almost absent from the Coastal Plain in Georgia.

Leaves – tardily deciduous, simple, alternate; blades elliptical to lance-shaped, tip usually acute, up to 5" long, ½–1½" wide, conspicuously veiny on both surfaces; both surfaces glabrous at maturity; fetid odor when bruised. Figure 379.

Twigs – slender, reddish brown, usually with unbranched thorns up to ¾" long, pubescent when young, glabrous with age; terminal bud absent, lateral buds minute; milky sap.

Bark – reddish brown to gray, with narrow fissures and scaly ridges, rather distinctive on older trees. Figure 380.

Flowers – similar to other species of *Bumelia*, numerous and clustered at leaf bases. Figure 379.

Fruit – drupe-like berry, purple-black, elliptical, about ½" in length; maturing in late summer. Figure 381.

RECOGNITION DIFFICULTIES WITH OTHER TAXA: *Bumelia lycioides* is distinguished from *B. tenax* or *B. lanuginosa* by its larger, glabrous leaves.

HABITAT: The species occurs on a variety of sites along borders of streams and sandy soils of the Coastal Plain and as a hardwood understory species on slopes and dry upland sites in the Piedmont and northward.

ECONOMIC, ORNAMENTAL AND OTHER USES: Buckthorn Bumelia is a rather attractive small tree, especially when the extremely large numbers of flower clusters are present. It is a desirable tree for naturalizing in some landscapes. The fruit is consumed by many species of birds.

Bumelia tenax (L.) Willd.

Tough Bumelia

DESCRIPTION: This species is a small, often scrubby tree, seldom over 20' tall. It is similar to *B. lanuginosa*, except that the leaves are conspicuously lustrous and have a coppery or golden appearance from the silky appressed hairs. The leaves are also considerably smaller than those of the Gum Bumelia. In Georgia, Tough Bumelia is commonly found on dry, sandy soils in the coastal counties and in a few interior counties on dry, upland pine-scrub oak sites. Figure 382, leaves—note copper hairs on under-surface.

EBENACEAE–EBONY FAMILY

Trees of the mostly tropical Ebenaceae are prized for their very hard and dark-colored heartwoods, particularly Ebony, *Diospyros ebenum* J. König ex Retz., which occurs in India and the East Indies. The Japanese Persimmon, *D. kaki* L.f., is grown commercially in California for its large, edible fruit. Two species of *Diospyros* are native to North America, *D. texana* Scheele and *D. virginiana* L. Only the latter occurs in Georgia.

Diospyros–Persimmon

Diospyros virginiana L.
Persimmon

DESCRIPTION: Persimmon is a small to medium-sized tree occasionally reaching 70–80′ tall. More often, it is a much smaller pioneer species occupying abandoned farm land or waste areas. On poorer sites, the stems are frequently twisted and contorted. Persimmon is found throughout the State, but it is more prevalent in the Piedmont and upper Coastal Plain.

    Leaves – deciduous, simple, alternate; blades oval or elliptic, acuminate tip, 2–6″ long, margins entire; the upper surface dark green, often with black marks; lower surface light green. Figure 383.

    Twigs – zigzag, conspicuous orange lenticels; terminal bud absent; lateral buds ⅛″ long or less, ovoid, with 2 lustrous, dark, deeply overlapping scales; leaf scars raised with prominent single bundle scar; pith weakly chambered.

    Bark – dark brown to almost black, thick, deeply furrowed into distinctive, scaly, block-like plates. Figure 384.

    Flowers – staminate and perfect, stamens in perfect flowers sterile, rendering plants functionally dioecious; yellow, urn-shaped; about ⅓″ long or less; staminate flowers in clusters; pistillate flowers solitary in leaf axils; appearing May–June. Figure 385.

    Fruit – pulpy berry, nearly globose, orange to purplish brown and sweet when ripe in autumn, up to 1½″ in diameter, persistent calyx; astringent taste when green. Figure 386.

RECOGNITION DIFFICULTIES WITH OTHER TAXA: Young Persimmon might be confused with Black Gum, particularly if the specimen is male or flowers and fruits are unavailable. However, the leaf margins of Persimmon are never toothed and those of Black Gum are often irregularly few-toothed. The single bundle scar and absence of a terminal bud also distinguish Persimmon from Black Gum, which has three bundle scars and a terminal bud. In winter conditions, the bark of Flowering Dogwood and Blackhaw Viburnum are similar to that of young Persimmon; however, these species have oppositely arranged leaves.

HABITAT: Persimmon is common throughout the State in a wide variety of habitats from deep, moist alluvial soils of valleys and stream bottoms to drier upland sites. Shade tolerant as an understory forest tree, it also thrives in full sun as an early successional species in abandoned fields and roadsides.

ECONOMIC, ORNAMENTAL AND OTHER USES: The wood of Persimmon is extremely hard, smooth and even textured. The dark heartwood resembles Ebony and is exceeded in hardness in North America only by Dogwood and Ironwood, and is used almost exclusively for heads of golf clubs. The sapwood is used for textile shuttles. The sweet fruit is edible when fully ripe and can be eaten raw or made into pudding. The green fruit is strongly astringent, bitter, and numbing to the mouth. Numerous mammals and birds feed upon the ripe fruits and serve in seed dispersal. Persimmon is occasionally planted as an ornamental and fruit tree, although its growth is rather slow on poor, upland sites.

STYRACACEAE–STORAX FAMILY

The Styracaceae is represented in Georgia by two genera, *Styrax* and *Halesia*. The five Georgia species are small trees or shrubs with simple, alternate, deciduous leaves with branched hairs. Several are used ornamentally for their conspicuous, white, bell-shaped flowers.

Halesia–Silverbells

SUMMER KEY TO SPECIES OF *HALESIA*
1. Corolla bell-shaped, slightly lobed; fruit 4 winged; leaves elliptic with gradual acuminate tips. 2
   2. Corolla about ¼" long; styles exerted; fruit usually about 1" long. . . . . *H. parviflora*
   2. Corolla up to 1" long; styles equal to corolla; fruit usually more than 1" long. . . . . *H. carolina*
1. Corolla divided nearly to the base; fruit 2 winged; leaves broadly ovate with abruptly acuminate tips. *H. diptera*

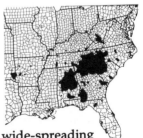

Halesia carolina L.

Carolina Silverbell

DESCRIPTION: Carolina Silverbell is an attractive wide-spreading small to medium-sized tree, occasionally as tall as 50–60' in mountain coves. It is common in the mountains, occasional in the Piedmont and rare in the Coastal Plain.

Leaves – deciduous, simple, alternate; blades elliptic-obovate, 3–6" long, finely toothed; branched hairs on lower surface. Figure 387.

Twigs – slender, often silky, shreddy, lenticels pale; terminal winter buds absent; lateral buds ovoid, small, uppermost bud of superposed buds triangular in shape and contiguous with bud beneath it; leaf scars half-round, single raised bundle scar; pith chambered or spongy.

Bark – reddish to brown with white-yellow streaks on young stems, thin, smooth, furrowed and scaly on older trunks. Figure 388, bark of young stem.

Flowers – perfect; white, occasionally pink, bell-shaped, 4 ciliated lobes, about 1" long, corolla narrowed below into a tube greater than half the length of petals; styles same length as corolla; in axillary fascicles of several flowers; appearing March–May. Figure 389.

Fruit – drupes, 4-winged, dry, about 1½–2" long, beaked; usually one seeded; maturing August–September. Figure 390.

RECOGNITION DIFFICULTIES WITH OTHER TAXA: *Halesia* can be distinguished from *Styrax* by the lateral buds, the uppermost bud of *Halesia* is triangular in shape and is contiguous with the lower bud, whereas the uppermost bud of *Styrax* is thumb-like and separate from the lower bud. In *Halesia diptera*, Two-wing Silverbell, the petals are united only at the base rather than more than half their length and the fruit is broadly two-winged rather than 4-winged.

HABITAT: Carolina Silverbell occurs on moist wooded slopes and fertile soils along streams chiefly in the Piedmont and mountains and rarely in the Coastal Plain.

ECONOMIC, ORNAMENTAL AND OTHER USES: *Halesia carolina* is often cultivated in the United States and in Europe for its showy, pendulous white flowers in early spring.

Halesia diptera Ellis

Two-wing Silverbell

DESCRIPTION: This species is smaller than Carolina Silverbell, usually less than 30' tall, and is restricted to the Coastal Plain. In Two-wing Silverbell the petals are united only at the base rather than more than half their length as for Carolina Silverbell and fewer flowers are produced. The leaves have an abrupt acuminate tip and the fruit is broadly two-winged, up to 2" long. The bark is thin, scaly, gray-brown, and lacks white streaks. This species occurs in swampy areas, bottomland forests and along river banks in scattered localities in the Coastal Plain. Figure 391, two winged fruit.

Halesia parviflora Michaux
Little Silverbell

DESCRIPTION: Little Silverbell is a small tree, or more commonly a shrub. The flowers are about ½" or less in length, and the styles are exerted. The narrowly 4-winged fruits are about 1" in length. The bark is dark brown and deeply furrowed. This species occurs sporadically in the Coastal Plain in dry sandy sites and in woodlands.

Styrax–Snowbells

SUMMER KEY TO SPECIES OF *STYRAX*
1. Leaves narrowly elliptic, up to 3" long; 1–4 flowered racemes . . . . *S. americanus*
1. Leaves broadly elliptic to obovate, 3–6" long; 5–20 flowered racemes . . . . *S. grandifolius*

Styrax americanus Lam.
American Snowbell

DESCRIPTION: American Snowbell is commonly a shrub, and rarely reaches tree dimensions in Georgia. It occurs in the Coastal Plain and Piedmont regions of the State.

Leaves – deciduous, simple, alternate; blades elliptic or oval, up to 3" long, margins irregularly toothed or mostly entire; lower surfaces glabrous to densely stellate pubescent. Figure 392.

Twigs – slender, slightly zigzag, young twigs with minute, stellate, white pubescence, by winter, hairless or nearly so; terminal winter buds absent; lateral buds naked; leaf scar with single bundle scar.

Bark – dark gray, thin, smooth.

Flowers – perfect; white, bell-shaped, 5-parted, ½" long;

occurring in racemes of 1–4 flowers, racemes up to 3" long; appearing in spring to early summer. Figure 392.

Fruit – drupes, globose, densely hairy, about ⅜" in diameter; maturing in September.

RECOGNITION DIFFICULTIES WITH OTHER TAXA: *Styrax americanus* can be distinguished from *Halesia* spp. by the shape of the lateral buds (see description of *Halesia carolina*). *Styrax americanus* can be separated from *S. grandifolius* by its smaller leaves and the shorter racemes with fewer flowers.

HABITAT: American Snowbell occurs in scattered localities, in moist to wet areas of the Piedmont and Coastal Plain.

ECONOMIC, ORNAMENTAL AND OTHER USES: This attractive species has ornamental potential for its showy white flowers.

Styrax grandifolius Aiton
Bigleaf Snowbell

DESCRIPTION: This is a small tree, up to 20' tall, but more commonly occurs as a large shrub with an open rounded crown. It occurs throughout the State.

Leaves – deciduous, simple, alternate; blade oval to obovate, tips abruptly pointed, 3–6" long, leaf margins entire or with few small teeth; upper surfaces dark green, glabrous; lower surfaces stellate-pubescent. Figure 393.

Twigs – slender, slightly zigzag, gray, scurfy with minute star-shaped hairs; terminal winter buds absent; lateral buds ⅛" long, naked, 2–3 at node, superposed, definite space between the upper two buds, the uppermost thumb-like in shape; leaf scars crescent-shaped; single protruding bundle scar, occasionally divided.

Bark – dark brown, streaked, thin, smooth.

Flowers – perfect; white, corolla 5-lobed, ¾" long, borne in leafy axillary racemes, 5–6" long, with 5–20 flowers; conspicuous; appearing early spring.

Fruit – drupes, globose, dry, ¼" in diameter; persistent calyx at base; maturing in autumn. Figure 393.

RECOGNITION DIFFICULTIES WITH OTHER TAXA: The foliage of *S. grandifolius* is similar to that of *Halesia diptera*, but can be distinguished by axillary buds (see description of *H. diptera*). *Styrax grandi-*

folius has larger leaves, longer racemes and more and larger flowers than *S. americanus.*

HABITAT: This species occurs in moist soils along streambanks, valleys and uplands throughout most of Georgia as an understory species in mixed hardwoods.

ECONOMIC, ORNAMENTAL AND OTHER USES: Bigleaf Snowbell is used occasionally as an ornamental, but has potential for more use in the horticultural trade as a small showy tree in natural areas, or as an understory tree of wooded, residential areas and parks.

SYMPLOCACEAE–SYMPLOCOS FAMILY

The Symplocaceae is composed of the single genus, *Symplocos,* comprising about 350 species found primarily in tropical Asia and America. About eight species of *Symplocos* extend northward into Mexico, but only *S. tinctoria* occurs in the United States.

Symplocos–Sweetleaf

Symplocos tinctoria (L.) L'Her

Horse-sugar, Sweetleaf

DESCRIPTION: Horse-sugar is a small tree usually 15–20' tall, occasionally reaching a height of 30' and 4–6" in diameter. Horse-sugar occurs throughout the State.

Leaves – tardily deciduous, simple, alternate; blades semi-leathery, elliptic, up to 6" long, tips short acuminate, margins entire or with fine shallow teeth; upper surfaces with short hairs; lower surfaces with more hairs; sweet to the taste; yellowish midrib later in season. Figure 394.

Twigs – moderately stout, reddish, with ashy bloom, ridged, with scattered hairs; terminal buds ovoid to conical, acute, brown, 1" long, 4 scaled, scales ciliate on margins; lateral leaf buds small, embedded in the twig; flower buds globose; leaf scar half-round to crescent-shaped; single bundle scar; pith chambered.

Bark – gray to light brown; thin, smooth to slightly furrowed, often with small warty or corky outgrowths.

Flowers – perfect; corollas cream to yellow, about ½" long; clustered in leaf axils or at the leafless nodes, on short stalks; appearing April–May before leaf emergence.

Fruit – cylindrical drupes, green when young, becoming dry and brownish at maturity, ½" in length; clustered on stem; maturing August–September.

RECOGNITION DIFFICULTIES WITH OTHER TAXA: The leaves of Horse-sugar may be confused with shrubby species such as *Lindera benzoin* (L.) Blume or *Ilex ambigua*. However, the firm, sweet-tasting leaves and the cylindric clusters of short-stalked fruits distinguish Horse-sugar. Other tree species with a single bundle scar and chambered pith include Silverbell which has reddish buds and Persimmon which has only 2, dark bud scales in contrast to the 4, brown, hairy-margined scales of Horse-sugar. Often, some leaves will be present throughout the winter and will aid in identification.

HABITAT: Horse-sugar occurs in the understory of moist, deciduous woods and along streams throughout the State.

ECONOMIC, ORNAMENTAL AND OTHER USES: Horse-sugar is eagerly fed upon by browsing wildlife, horses or livestock because of the sweet foliage, hence the common names. In colonial days, a bright yellow dye was obtained from boiling the leaves and inner bark in water.

OLEACEAE–OLIVE FAMILY

The Oleaceae is a large family of trees and shrubs containing 22 genera and over 500 species found in temperate and tropical regions. The family is of considerable economic importance for food, timber and ornamental uses. The Olive (*Olea*) is a valuable source of food, and oil expressed from the fruit is used worldwide. Ash lumber (*Fraxinus*) is widely utilized. Several genera contain important ornamental plants, notably the Lilac (*Syringa*), Privet (*Ligustrum*), Yellow Bells (*Forsythia*), Jasmine (*Jasminum*), and many others.

The family is represented in Georgia by four native arborescent genera, *Fraxinus* (ashes), *Forestiera* (Swamp Privet), *Chionanthus* (Fringe Tree), and *Osmanthus* (Devilwood). Some of the ornamental genera introduced into the United States from Asia have become naturalized and present many silvicultural problems as weed species, especially *Ligustrum sinense* Lour. (Chinese Privet).

The genus *Fraxinus* contains five species that occur in Georgia. With the exception of *F. quadrangulata* Michaux, the fruit is usually needed for reliable identification of *Fraxinus* species.

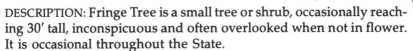

Chionanthus–Fringe Tree

Chionanthus virginicus L.
Fringe Tree, Old-man's-beard

DESCRIPTION: Fringe Tree is a small tree or shrub, occasionally reaching 30' tall, inconspicuous and often overlooked when not in flower. It is occasional throughout the State.

Leaves – deciduous, simple, opposite; blades oblong to oval, up to 6" long, 2–3" broad, margins entire; upper surfaces glabrous; the lower surfaces glabrous to densely hairy; petioles maroon or blackish purple; turning yellow in autumn. Figure 395.

Twigs – stout, gray to brown, slightly hairy, lenticels conspicuous, warty; terminal bud ovoid, pointed, brown, about ⅓" long, 6–8 scales; lateral buds often superposed; bud scales keeled; leaf scars half-round, elevated; bundle scars solitary and U-shaped.

Bark – gray to brown, developing thin exfoliating scales with age.

Flowers – perfect or functionally unisexual; the plants dioecious or polygamous; white, linear, 4 petals, about ¾–1" long; occurring in pendant axillary panicles, 4–10" long; appearing April–May. Figure 396.

Fruit – drupes, bluish-black, ovoid, about ¾" long; maturing July–Sept. Figure 397.

RECOGNITION DIFFICULTIES WITH OTHER TAXA: In flower, Fringe Tree is easily recognized by its conspicuous cluster of white, fringe-like flowers. At other seasons, it is recognized by opposite leaves with purplish petioles, enlarged nodes and large, rough lenticels. Fringe Tree might be confused with *Osmanthus americanus*, which also has opposite leaves. However, the leaves of Fringe Tree are deciduous and those of *Osmanthus* are thick, leathery and evergreen. In winter condition, Fringe Tree can be separated from ashes which have more than one bundle scar. It can be separated from *Viburnum* by the buds, those of *Chionanthus* with six to eight scales and those of *Viburnum* with two valvate scales.

HABITAT: Fringe Tree occurs in rich, deciduous woods and often is abundant along the edges of granitic outcrops.

ECONOMIC, ORNAMENTAL AND OTHER USES: This species is often used as an ornamental because of its showy cluster of flowers and is most effective in borders or in groups near buildings. The autumn foliage is bright to dark yellow. No serious disease or pest problems are associated with this species.

Forestiera–Forestiera

Forestiera acuminata (Michaux) Poiret

Swamp-privet

DESCRIPTION: This is most often a weak, leaning shrub or small tree seldom over 30' tall, widely scattered in a few localities in the Coastal Plain.

Leaves – deciduous, simple, opposite; blades oblong to diamond-shaped, tapering at both ends, up to 3" long, about 1" broad, margins almost entire or serrate from the middle to the tip; glabrous or slightly pubescent; petiole about 1" long. Figure 398.

Twigs – slender, light brown, warty, lenticels white; terminal bud ovoid, about 1/16" long, 4–6 scales; lateral buds globose, often superposed; leaf scars small, circular to half-round; bundle scars single, U-shaped.

Bark – dark brown, slightly ridged and flaky with age.

Flowers – perfect or functionally unisexual; the plant dioecious or polygamous; small, petals absent, greenish; staminate with 4 stamens, in stalked clusters; pistillate in panicles 1" long; appearing in March before the leaves. Figure 399, clusters of staminate flowers.

Fruit – drupes, brownish to purple, ellipsoid, wrinkled, fleshy, about ½" long. Figure 400.

RECOGNITION DIFFICULTIES WITH OTHER TAXA: In fruit, Swamp-privet is distinctive. The fruit of the shrubby species *Forestiera ligustrina* (Michaux) Poiret is globose and the leaves are typically 1–2" long; whereas, the fruit of *F. acuminata* is elongated in shape and the leaves are up to 3" long. Another species, *F. segregata* (Jacq.) Krug & Urban, is evergreen. The long petiole distinguishes Swamp-Privet from the introduced and naturalized Chinese Privet, *Ligustrum sinense*, which has a petiole less than ⅛" long. Additionally, *Ligustrum* has terminal clusters of flowers and fruits and numerous leaves per branchlet, in contrast to axillary flowers and more sparse leaf arrangement of *Forestiera acuminata*.

HABITAT: This species is occasional in river bottom floodplains or on moist soils near streams and margins or swamps.

ECONOMIC, ORNAMENTAL AND OTHER USES: Swamp-Privet is of no commercial value. Wild ducks and other birds feed upon its fruit.

Fraxinus–Ashes

SUMMER KEY TO SPECIES OF *FRAXINUS*

1. Twigs 4-angled and winged.................... *F. quadrangulata*
1. Twigs not 4-angled, and not winged......................... 2
   2. Leaf scar deeply concave; samara winged only at terminal end of fruit body.................................... *F. americana*
   2. Leaf scar half-round or slightly concave; samara winged to middle of the fruit body or beyond 3
      3. Samara winged to the base, fruit body flattened... *F. caroliniana*
      3. Samara not winged to base, fruit body plump 4
         4. Twigs densely hairy when young; fruit wing ⅓" or more wide; leaflets not decurrent-winged along stalk, or only slightly at base.......................... *F. profunda*
         4. Twigs glabrous; fruit wing less than ⅓" wide; leaflets decurrent-winged along entire length of stalk..........
        .... *F. pennsylvanica*

Fraxinus americana L.

White Ash

DESCRIPTION: White Ash is a large tree often exceeding 80' in height and 2–3' in diameter. In Georgia, it is most abundant in the Piedmont and mountains.

    Leaves – deciduous, compound, opposite; 5–9 leaflets (usually 7), entire or obscurely toothed margins; upper surface of leaflets dark green; lower surface of leaflets paler. Figure 401.

    Twigs – moderately stout, flattened at nodes, gray-brown, lenticels large, pale; terminal bud rounded, brownish to black, with 4–8 scales; leaf scars narrow and deeply concave, partly surrounding the bud; bundle scars numerous, indistinct to crescent-shaped.

    Bark – gray, thick, rough, becoming deeply and narrowly fissured with forking, interlacing ridges forming a somewhat diamond-shaped pattern. Figure 402.

    Flowers – usually imperfect, plants usually dioecious; purplish, without petals, small, ¼" long; arranged in compound clusters on the previous season's growth; opening prior to leaf emergence. See Figure 409 of female flowers in Green Ash.

    Fruit – samara, about 1–2" long; terminal wing scarcely extends down side of fruit body; appearing late summer to autumn. Figure 403.

RECOGNITION DIFFICULTIES WITH OTHER TAXA: *Fraxinus americana* is a highly variable species. Numerous varieties and ecotypes have been described, but generally are considered to intergrade. *Fraxinus americana* can be distinguished from *F. pennsylvanica*, with which it occasionally occurs, by its deeply notched leaf scars and terminally winged samaras.

HABITAT: White Ash occurs in deciduous moist, upland or lowland forests throughout the State, usually in rich, well-drained soils, mostly in the mountains and Piedmont.

ECONOMIC, ORNAMENTAL AND OTHER USES: White Ash is a valuable timber tree, used for furniture, veneer, interior finish, baseball bats, railroad ties, tool handles and for fuel. Because of its large crown when open grown, White Ash makes an excellent shade and park tree. It is, however, plagued with numerous leaf pests late in the season.

Fraxinus caroliniana Miller

Carolina Ash

DESCRIPTION: This is a small to medium-sized tree 40–50' in height, usually less than 12" in diameter, restricted to the Coastal Plain.

    Leaves – deciduous, compound, opposite; up to 12" long; leaflets variable in size and shape, 5–9, margins entire or irregularly toothed. Figure 404.

    Twigs – slender, slightly flattened at nodes; light green-brown; pubescent when young; leaf scars half-round.

    Bark – gray, shallowly fissured and irregularly scaly. Figure 405.

    Flowers – similar to other ashes.

    Fruit – samara, variable in shape and size; fruit bodies flat or concave; wing broad, elliptical, extending to the base of the fruit body; appearing late summer and autumn. Figure 406.

RECOGNITION DIFFICULTIES WITH OTHER TAXA: *Fraxinus caroliniana* might be confused with *F. pennsylvanica* or *F. profunda*, all of which might be found in inundated areas of the Coastal Plain. To separate satisfactorily, these species should have fruits. The combination of characteristics used to distinguish *F. caroliniana* include: a broad wing extending to the base of the fruit body of the samara; the fruit body flat or concave; and often with several trunks.

HABITAT: Carolina Ash occurs on wet sites which may be inundated for long periods of time, such as river swamps, wet depressions in flatwoods and pond margins.

ECONOMIC, ORNAMENTAL AND OTHER USES: Due to its small size and poor quality, this tree is of little commercial value.

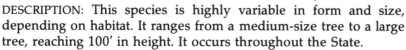

Fraxinus pennsylvanica Marshall

Green Ash

DESCRIPTION: This species is highly variable in form and size, depending on habitat. It ranges from a medium-size tree to a large tree, reaching 100' in height. It occurs throughout the State.

Leaves – deciduous, compound, opposite; leaflets ovate to elliptical, 5–9 (usually 7), margins entire or remotely toothed; upper surfaces dark green; lower surfaces paler, pubescent along veins; leaflet stalks ⅛–½" long, winged nearly their entire length by the extended leaflet bases. Figure 407.

Twigs – moderately stout, often flattened at the node, grayish green, glabrous; terminal buds with 4, pubescent, rusty brown scales; leaf scars half-round, usually straight across at the top rather than notched.

Bark – gray-brown, with narrow fissures separated by interlacing ridges; sometimes resemble young Black Walnut trees. Figure 408.

Flowers – similar to *F. americana*. Figure 409, female flowers.

Fruit – samara, 1–2" long; fruit body less than ⅛" broad, round in cross section; long, narrow wings extend about half way down the sides of the fruit body, less than ⅓" long; maturing late summer and autumn. Figure 410.

RECOGNITION DIFFICULTIES WITH OTHER TAXA: In the Piedmont, Green Ash might occur in the same habitat with White Ash on moist sites. The two can be distinguished by the leaf scar of Green Ash which is half-round rather than deeply notched and by the wing of the samara which extends about ⅓–½ way down the body of the fruit rather than being terminal. In the lower Piedmont or Coastal Plain, Green Ash may occur with either Pumpkin Ash or Carolina Ash. Green Ash can be recognized from Carolina Ash by its samaras with a fruit body that is round in cross section and not winged to the base, whereas, Carolina Ash samaras have a flat fruit body, winged to the base. Green Ash differs from Pumpkin Ash by its nearly glabrous twigs, winged leaflet stalks and samara with fruit body less than ⅛" broad.

HABITAT: Green Ash most often occurs along streams and in alluvial floodplains where frequent inundation occurs in winter and spring. It is tolerant of flooding for extended periods, but is also found scattered on dry, severe, upland sites, especially around granitic outcrops in the Georgia Piedmont.

ECONOMIC, ORNAMENTAL AND OTHER USES: The wood of Green Ash is inferior to that of White Ash, being more brittle and less resilient. However, it is frequently mixed with the latter and used for the same purposes. Because of its fast seedling growth, it is often used in reforesting spoil banks following strip mining in the Southeast and for shelterwood planting in the Great Plains. It is often used locally for lawn and shade trees because of its initial rapid growth and site adaptability.

Fraxinus profunda (Bush) Bush
Pumpkin Ash

DESCRIPTION: This is a large tree, occasionally over 80' tall and 2–3' in diameter. It commonly forms large buttressed bases in deep river swamps. Pumpkin Ash occurs infrequently in the lower Piedmont and Coastal Plain along the Coast.

Leaves – deciduous, compound, opposite; leaflets variable in size and shape, often rounded base, 5–9 (usually 7) leaflets; lower surfaces pubescent along midribs or principal veins; leaflet stalks ¼–1" long, without wings.

Twigs – stout, light gray, often pubescent when young.

Bark – gray, thick, interlacing ridges and furrows forming a diamond pattern similar to White Ash.

Flowers – similar to other ashes.

Fruit – samara, 2–3" long; fruit body more than ⅛" broad; wing elliptical, more than ⅓" wide, extending nearly to base of the fruit body; maturing late summer to autumn.

RECOGNITION DIFFICULTIES WITH OTHER TAXA: *Fraxinus profunda* is distinguished from other species of ash by its dense pubescence along the mid-rib and principal veins on the undersurface of leaves, the wingless leaflet stalks, and the fruit body of the samara that is round in cross section with elliptical wings.

HABITAT: Pumpkin Ash is scattered in river swamps and floodplains in only a few counties in the Coastal Plain and lower Piedmont.

ECONOMIC, ORNAMENTAL AND OTHER USES: The wood of this species is similar to that of Green Ash, but because it is scattered, is of little economic importance.

Fraxinus quadrangulata Michaux

Blue Ash

DESCRIPTION: Blue Ash is a medium sized tree that may reach 70' in height in some parts of its range, but it is usually much smaller on the sites where it occurs in the northwestern portion of the State.

Leaves – deciduous, pinnately compound, opposite; leaflets; variable in length, 7–11; turning pale yellow in autumn. Figure 411.

Twigs – moderately stout, 4-angled, noticeably winged, brown to gray. Figure 412.

Bark – gray, furrowed into flattened scaly, plates.

Flowers – similar to other ashes.

Fruit – samara, 1–2" long; fruit body flattened; broad wing extending to base of fruit body; maturing in autumn.

RECOGNITION DIFFICULTIES WITH OTHER TAXA: Blue Ash is readily identified by its 4-angled, winged twigs.

HABITAT: In Georgia, only two localities for this species have been documented, both in limestone areas of the Ridge and Valley and Cumberland Plateau on dry, rocky, hardwood slopes.

ECONOMIC, ORNAMENTAL AND OTHER USES: The sap of the inner bark was used by early settlers to produce a blue dye for cloth.

Osmanthus–Osmanthus

Osmanthus americanus (L.) Gray

Devilwood

DESCRIPTION: Devilwood is a semi-evergreen, small to medium-sized tree of the Coastal Plain, occasionally reaching 30–40' in height.

Leaves – persistent to evergreen, simple, opposite; blades leathery, elliptic to oblanceolate, 4–9" long, about 2" broad, margins entire, revolute; upper surfaces dark green, lustrous; lower surface paler. Figure 413.

Twigs – brown, lenticels minute; terminal buds lance-shaped, red-brown, with 2 valvate scales, ½" long; lateral buds smaller, sometimes superposed; leaf scars elevated; ring of small bundle scars.

Bark – grayish brown, exfoliating in scales and exposing reddish inner bark.

Flowers – mostly imperfect; white to greenish, bell-shaped, small, 3/16" wide; clustered on twigs; flowers fragrant; flower buds appearing in autumn and winter; opening in February–March.

Fruit – drupes, dark blue, globose, about ½" long; on a jointed fruiting stalk; often persistent through following year; maturing August through October. Figure 413.

RECOGNITION DIFFICULTIES WITH OTHER TAXA: Other species that might be confused with Devilwood include Viburnums, which also have simple, opposite leaves with valvate buds; but Viburnum flowers are borne in terminal cymes and the buds are rusty-pubescent. The leaves of *Symplocos* are similar to those of *Osmanthus*, but are alternately arranged. The distinctive, olive-like fruits of *Osmanthus* occur in jointed, bracted panicles which are often persistent for several seasons.

HABITAT: Devilwood is found on a wide range of sites in the Coastal Plain, including dry woods, maritime forests and rich woodlands.

ECONOMIC, ORNAMENTAL AND OTHER USES: *Osmanthus americanus* is occasionally utilized as an ornamental evergreen shrub. It is referred to as "Devilwood" because the wood is fine-textured, difficult to split and hard to work.

BIGNONIACEAE–BIGNONIA FAMILY

The Bignoniaceae is a large, mostly tropical family of trees, shrubs, and vines comprising approximately 110 genera. Members of the family are of considerable economic importance for both timber and cultivated ornamental plants. Among the most notable trees in the family are the South African Sausage Tree (*Kigelia*) now widely planted in many tropical areas, and the hardy Princess Tree of China [*Paulownia tomentosa* (Thunberg) Steudel] which has been widely planted throughout much of the Southeast as an attractive ornamental tree with exceptionally large leaves and showy, bluish-purple flowers. *Paulownia tomentosa* is a prolific seed producer and it has now become naturalized in many local areas. There are five tree species in the Bignoniaceae native to North America, but only *Catalpa bignonioides* Walter is indigenous to Georgia.

Trees in this family characteristically have opposite or whorled leaves and large clusters of showy, 2-lipped flowers. The fruits of *Catalpa* are distinctive, elongated capsules often referred to as Indian-beans or monkey cigars.

Catalpa–Catalpa

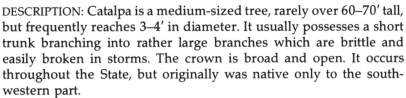

Catalpa bignonioides Walter
Southern Catalpa, Indian-bean

DESCRIPTION: Catalpa is a medium-sized tree, rarely over 60–70' tall, but frequently reaches 3–4' in diameter. It usually possesses a short trunk branching into rather large branches which are brittle and easily broken in storms. The crown is broad and open. It occurs throughout the State, but originally was native only to the south-western part.

Leaves – deciduous, simple, opposite or in whorls of 3; blades ovate or heart-shaped with long pointed tips, 5–11" long, 4–8" wide, margins entire or wavy; upper surfaces dark green; lower surfaces paler, pubescent; petioles 5–6" long. Figure 414.

Twigs – stout, brittle, lenticels conspicuous, pale; terminal bud absent, lateral buds globose and small, about 1/16 " long; leaf scars large with depressed center; bundle scars numerous in a closed, elliptical ring.

Bark – gray to reddish brown, separating into long, thin irregular scales.

Flowers – perfect; showy, white with purplish and orange blotches and stripes in the throat, up to 2" long, corolla tubular, in many-flowered panicles, up to 10" across; appearing late spring after the leaves. Figure 415.

Fruit – capsules, elongate, dark brown with two valves, 6–18" long, ¼" wide; seeds flat winged with fringed edges; maturing in October and persisting until spring. Figure 416.

RECOGNITION DIFFICULTIES WITH OTHER TAXA: Southern Catalpa is difficult to separate from the closely related Northern Catalpa, *C. speciosa* Warder ex Engelm., which is not native to Georgia, but has been extensively planted in many localities as an ornamental. The most consistent feature for separating the two taxa is the relative thickness of the fruit wall. *Catalpa speciosa* fruit walls are considerably thicker than those of *C. bignonioides*. Southern Catalpa somewhat resembles the exotic, but naturalized Princess Tree, *Paulownia tomentosa*. However, Southern Catalpa has a white flower and an elongate capsule up to 20" long, whereas Princess Tree has a large, pubescent, lavender flower and the fruit is a globose, beaked capsule, about 1–2" in length. The leaves of both genera are large, entire and heart-shaped; however, the leaves of Southern Catalpa are opposite or in whorls of three and Princess Tree has all opposite leaves. The twigs of Southern Catalpa have a homogeneous pith, solitary lateral buds and crater-shaped leaf scars. Princess Tree is characterized by a chambered or hollow pith, superposed lateral buds and notched leaf scars.

HABITAT: Moist soils, especially in open areas around the margins of streams, fields and roadsides.

ECONOMIC, ORNAMENTAL AND OTHER USES: Formerly, Southern Catalpa was restricted to only a few counties in the Coastal Plain of Southwest Georgia, but it is now widespread throughout the State because it has been planted extensively as an ornamental tree and also for the culture of "catalpa worms," a large black caterpillar, which is highly prized as fishbait. The wood is of little commercial importance, although it is highly durable in contact with the soil and was once widely used for fence posts. The tree makes fast growth on moist sites. Remarkably, it may be completely defoliated by caterpillars in early summer year after year, regenerate a new set of leaves in mid-summer, which may also be partly defoliated, and still survive.

RUBIACEAE–MADDER FAMILY

The Rubiaceae comprises a large group of tropical and sub-tropical plants with nearly 400 genera and about 5000 species. This family is of much economic importance, primarily for several tropical crops such as Coffee (*Coffea*), Quinine (*Cinchona*), and numerous ornamental taxa grown in North America including *Gardenia*, *Rubia*, *Galium*, and others. In Georgia, only two tree species of the Rubiaceae occur, *Cephalanthus occidentalis* L. and *Pinckneya bracteata* (Bartram) Raf. Both are small trees with opposite leaves and tubular perfect flowers.

Cephalanthus–Buttonbush

Cephalanthus occidentalis L.
Buttonbush

DESCRIPTION: In much of its range, Buttonbush occurs as a multibranched, sprawling shrub; however, in some localities it becomes tree size reaching heights of 25–30' and diameters of 4–5". It occurs throughout Georgia.

Leaves – often persistent, simple, opposite or occasionally in whorls of 3–4; blades elliptical, 3–7" long, 1½–3" wide, margins entire; dark green above; paler and pubescent beneath; minute triangular stipules between the petioles leaving stipular scars. Figure 417.

Twigs – red-brown, smooth or pubescent, dead shoots persisting, lenticels conspicuously raised, pale; winter terminal buds absent; lateral buds small and partly concealed in the bark; leaf scars crescent shaped or triangular; bundle scars solitary, usually crescent-shaped, occasionally broken into several scars in a U-shaped line; stipules persistent, scars leaving stipular line connecting petioles.

Bark – gray to brown, thin, fissured on older stems into narrow scaly ridges.

Flowers – perfect; white, tubular, small; in dense globose heads, about 1½" across; appearing sporadically all summer. Figure 418.

Fruit – nutlets, angular, in compact, globose, dark-reddish brown heads, about ¾" in diameter; maturing June–September. Figure 419.

RECOGNITION DIFFICULTIES WITH OTHER TAXA: Buttonbush should not be confused with other species in the State. It is distinctive by its opposite or whorled leaves, single bundle scar, conspicuous globose flowers and fruits and occurrence along streams or swamps.

HABITAT: Buttonbush is common in moist sites along streams, swamps, flood plains, and margins of ponds where it often forms thickets. It occurs throughout the State.

ECONOMIC, ORNAMENTAL AND OTHER USES: The foliage of Buttonbush is poisonous to cattle and it becomes a troublesome "weed" in low lying pastureland. The species has been used as an ornamental shrub because of its uniquely attractive flower heads and dark red to maroon colored fruits. Buttonbush is restricted to natural moist sites or poorly drained areas, and is not suitable for dry sites. Numerous species of water fowl and birds feed upon the seeds.

Pinckneya–Pinckneya

Pinckneya bracteata (Bartram) Raf.
(*Pinckneya pubens* Michaux)

Pinckneya, Fever-tree

DESCRIPTION: This is a small, vigorous tree or large shrub which occurs sporadically on wet sites throughout the Coastal Plain. It may occur in abundance in some localities because it sprouts profusely from lateral roots.

Leaves – deciduous, simple, opposite; blades elliptic or ovate, 4–8″ long, margins entire; upper surfaces dark green, slightly pubescent; lower surfaces pale, downy pubescent. Figure 420.

Twigs – young twigs, pubescent, becoming glabrous, triangular stipules deciduous, leaving stipular lines on each side of the twig between the petioles; terminal buds ½″ long, oval with slender point, covered by rusty stipules of previous year's leaves; axillary buds inconspicuous and embedded in the bark; leaf scars shield-shaped to round with single bundle scar.

Bark – light brown, becoming lightly fissured into thin, appressed scales.

Flowers – perfect; corolla yellowish green with maroon splotches, 5-lobed, tubular, about 1″ long; calyx 5-lobed, one or more sepals becoming enlarged and petaloid, creamy to rose colored, conspicuous; borne in terminal clusters; appearing early summer. Figure 421.

Fruit – capsules, subglobose, splitting into 2 parts, about ½″ across, pubescent, marked by pale spots and by the scars of the perianth; seeds numerous flat, light brown, broad winged; maturing in late summer and persisting during the winter. Figure 422.

RECOGNITION DIFFICULTIES WITH OTHER TAXA: Fever-tree is easily distinguished by its conspicuous inflorescence of rose-pink, petal-like sepals, large opposite leaves, its persistent, spotted capsules and twigs with downy pubescence and stipular lines between the opposite leaf scars.

HABITAT: Pinckneya occurs along wet margins of swamps and on poorly drained sites of the Coastal Plain.

ECONOMIC, ORNAMENTAL AND OTHER USES: Pinckneya is one of the most showy and attractive native trees in Georgia when in full bloom. The enlarged calyx lobes range in color from creamy white to almost brilliant red on individual plants or clones. The species is gaining much attention as a valuable ornamental plant, but unfortunately, its use is restricted to permanently moist sites or areas inundated during part of the year. A home medicine made from the inner bark was used in earlier days in treating malaria and other fevers, hence, the common name "fevertree."

CAPRIFOLIACEAE–HONEYSUCKLE FAMILY

The Caprifoliaceae is a family of 18 genera and over 300 species of mostly shrubs, vines and small trees, primarily restricted to the north temperate regions of Asia and North America. The North American arborescent species which occur in the Southeast are found in two genera, *Sambucus* and *Viburnum*. Economically, the family is important for its large number of ornamental species; over 100 taxa in 13 genera are currently offered in the horticultural trade in the United States. One well-known cultivated shrub in this family is *Viburnum triloba* Marshall. Japanese honeysuckle, *Lonicera japonica* Thunberg, was introduced into this country from Asia and has become a naturalized, noxious weed throughout much of the eastern United States, particularly in the Southeast.

Sambucus–Elder

Sambucus canadensis L.
Elderberry, American Elder

DESCRIPTION: Elderberry only occasionally reaches tree size (20' tall and 5–6" in diameter). Most often it is a thicket-forming shrub and is common throughout the State.

Leaves – deciduous, pinnately compound, opposite; 5–9" long; leaflets elliptical, 5–7 pairs, 1½–4" long, sharply serrate, short leaflet stalks; upper surfaces shiny green; lower surfaces lighter, slightly pubescent along midvein. Figure 423.

Twigs – stout, light green-gray, lenticels numerous; terminal bud usually lacking; lateral buds small, ⅛" long, several scales; leaf scars broadly crescent-shaped and often transversely connected, forming ringed nodes; bundle scars 3, 5 or 7; pith large, white; disagreeable odor when crushed.

Bark – light gray thin, smooth, with raised protuberances from lenticels, later becoming slightly fissured and rough.

Flowers – perfect; small, ¼" wide; in slightly convex clusters 6–12" wide, clusters usually profuse, covering entire crown; appearing early to mid-summer. Figure 424.

Fruit – berry-like drupe, purple-black, about ¼" in diameter, juicy and slightly sweet; occur in drooping clusters; maturing late summer through early autumn. Figure 425.

RECOGNITION DIFFICULTIES WITH OTHER TAXA: Elderberry should

be easy to separate from other species, although at a distance, its pinnately compound leaves resemble those of young sumacs. It is very distinctive in flower and fruit. Its stout twigs have an exceptionally large pith and have a disagreeable acrid odor when crushed.

HABITAT: Elderberry is common on wet or moist sites, usually along streams, drainage areas and bottomlands or in moist areas near the margins of fields and forests.

ECONOMIC, ORNAMENTAL AND OTHER USES: The fruit of Elderberry is occasionally used for making jelly, pies, and wine. Numerous game and song birds and mammals consume the fruit. Although quite showy in full bloom, it has limited use as an ornamental because of its spreading, sprawling unkempt growth habit.

Viburnum–Viburnums

SUMMER KEY TO SPECIES OF *VIBURNUM*
1. Leaves finely toothed, not wavy 2
    2. Petioles and lower leaf surfaces rusty-hairy; leaves lustrous above .... *V. rufidulum*
    2. Petioles and lower leaf surfaces smooth or nearly so; leaves dull above...................................... *V. prunifolium*
1. Leaves entire, or wavy....................................... 3
    3. Leaves small, about ½–2" long; flower cluster nearly sessile...
    .... *V. obovatum*
    3. Leaves about 2¼–6" long; flower cluster with long stalk ......
    .... *V. nudum*

Viburnum nudum L.

Possumhaw Viburnum

DESCRIPTION: Possumhaw is a small tree, occasionally 15–20' tall, most often a large shrub with an open crown of spreading branches. The species occurs scattered throughout the State.

    Leaves – deciduous, simple, opposite; blades usually broadest near, or above the middle, up to 6" long, 1½–2" wide, margins entire or slightly wavy and revolute; upper surfaces lustrous green; lower surfaces paler, rusty-scurfy with conspicuous raised veins beneath; short petioles covered with rust-colored hairs. Figure 426.

Twigs – slender, brown, rusty-scurfy when young; lateral buds ½" long with several scales; flower buds terminal, long, narrow, covered with rusty hairs, two scales; leaf scars U- to V-shaped, encircling young twig; bundle scars 3.

Bark – gray to brown, smooth, becoming somewhat blocky and scaly on older stems.

Flowers – perfect; creamy white, small, corolla lobes 5; in terminal flat-topped clusters, 2½–5" wide; cluster stalked, with 4–5 principal branches arising from main stalk; appearing April–June. Figure 426.

Fruit – drupes, during maturation varying from pink to red, at maturity dark blue, globose to elliptical, ¼" in diameter; maturing in September–October. Figure 427.

RECOGNITION DIFFICULTIES WITH OTHER TAXA: Possumhaw might be confused with *V. rufidulum* which also has rusty hairs on the leaves. However, the latter has smaller, thick, lustrous, finely toothed leaves unlike those of *V. nudum* which have entire or wavy margins.

HABITAT: Possumhaw frequently occurs along streams, margins of swamps and low moist slopes of uplands throughout most of Georgia.

ECONOMIC, ORNAMENTAL AND OTHER USES: The species is occasionally used as an ornamental on moist to poorly drained sites. Possumhaw fruit is a food source for many species of birds and mammals. Deer frequently browse leaves and twigs.

Viburnum obovatum Walter
Viburnum, Small-leaf Viburnum

DESCRIPTION: *Viburnum obovatum* is a small evergreen tree up to 20' tall, often with branches near the ground. It is found occasionally throughout much of the Coastal Plain.

Leaves – evergreen, simple, opposite; blades broadest at or above the middle, 1–2½" long, ¼–1¼" wide, margins revolute, entire or irregularly toothed; upper surfaces glabrous; lower surface shiny, dark green with scurfy-glandular dots; nearly sessile; strong odor when crushed. Figure 428.

Twigs – stubby, numerous spur shoots; terminal buds narrow, pubescent, reddish brown, ¼" long or less, valvate; bundle scars 3; strong odor when crushed.

Bark – dark brown to black, furrowed into angular blocks.

Flowers – small, 5 corolla lobes; flower clusters 1½–2½" wide, sessile or with a very small stalk, 2–5 primary branches; appearing in early spring as new leaves emerge.

Fruit – drupes, turning red to shiny black with maturity in summer, spherical to ovoid, about ¼" diameter; persisting into late autumn. Figure 428.

RECOGNITION DIFFICULTIES WITH OTHER TAXA: Small leaves distinguish Small-leaf Viburnum from other species of *Viburnum*. The leaves may resemble those of *Ilex decidua*, except that the leaves of *Ilex* are alternate rather than opposite, and *Ilex* bark is light gray rather than dark.

HABITAT: *Viburnum obovatum* is locally common in floodplains, low woods and stream banks of the Coastal Plain.

ECONOMIC, ORNAMENTAL AND OTHER USES: *Viburnum obovatum* is similar to the other *Viburnum* species, but not as showy and seldom used as an ornamental.

Viburnum prunifolium L.

Blackhaw

DESCRIPTION: Blackhaw is a small tree occasionally reaching 20–25' in height, with a short trunk and spreading, irregular crown. It is found intermittently in the Piedmont and across the northern part of the State, and less frequently in the upper Coastal Plain.

Leaves – deciduous, simple, opposite; blades 1–3" long, margins finely serrate; upper surfaces dull green; lower surfaces paler, glabrous or nearly so; petioles red. Figure 429.

Twigs – slender, gray to brown, smooth with orange lenticels; slender spine-like spur shoots; lateral buds narrow, blunt-pointed, brown to red-gray, about ¼", appressed, smooth or scurfy; flower bud terminal, about ½" long, bases swollen; bundle scars 3.

Bark – dark, reddish brown, broken into small, scaly blocks on lower trunk, often resembling young Flowering Dogwood.

Flowers – perfect; creamy white, corolla lobes 5, small, ¼" wide; in flat-topped clusters 2½–4" wide; clusters stalkless or nearly so with 3–5 primary branches; appearing with the leaves in April. Similar to *V. nudum* in overall appearance.

Fruit – drupes, dark blue to black, globose to ellipsoid, about ½" long; in drooping clusters, with red stalks; maturing in mid to late summer.

RECOGNITION DIFFICULTIES WITH OTHER TAXA: *Viburnum prunifolium* somewhat resembles and may even hybridize with *V. rufidulum*, which has lustrous leaves with woolly, rusty red hairs.

HABITAT: Blackhaw occurs around margins of swamps or on the moist upland slopes of deciduous forests as an understory species. It is found predominantly in the Piedmont and mountain regions.

ECONOMIC, ORNAMENTAL AND OTHER USES: Blackhaw is infrequently used as an ornamental. Its use for this purpose should increase as more nurseries become aware of using native plants.

Viburnum rufidulum Raf.
Rusty Blackhaw

DESCRIPTION: Rusty Blackhaw is a small tree, seldom more than 25' tall and 4–5" in diameter. It occurs as an occasional tree throughout the State.

    Leaves – deciduous, simple, opposite; blades ½–3" long, 1–1½" wide, margins finely toothed; upper surfaces lustrous, lower surface rusty-hairy; petioles rusty hairy, grooved, sometimes winged. Figure 430.

    Twigs – slender, reddish brown to gray; hairy when young, smooth with age; flower buds with swollen bases, up to ½" long, 2 scales, covered with rusty-woolly hairs; leaf scars similar to other species.

    Bark – reddish brown to almost black, with blocky plates on larger trunks; resembling that of Flowering Dogwood.

    Flowers – perfect; creamy white, similar to other species, but the flower clusters are usually larger, up to 6" wide; flower clusters stalk-less; appearing with the leaves in early spring, April–May. Figure 431.

    Fruit – drupes, purple to dark blue, globose to ellipsoid, about ½" long; borne on drooping reddish stalks; maturing mid to late summer. Figure 432.

RECOGNITION DIFFICULTIES WITH OTHER TAXA: See *V. prunifolium*.

HABITAT: *Viburnum rufidulum* occupies a wide range of sites from moist lower slopes to drier uplands, around the edge of forest openings, and as an understory species throughout the State.

ECONOMIC, ORNAMENTAL AND OTHER USES: Rusty Blackhaw is used occasionally as an ornamental, but deserves much more attention as a specimen plant for residential landscapes because of its showy cluster of flowers, lustrous dark green foliage, and attractive bronze to red autumn coloration.

Winter Key to Genera of Flowering Trees

KEY TO SUBGROUPS OF ANGIOSPERMS

1. Leaves fan-like, up to 7' long . . . . *Sabal palmetto*
1. Leaves not fan-like, much less than 7' long. 2
   2. Foliage evergreen . . . . **Group A**
   2. Foliage deciduous. 3
      3. Leaf scars opposite or 3 per node. . . . . **Group B**
      3. Leaf scars alternate 4
         4. Twigs armed with spines or thorns . . . . **Group C**
         4. Twigs not armed with spines or thorns. . . . . **Group D**

KEY TO GROUP A (Evergreen trees)

1. Leaves opposite. 2
   2. Leaves 4–9" long, petiole stout. . . . . *Osmanthus americanus*
   2. Leaves ½–2" long, sessile. . . . . *Viburnum* (in part)
1. Leaves alternate 3
   3. Leaves spicy aromatic. 4
      4. Petioles red, leaves thick, nearly fleshy; buds glabrous. . . . .
      . . . . *Illicium floridanum*
      4. Petioles not red, leaves leathery, but not fleshy; buds densely
      hairy, or with resin dots. 5
         5. Leaves irregularly serrate, resinous dotted, 2–4" long . . .
         . . . . *Myrica* (in part)
         5. Leaves entire, not resinous dotted, 2–8" long . . . .
         . . . . *Persea borbonia*
   3. Leaves not spicy aromatic. 6
      6. Buds naked with lustrous silky hairs, leaves serrate. . . . .
      . . . . *Gordonia lasianthus*
      6. Buds with single to numerous scales, leaves entire or serrate
      only at apex 7
         7. Terminal bud absent 8
            8. Lateral buds embedded in twig; twig usually thorny, spur
            shoots present, milky sap when cut . . . . *Bumelia* (in part)
            8. Lateral buds not embedded in twig; lacking thorns and
            spur shoots, without milky sap. 9
               9. Leaves finely glandular dotted; fruits olive-brown. . .
               . . . . *Myrica* (in part)
               9. Leaves not glandular dotted; fruits black. . . . .
               . . . . *Vaccinium arboreum*
         7. Terminal bud present 10
           10. Bud with single caplike scale . . . . . *Magnolia* (in part)
           10. Bud with 2 or more scales 11

11. Buds clustered toward tips of twigs 12
12. Bundle scars numerous; fruit an acorn . . . . . .
. . . . *Quercus* (in part)
12. Bundle scar one (sometimes broken into several); fruit not an acorn 13
13. Leaves 3½–12″ long; persistent capsules ½–¾″ long . . . . *Rhododendron*
13. Leaves 1–4″ long; persistent capsules ¼″ long. 14
14. Leaves rusty scaly beneath. . . . .
. . . . *Lyonia ferruginea*
14. Leaves glabrous beneath. . . . .
. . . . *Kalmia latifolia*
11. Buds not clustered at end of twig 15
15. Leaf scars with 3 bundle scars. . . . .
. . . . *Prunus* (in part)
15. Leaf scar with single bundle scar 16
16. Pith chambered; twigs ridged with scattered hairs. . . . . *Symplocos tinctoria*
16. Pith homogeneous 17
17. Leaf scars half-round or crescent-shaped; fruit solitary or small clusters in axils of leaves. . . . . . . *Ilex* (in part)
17. Leaf scars shield shaped; fruit in racemes. 18
18. Leaves 2–4″ long; leaf scar fringed; fruits not winged, racemes borne just below previous season growth . . . . *Cyrilla racemiflora*
18. Leaves 1–2″ long; leaf scars not fringed; fruits 2–4 winged, racemes borne terminally . . . . . .
. . . . *Cliftonia monophylla*

KEY TO GROUP B (Leaves deciduous, leaf scars opposite)

1. Buds with valvate scales (or appearance of single pair scales only) . . 2
2. Lateral buds long stalked. . . . . *Acer* (in part)
2. Lateral buds not long stalked 3
3. Young twigs green, red or maroon; buds ¼″ or less long . . . . . .
. . . . *Cornus* (in part)
3. Young twigs gray to brown; buds (at least flower buds) up to ½″ long . . . . *Viburnum* (in part)
1. Buds with 4 or more scales 4
4. Terminal bud lacking 5
5. Twigs stout; leaf scars large. 6
6. Leaf scars round-elliptical with depressed centers, 3 per node; bundle scars numerous, in elliptical pattern; twigs lacking disagreeable odor; persistent fruit a capsule, 6–18″ long. . . . . *Catalpa bignonioides*
(Figure 23, Plate 83)

      6. Leaf scars crescent-shaped, 2 per node, bundle scars 3, 5, or 7; twigs with disagreeable odor; fruit a berry-like drupe, not persistent all winter .... *Sambucus canadensis*
                                   (Figure 79, Plate 90)
   5. Twigs moderate to slender; leaf scars small.............. 7
      7. Bundle scars 3, 5, or 7, elliptical; stipule scars half round or elongated .... *Staphylea trifolia*
                                   (Figure 82, Plate 91)
      7. Bundle scar 1, crescent or U-shaped; stipule scars connecting leaf scars .... *Cephalanthus occidentalis*
                                   (Figure 25, Plate 84)
 4. Terminal bud present..................................... 8
  8. Bundle scar single (or compound in U-shaped pattern) ... 9
   9. Terminal bud 1/16″ long .... *Forestiera acuminata*
                              (Figure 36, Plate 85)
   9. Terminal bud longer than 1/16″.................... 10
     10. Terminal bud ½″ long, slender pointed; stipule scars on both sides of twig .... *Pinckneya bracteata*
                         (Figure 59, Plate 88)
     10. Terminal bud less than ½″ long, ovoid; stipule scars lacking 11
       11. Bud scales purplish, not keeled; twigs without warty lenticels .... *Euonymus atropurpureus*
       11. Bud scales brownish, prominently keeled; twigs with warty lenticels .... *Chionanthus virginicus*
                          (Figure 27, Plate 84)
  8. Bundle scars 3 or more 12
     12. Terminal bud more than ⅔″ long (exception: *A. parviflora* ¼″); leaf scars triangular to round.......... *Aesculus*
     12. Terminal bud less than ½″ long; leaf scars crescent shaped, half circles, or V-shaped................ 13
      13. Twigs often flattened at nodes; bundle scars numerous, sometimes indistinct, crescent-shaped; opposite leaf scars not connected .... *Fraxinus*
      13. Twigs not flattened at nodes; bundle scars 3; opposite leaf scars connected by transverse ridge..........
                                 Acer (in part)

KEY TO GROUP C (Leaves deciduous, leaf scars alternate, twigs armed)

1. Terminal bud absent 2
  2. Spines on twigs paired at nodes .... *Robinia pseudoacacia*
                              (Figure 77, Plate 90)
  2. Thorns, or sharp pointed spur shoots on twigs 3
   3. Thorns 2–3 or many branched.................... *Gleditsia*
   3. Thorns not branched, or spur shoots sharp.............. 4
    4. Twigs with milky sap .... *Bumelia*
    4. Twigs lacking milky sap .... *Prunus* (in part)
1. Terminal bud present...................................... 5

5. Spines or prickles distributed over surface of twig 6
  6. Twigs very stout; leaf scars nearly encircling twig ....
      .... *Aralia spinosa*
                            (Figure 8, Plate 81)
  6. Twigs slender; leaf scars C-shaped or triangular. ....
      .... *Zanthoxylum* (in part)
5. Spines or thorns at nodes of twig or at tip of spur shoots. ... 7
  7. Spines paired at nodes .... *Zanthoxylum* (in part)
  7. Thorns single at nodes or tips of spur shoots 8
    8. Thorns single at nodes, buds glabrous .... *Crataegus*
                              (Figure 32, Plate 84)
    8. Thorns at tip of spur shoots, buds hairy .... *Malus*

KEY TO GROUP D (Leaves deciduous, alternate, twigs not armed)
1. Pith diaphragmed, or chambered, or chambered only at nodes 2
  2. Terminal buds lacking 3
    3. Lateral buds superposed, the uppermost triangular .... *Halesia*
    3. Lateral buds not superposed. 4
      4. Buds with 4 or more scales; bundle scars 3; bark smooth to
         warty. .... *Celtis*
      4. Buds with 2 scales; single bundle scar; bark rough,
         blocky. .... *Diospyros virginiana*
                              (Figure 33, Plate 85)
  2. Terminal bud present. 5
    5. Buds naked .... *Asimina triloba*
                              (Figure 9, Plate 82)
    5. Buds with 1 or more scales. 6
      6. Terminal bud with single cap-like scale .... *Magnolia*
      6. Terminal bud with 2 or more scales 7
        7. Lateral buds of 2 sizes .... *Symplocos tinctoria*
                              (Figure 85, Plate 91)
        7. Lateral buds all essentially same size. 8
          8. Terminal bud flattened, with 2 valvate scales .....
              .... *Liriodendron tulipifera*
                              (Figure 48, Plate 86)
          8. Terminal buds not flattened, scales overlapping ... 9
            9. Terminal bud hairy, greater than ⅓"; bundle scars
               numerous in 3 U-shaped clusters ...... *Juglans*
            9. Terminal bud glabrous, about ⅛–¼" long, bundle
               scars 3 .... *Nyssa*
1. Pith continuous (not diaphragmed or chambered) 10
  10. Buds with single scale, naked, or indistinctly scaly 11
    11. Terminal bud present 12
      12. Buds with single scale. .... *Magnolia* (in part)
      12. Buds naked 13
        13. Buds not stalked .... *Rhamnus caroliniana*
                              (Figure 73, Plate 90)
        13. Buds stalked .... *Hamamelis virginiana*
                              (Figure 42, Plate 86)

11. Terminal bud not present. 14
14. Bundle scar 1; twigs with minute stellate hairs . . . . *Styrax*
14. Bundle scars more than 1; twigs lacking stellate hairs . . 15
15. Lateral bud scale cap-like; not woolly or silky 16
16. Leaf scars narrow, V-shaped; bundle scars 3; buds small; bark not peeling in large plates. . . . .
. . . . *Salix*
16. Leaf scars ring-like, encircling bud; bundle scars 5–9; buds large; bark peeling in large plates exposing mottled white to greenish layers beneath . . . . *Platanus occidentalis*
(Figure 61, Plate 88)
15. Lateral buds appearing naked; woolly or silky. . . . 17
17. Buds silky; bark with wart-like growths; twigs with rank odor . . . . *Ptelea trifoliata*
(Figure 65, Plate 89)
17. Buds woolly; bark without warty growths; twigs lacking rank odor. 18
18. Lateral buds superposed (sometimes appearing as single bud); petiole base often persistent and covering buds . . . .
. . . . *Cladrastis kentukea*
(Figure 28, Plate 84)
18. Lateral buds not superposed; petiole base never persistent. . . . . *Rhus*
10. Buds with 2 to numerous scales. 19
19. Leaf scars two-ranked 20
20. Leaf scars fringed; buds often superposed; twigs reddish; leaf bud scales 2 . . . . *Cercis canadensis*
(Figure 26, Plate 84)
20. Leaf scars not fringed; buds not superposed; twigs grayish; buds with more than 2 scales 21
21. Buds stalked. . . . . *Alnus serrulata*
(Figure 6, Plate 81)
21. Buds not stalked 22
22. Buds ½" long or longer 23
23. Buds green-red, ½–¾" long; all leaves dropping before winter . . . .
. . . . *Amelanchier arborea*
(Figure 7, Plate 81)
23. Buds lustrous tan, 1" long; some dead leaves remaining all winter . . . . . *Fagus grandifolia*
(Figure 35, Plate 85)
22. Buds less than ½" long. 24
24. Twigs with milky sap, bundle scars numerous. . . . . *Morus rubra*
(Figure 54, Plate 87)
24. Twigs with watery sap, bundle scars 3, sometimes indistinct 25

25. Buds minute, about 1/16", rounded; bark of older trees with large scales that flake off to expose reddish inner bark......
.... *Planera aquatica*
(Figure 60, Plate 88)
25. Buds ⅛" or longer, pointed; bark not as above 26
    26. Bark separating into papery layers; lenticels horizontally elongated; spur shoots common .... *Betula*
    26. Bark smooth, or furrowed, or with thin shreddy scales; lenticels not horizontally elongated; spur shoots lacking ...
.... 27
        27. Leaf scars with corky layer, often positioned to side of bud .... *Ulmus*
        27. Leaf scars lacking corky layer, positioned directly below bud.. 28
            28. Catkins often present in winter, trunk round, bark with thin, shreddy scales .... *Ostrya virginiana*
(Figure 57, Plate 88)
            28. Catkins not present in winter, trunk fluted, bark smooth .... *Carpinus caroliniana*
(Figure 15, Plate 82)
19. Leaf scars not 2-ranked 29
29. Bundle scar 1 30
    30. Leaf scars raised as a shelf; persistent fruit a berry, about 1½" in diameter....................... *Diospyros virginiana*
(Figure 33, Plate 85)
    30. Leaf scars not raised; fruit not a berry or less than ¾" long ..
.... 31
        31. Spur shoots common; leaf scars densely crowded...
.... *Ilex* (in part)
        31. Spur shoots absent; leaf scars not densely crowded.. 32
            32. Twigs bright green, spicy odor when crushed...
.... *Sassafras albidum*
(Figure 80, Plate 90)
            32. Twigs not bright green, lacking spicy odor.... 33
            33. Terminal bud ¼–½" long, outer bud scales as long as bud.............. *Clethra acuminata*
(Figure 29, Plate 84)
            33. Terminal bud absent or less than ¼", outer bud scales not as long as bud................ 34
                34. Bark shreddy; persistent capsule about ½" long or longer, solitary .... *Stewartia*
                34. Bark furrowed; persistent capsules ½" long or less, in racemes................... 35
                  35. Lateral buds partially embedded in bark; fruit racemes one-sided.......
.... *Oxydendrum arboreum*
(Figure 58, Plate 88)
                  35. Lateral buds not embedded in bark; racemes not one-sided............
.... *Elliottia racemosa*
(Figure 34, Plate 85)

29. Bundle scars 3 or more 36
   36. Buds clustered at tip of twigs; twigs gray to brown......
    .... *Quercus* (in part)
   36. Buds not clustered at tips of twigs, or if clustered, twig is also
    bright red....................................... 37
     37. Some twigs corky-winged; persistent fruit in spiny
     globose heads; bundle scars light with dark center ..
     .... *Liquidambar styraciflua*
     (Figure 47, Plate 86)
     37. Twigs not corky-winged; fruit not persistent or if persis-
     tent, not in spiny heads; bundle scars not as above 38
      38. Lateral buds obliquely asymmetrical, divergent..
      .... *Tilia americana*
      (Figure 86, Plate 91)
      38. Lateral buds not as above................... 39
       39. Terminal buds ⅓–1" long.............. 40
        40. Bundle scars more than 7; buds not
        resinous................ *Carya* (in part)
        40. Bundle scars 3, 5, or 7; buds resinous.. 41
         41. Terminal bud with curved tip; persis-
         tent fruit a pome, orange-red, ¼"
         across; bark warty .. *Sorbus americana*
         (Figure 81, Plate 91)
         41. Terminal bud without curved tip; fruit
         not persistent; bark not warty ......
         .... *Populus*
       39. Terminal buds less than ⅓" long, or absent.. 42
        42. Terminal bud absent............... 43
         43. Bark usually with wart-like growths;
         pith round lateral buds often super-
         posed 44
          44. Persistent fruit a berry, ¾" in diam-
          eter; leaf scar shield-shaped or 3-
          lobed .... *Sapindus marginatus*
          44. Persistent fruit a samara, 1" in
          diameter; leaf scar horseshoe-
          shaped.......... *Ptelea trifoliata*
          (Figure 65, Plate 89)
         43. Bark without warts; pith 5-angled ...
         .... *Castanea*
        42. Terminal bud present.............. 45
         45. Twigs with free flowing gummy sap;
         lenticels corky; leaf scar with minute
         folds .... *Cotinus obovatus*
         45. Twigs, lenticels and leaf scars not as
         above 46

46. Leaf scars crowded toward tip of twig. 47
   47. Bud scales 2; flower buds not enlarged; twigs with rank odor
      when bruised, lenticels not conspicuous . . . .
      . . . . *Cornus* (in part)
   47. Bud scales more than 2; flower buds larger than leaf buds;
      twigs without rank odor, lenticels conspicuous . . . .
      . . . . *Leitneria floridana*
      (Figure 46, Plate 96)
46. Leaf scars not crowded toward tip of twig 48
   48. Terminal bud with 2 purple scales; sap becoming black with
      exposure to air (very poisonous) . . . . *Toxicodendron vernix*
      (Figure 87, Plate 91)
   48. Terminal bud with more than 2 scales, not purplish; sap not
      blackening with exposure. 49
      49. Bark black or reddish, thin scaly, twigs with bitter
         almond taste. . . . . *Prunus* (in part)
      49. Bark gray, fissured, or furrowed or shaggy, but not thin
         scaly; twigs lacking bitter almond taste . . *Carya* (in part)

Winter Key to Species of Flowering Trees

(Genera in alphabetical order)

Acer

1. Bud scales 2, lateral buds long-stalked, pith brown............ 2
   2. Terminal buds ½″ long, twigs stout, glabrous; trunks with white longitudinal streaks...................... *A. pensylvanicum*
                    (Figure 2, Plate 81)
   2. Terminal buds ⅛–¼″ long, twigs slender, minutely pubescent; trunks without white longitudinal streaks.......... *A. spicatum*
1. Bud scales more than 2, lateral buds not long-stalked, pith white.... 3
   3. Twigs green (or reddish); buds densely hairy...... *A. negundo*
                    (Figure 1, Plate 81)
   3. Twigs and buds not as above........................... 4
      4. Terminal bud pointed, buds brown or black, twigs red-brown or tan...
      ....*A. saccharum* or *A. nigrum* or *A. barbatum* or *A. leucoderme*
                    (Figure 4, Plate 81)
      4. Terminal bud blunt, buds reddish orange; twigs bright glossy red or dark red........................... 5
         5. Crushed twigs lacking rank odor......... *A. rubrum*
                    (Figure 3, Plate 81)
        5. Crushed twigs with definite rank odor... *A. saccharinum*

Aesculus

1. Buds up to ¼″ long; fruit stalks persistent; shrubby...... *A. parviflora*
1. Buds longer than ¼″; fruit stalks not persistent; tree........... 2
   2. Bark rough, breaking into corky plates; twigs with ill scent when crushed; bud scales usually keeled; fruit spiny....... *A. glabra*
                    (Figure 5, Plate 81)
   2. Bark smooth and firm; twigs lacking ill scent when crushed; bud scales not keeled; fruit not spiny........................ 3
      3. Terminal buds about ⅔″ long; fruit 2–3″ in diameter... *A. flava*
      3. Terminal buds up to ½″ long; fruit 1–2″ in diameter......
      ....*A. sylvatica* or *A. pavia*

Betula

1. Mature bark pinkish to gray-brown, papery layers of scales; buds frequently with hook at tip; twigs without wintergreen taste . . . . .
. . . . *B. nigra*
(Figure 12, Plate 82)
1. Mature bark yellowish and papery or nearly black and not exfoliating in large scales; buds not hooked; twigs with wintergreen taste. 2
    2. Mature bark golden-gray to bronze-gray, exfoliating in papery curls; twigs greenish brown. . . . . *B. alleghaniensis*
(Figure 10, Plate 82)
    2. Mature bark and twigs dark brown to black with scaly plates. . . . . .
. . . . *B. lenta*
(Figure 11, Plate 82)

Bumelia

1. Leaves deciduous; bark with small flat plates, red-brown; buds glabrous . . . . *B. lycioides*
(Figure 14, Plate 82)
1. Leaves evergreen or persistent; bark with narrow ridges, grayish brown; buds hairy 2
    2. Leaves with lustrous coppery hairs below . . . . *B. tenax*
    2. Leaves with dull white or rusty hairs below . . . . . . *B. lanuginosa*
(Figure 13, Plate 82)

Carya

1. Terminal buds elongated, 4–6 valvate scales (sometimes appearing naked); fruit husks winged along sutures. 2
    2. Terminal buds distinctly yellow, about ½" long; fruit globose. . . . .
. . . . *C. cordiformis*
(Figure 16, Plate 82)
    2. Terminal buds yellowish brown, about ¼–½" long; fruit strongly flattened . . . . *C. aquatica*
1. Terminal buds ovoid, 6 or more imbricate scales; fruit husks not winged along sutures. 3
    3. Bark with long shaggy plates 4
        4. Buds glabrous, scales shiny black. . . . . . . *C. ovata* var. *australis*
(Figure 19, Plate 83)
        4. Buds hairy, scales chestnut brown or dark brown 5
            5. Buds chestnut brown, ¾" long; nut almost round, 1–1½" long; husk about ¼–⅜" thick; twigs dark brown . . . . . .
. . . . *C. ovata* var. *ovata*
(Figure 18, Plate 83)
            5. Buds brown, ¾–1" long; nut oblong, 1½–2" long; husk about ¼" thick; twigs buff to orange-brown. . . . . *C. laciniosa*
    3. Bark tight, lacking conspicuous shaggy plates, or only slightly scaly. 6

6. Terminal buds ½–¾" long; nut 1–1½" long, elliptical, husk ¼–⅓" thick; bark in anastomosing ridges; twigs stout . . . .
. . . . *C. tomentosa*
(Figure 20, Plate 83)

6. Terminal buds less than ½"; nut ¾–1" long; husk ⅛" thick or less; bark not in anastomosing ridges; twigs moderate-slender. 7

   7. Bud scales dotted with silvery or yellow scales; fruit husk with silvery scales . . . . *C. pallida*

   7. Bud scales and fruit husk lacking silvery scales. 8

      8. Bark slightly shaggy or scaly; fruit nearly globose, husks splitting to base . . . . *C. ovalis*
(Figure 17, Plate 83)

      8. Bark tight, not scaly; fruit pear-shaped with neck-like extension at base, husk indehiscent or splitting part way at maturity. . . . . *C. glabra*

Castanea

1. Buds and twigs pubescent . . . . *C. pumila*
(Figure 22, Plate 83)

1. Buds and twigs glabrous. . . . . *C. dentata*
(Figure 21, Plate 83)

Celtis

Species of *Celtis* are not easily distinguishable in winter condition.

1. Buds about ¼" long . . . . *C. occidentalis*
1. Buds 1/16–⅛" long 2

   2. Twigs glabrous; medium-sized tree . . . . *C. laevigata*

   2. Twigs rough-hairy; scrubby small tree or large shrub. . . . .
. . . .*C. tenuifolia*
(Figure 24, Plate 83)

Cornus

1. Branching pattern and leaf scars alternate; twigs with fetid odor if bruised . . . . *C. alternifolia*
(Figure 30, Plate 84)

1. Branching pattern and leaf scars opposite; twigs without fetid odor . 2

   2. Terminal flower buds globe-shaped; leaf buds with 2 valvate scales; twigs green or purple with small dark lenticels; mature bark breaking into square scaly blocks. . . . . *C. florida*
(Figure 31, Plate 84)

   2. Terminal flower buds slender; leaf buds with 2–3 overlapping, visible scales; twigs reddish brown with large light lenticels; mature bark thin, red-brown, becoming ridged 3

      3. Twigs hairy; fruits white . . . . *C. drummondii*

      3. Twigs not hairy or sparsely so near the tips; fruits blue . . . .
. . . .*C. stricta*

Fraxinus

1. Twigs 4-angled and winged...................... *F. quadrangulata*
   (Figure 39, Plate 85)
1. Twigs round, sometimes flattened at nodes, but not 4-angled, not winged 2
   2. Bark deeply fissured with narrow interlacing ridges; trunks not buttressed... 3
      3. Leaf scar narrow, deeply U-shaped............ *F. americana*
         (Figure 37, Plate 85)
      3. Leaf scar half-round..................... *F. pennsylvanica*
         (Figure 38, Plate 85)
   2. Bark shallowly fissured with narrow, longitudinal scaly ridges, trunk buttressed 4
      4. Twigs slightly pubescent .... *F. caroliniana*
      4. Twigs decidedly pubescent................... *F. profunda*

Gleditsia

G. triacanthos and *G. aquatica* are not separable in winter condition, except by fruit which is persistent for a while.

1. Fruit 12–18" long, pulpy .... *G. triacanthos*
   (Figure 40, Plate 85)
1. Fruit 1–2" long, not pulpy .... *G. aquatica*

Halesia

1. Bark of young stems with white streaks.............. *H. carolina*
   (Figure 41, Plate 86)
1. Bark of young stems lacking white streaks 2
   2. Trunk bark deeply furrowed, dark brown; fruit 4-winged .....
      .... *H. parviflora*
   2. Trunk bark thin, scaly, gray-brown; fruit 2-winged ... *H. diptera*

Ilex

1. Leaves evergreen 2
   2. Margins of the leaves with sharp, coarse teeth; each tooth with stiff, sharp spines.. *I. opaca*
   2. Margins of the leaves entire, or with rounded or fine teeth, lacking a stiff, sharp spine....................................... 3
      3. Leaves crenate along entire leaf margin......... *I. vomitoria*
      3. Leaves not as above 4
         4. Leaves less than 1½" long, and less than ¼" wide; linear to linear-oblong............................... *I. myrtifolia*
         4. Leaves usually exceeding 1½" in length and ¼" wide; not linear 5

Fig. 49
Magnolia acuminata

Fig. 50
Magnolia fraseri

Fig. 51
Magnolia macrophylla

Fig. 52
Magnolia virginiana

Fig. 53
Malus angustifolia

Fig. 54
Morus rubra

Fig. 55
Nyssa aquatica

Fig. 56
Nyssa sylvatica

PLATE 87

Fig. 57	Fig. 58	Fig. 59	Fig. 60
Ostrya virginiana	*Oxydendrum arboreum*	*Pinckneya bracteata*	*Planera aquatica*

Fig. 61	Fig. 62	Fig. 63	Fig. 64
Platanus occidentalis	*Populus deltoides*	*Prunus serotina*	*Prunus umbellata*

PLATE 88

Fig. 65
Ptelea trifoliata

Fig. 66
Quercus alba

Fig. 67
Quercus coccinea

Fig. 68
Quercus laevis

Fig. 69
Quercus marilandica

Fig. 70
Quercus nigra

Fig. 71
Quercus stellata

Fig. 72
Quercus velutina

PLATE 89

Fig. 73
Rhamnus caroliniana

Fig. 74
Rhus copallina

Fig. 75
Rhus glabra

Fig. 76
Rhus typhina

Fig. 77
Robinia pseudoacacia

Fig. 78
Salix nigra

Fig. 79
Sambucus canadensis

Fig. 80
Sassafras albidum

Fig. 81
Sorbus americana

Fig. 82
Staphylea trifolia

Fig. 83
Stewartia ovata

Fig. 84
Styrax qrandifolius

Fig. 85
Symplocus tinctoria

Fig. 86
Tilia americana

Fig. 87
Toxicodendron vernix

Fig. 88
U   's alata

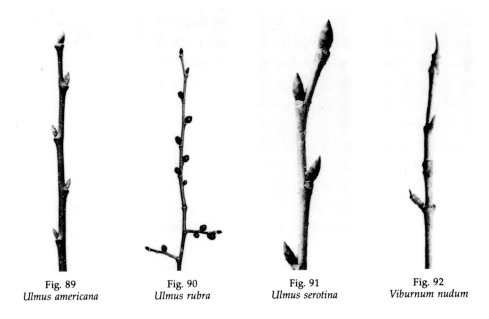

Fig. 89
Ulmus americana

Fig. 90
Ulmus rubra

Fig. 91
Ulmus serotina

Fig. 92
Viburnum nudum

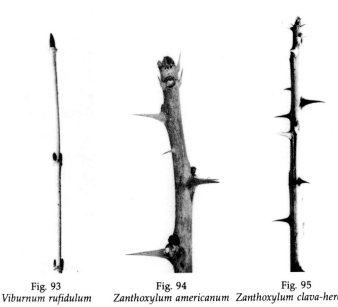

Fig. 93
Viburnum rufidulum

Fig. 94
Zanthoxylum americanum

Fig. 95
Zanthoxylum clava-herculis

PLATE 92

Fig. 17
Carya ovalis

Fig. 18
Carya ovata
var. *ovata*

Fig. 19
Carya ovata
var. *australis*

Fig. 20
Carya tomentosa

Fig. 21
Castanea dentata

Fig. 22
Castanea pumila

Fig. 23
Catalpa bignonioides

Fig. 24
Celtis tenuifolia

PLATE 83

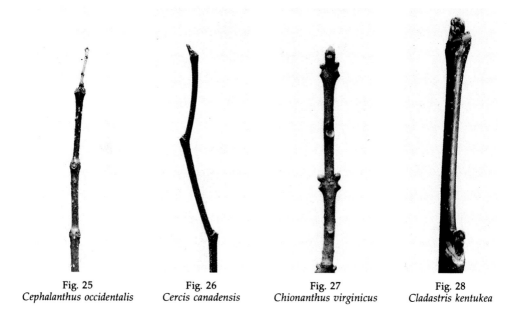

Fig. 25
Cephalanthus occidentalis

Fig. 26
Cercis canadensis

Fig. 27
Chionanthus virginicus

Fig. 28
Cladastris kentukea

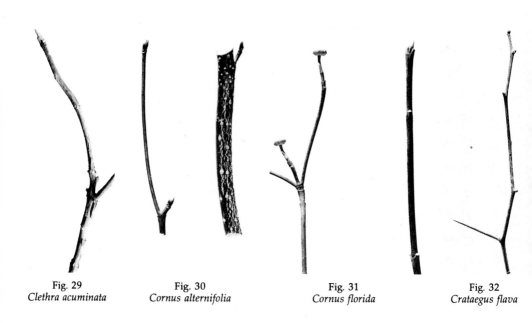

Fig. 29
Clethra acuminata

Fig. 30
Cornus alternifolia

Fig. 31
Cornus florida

Fig. 32
Crataegus flava

PLATE 84

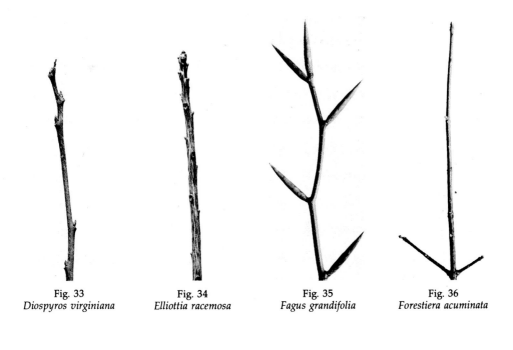

Fig. 33	Fig. 34	Fig. 35	Fig. 36
Diospyros virginiana	*Elliottia racemosa*	*Fagus grandifolia*	*Forestiera acuminata*

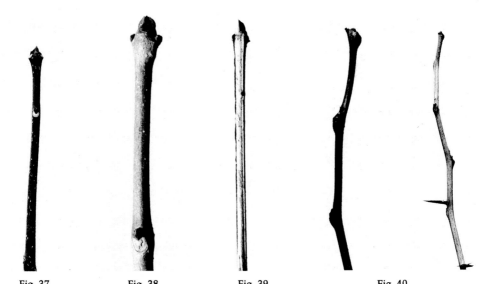

Fig. 37	Fig. 38	Fig. 39	Fig. 40
Fraxinus americana	*Fraxinus pennsylvanica*	*Fraxinus quadrangulata*	*Gleditsia triacanthos*

PLATE 85

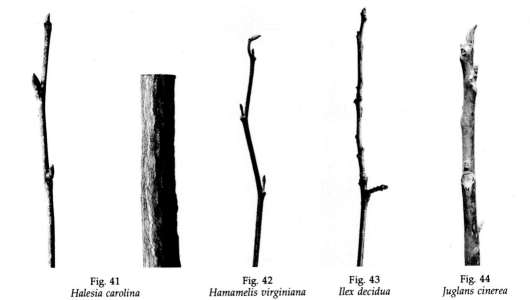

Fig. 41
Halesia carolina

Fig. 42
Hamamelis virginiana

Fig. 43
Ilex decidua

Fig. 44
Juglans cinerea

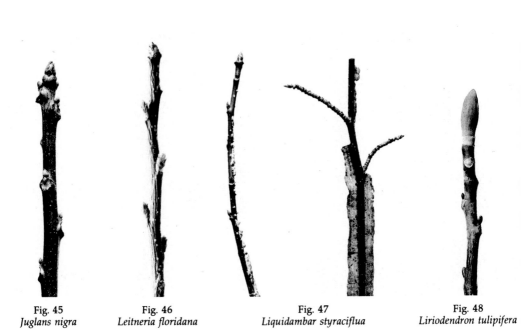

Fig. 45
Juglans nigra

Fig. 46
Leitneria floridana

Fig. 47
Liquidambar styraciflua

Fig. 48
Liriodendron tulipifera

PLATE 86

5. Leaves entire, or with bristly teeth above the middle of the blade, and projecting outward from the blade; blades usually less than 2 × as long as broad; fruit black. . . .
. . . . *I. coriacea*

5. Leaves entire, or with a few, small teeth near the apex which are incurved; blades usually over 2× longer than wide; fruit red . . . . *I. cassine*

1. Leaves deciduous . . . . species not easily separated in winter.
(Figure 43, Plate 86)

Juglans

1. Leaf scar notched, lacking hairy fringe; terminal bud ⅓" long or less; fruit spherical, nearly black; bark dark brown-black with interlacing ridges. . . . . *J. nigra*
(Figure 45, Plate 86)

1. Leaf scar not notched, hairy fringe above scar; terminal bud ½–¾" long; fruit oblong, greenish brown; bark with grayish ridges and darker furrows . . . . *J. cinerea*
(Figure 44, Plate 86)

Magnolia

1. Leaves evergreen or persistent 2
2. Leaves thick, lower surface rusty woolly or greenish, but not glaucous; up to 12" long . . . . *M. grandiflora*
2. Leaves thin, lower surface glaucous, silvery pubescent, up to 6½" long . . . . *M. virginiana*
(Figure 52, Plate 87)

1. Leaves deciduous 3
3. Terminal buds 1" or longer 4
4. Buds densely white hairy . . . . *M. macrophylla*
(Figure 51, Plate 87)
4. Buds glabrous, purplish 5
5. Leaf scars all along twig; remnant fruit cones 3–4½" long, oblong, symmetrical, bright red . . . .
. . . . *M. fraseri* or *M. pyramidata*
(Figure 50, Plate 87)
5. Leaf scars clustered at end of twig; remnant fruit cones 2–3" long, conical-cylindrical, lop-sided, rose-colored. . . . .
. . . . *M. tripetala*
3. Terminal buds ¾" or less . . . . *M. acuminata*
(Figure 49, Plate 87)

Malus

Species of *Malus* are not reliably separated in winter. (Figure 53, Plate 87)

Myrica

1. Leaves leathery, not reduced in size toward tip of twig; crushed twigs not fragrant; fruit more that ¼" in diameter, with conspicuous rough protuberances . . . . M. inodora
1. Leaves not leathery, reduced in size toward tip of twig; crushed twigs fragrant; fruit ⅛" or less in diameter, with thick blue wax 2
   2. Glands on upper leaf surface dense . . . . M. cerifera
   2. Glands on upper leaf surface absent or sparse . . . . . M. heterophylla

Nyssa

1. Buds pointed, terminal buds about ¼" long, lateral buds ⅛" long; fruit ¼–½" long . . . . N. sylvatica
   (Figure 56, Plate 87)
1. Buds blunt, terminal bud up to ⅛" long, lateral buds minute; fruit greater than 1" long. 2
   2. Fruit red; multi-stemmed tree. N. ogeche
   2. Fruit purple; single-stemmed tree. . . . . N. aquatica
   (Figure 55, Plate 87)

Prunus

1. Leaves evergreen . . . . P. caroliniana
1. Leaves deciduous 2
   2. Terminal bud absent; twigs often with thorn-like spur shoots. . . . .
   . . . . P. americana, P. angustifolia, or P. umbellata
   (Figure 64, Plate 88)
   2. Terminal bud present; twigs lacking thorn-like spur shoots. . . 3
      3. Bark on mature trees nearly black, fissured and scaly; twigs red-brown, lenticels small, dot-like . . . . P. serotina
      (Figure 63, Plate 88)
      3. Bark on mature trees red-brown to gray, smooth, fissured into flat plates and peeling at base of trunks; twigs bright red, with pronounced horizontal lenticels . . . . P. pensylvanica

Populus

1. Twigs yellowish gray; terminal buds acute, ¾–1" long, green-brown, highly resinous . . . . P. deltoides
   (Figure 62, Plate 88)
1. Twigs dark reddish brown; terminal buds broadly ovoid, ⅓–½" long, reddish brown, slightly resinous . . . . P. heterophylla

Quercus

Immature acorns not present; inner surface of mature acorn shell glabrous (use knife to open shell); remnant leaves lacking bristle tips; bark of most species light gray or whitish . . . . White Oaks . . . . Group A

Immature acorns present; inner surface of mature acorn shell pubescent; remnant leaves bristly tipped; bark dark gray . . . Red Oaks . . . Group B

KEY TO GROUP A (White Oaks)

1. Leaves evergreen 2
    2. Leaf margins distinctly revolute, lower surface wrinkled with conspicuous raised veins . . . . *Q. geminata*
    2. Leaf margins sometimes thickened, but not distinctly revolute, lower surface without conspicuously raised veins. . . . *Q. virginiana*
1. Leaves deciduous 3
    3. Larger buds up to ½" long; buds silky hairy . . . . *Q. prinus*
    3. Larger buds ¼" or less; buds not silky hairy 4
        4. Twigs stout, hairy . . . . *Q. stellata*
                                            (Figure 71, Plate 89)
        4. Twigs slender to moderately stout, glabrous 5
            5. Buds up to ¼" long. 6
                6. Bud scales red-brown, lacking gray margin; acorn 1–1½" long . . . . *Q. michauxii*
                6. Bud scales with gray margin; acorn up to ¾" long. . .
                   . . . . *Q. muehlenbergii*
            5. Buds ⅛" or less long 7
                7. Buds hairy; acorn nearly enclosed in cup. . . . *Q. lyrata*
                7. Buds glabrous; acorn not nearly enclosed in cup . . . 8
                    8. Bark rough, reddish brown to gray. . . *Q. margaretta*
                    8. Bark scaly, silver gray 9
                        9. Acorn cup enclosing ½ of nut; shrubby; leaves somewhat persistent. . . . . *Q. chapmanii*
                        9. Acorn cup enclosing less than ½ of nut; large tree; leaves deciduous. 10
                            10. Acorn about ¾" long or longer; cup scales knobby. . . . . *Q. alba*
                                            (Figure 66, Plate 89)
                            10. Acorn less than ¾" long; cup scales thin. . . 11
                                11. Acorn conical; epicormic branching not common. . . . . *Q. austrina*
                                11. Acorn nearly globose; epicormic branching common . . . . *Q. oglethorpensis*

KEY TO GROUP B (Red Oaks)

1. Leaves evergreen 2
    2. Leaves up to 2" long, margins revolute, apex rounded, usually lacking bristly tip; usually shrubby. . . . . *Q. myrtifolia*
    2. Leaves up to 5" long, margins not revolute, apex usually pointed and bristle-tipped; tree. . . . . *Q. hemisphaerica*

1. Leaves not evergreen (some tardily deciduous)............... 3
   3. Buds angled in cross section............................. 4
      4. Bud scales light brown, glabrous .... *Q. shumardii*
      4. Bud scales brown-gray, pubescent...................... 5
         5. Bud scales with whitish pubescence only on tips; acorn usually with concentric circles at tip .... *Q. coccinea*
              (Figure 67, Plate 89)
         5. Buds hairy, acorns lacking concentric circles at tip..... 6
           6. Buds gray-brown, woolly; twigs shiny, scales of acorn cups fringed .... *Q. velutina*
               (Figure 72, Plate 89)
           6. Buds with reddish hairs; twigs hairy, or if lacking hairs, twigs dull; scales of acorn cup not fringed........ 7
             7. Buds less than ¼" long; twigs slender, glabrous; bark smooth .... *Q. nigra*
                 (Figure 70, Plate 89)
             7. Buds ¼" long or longer; twigs stout, hairy; bark deeply fissured .... *Q. marilandica*
                 (Figure 69, Plate 89)
   3. Bud not angled in cross section........................... 8
      8. Margin of acorn cups conspicuously rolled inward; buds ½" long .... *Q. laevis*
              (Figure 68, Plate 89)
      8. Margin of acorn cups not rolled inward or only slightly so; buds less than ½" long 9
         9. Acorns 1" or greater in length, oblong to ovoid; bark of upper trunk with conspicuous lighter gray vertical streaks .... *Q. rubra*
         9. Acorns smaller, subglobose; bark without light streaks ..10
           10. Persistent leaves nearly as broad as long, shallowly lobed only at tip; acorn pubescent ..... *Q. arkansana*
           10. Persistent leaves longer than broad or deeply lobed; acorn not pubescent or minutely so............ 11
             11. Twigs densely hairy; acorns often striped ....
                .... *Q. incana*
             11. Twigs glabrous by second year or sparsely pubescent; acorns not striped 12
             12. Buds hairy 13
               13. Bark lightly fissured, scaly, resembling Black Cherry .... *Q. pagoda*
               13. Bark deeply fissured, not scaly ... *Q. falcata*
             12. Buds not hairy........................ 14
               14. Persistent leaves lacking bristle tip at apex; acorn greater than ½" long ... *Q. laurifolia*
               14. Persistent leaves bristle tipped; acorn less than ½" long 15
                15. Bark dark gray, shallowly fissured on older trunks; persistent leaves not lobed, tapered at both ends; large tree......
                  .... *Q. phellos*

15. Bark light gray, smooth or scaly; persistent leaves lobed; small tree.........
.........................Q. *georgiana*

Rhododendron

1. Leaves 4–12″ long, pointed at the tips, tapered at the base.......
....R. *maximum*
1. Leaves 3½–6″ long, blunt at the tip, rounded at the base ....
....R. *catawbiense*

Rhus

1. Leaf scars broadly crescent-shaped, not nearly surrounding the bud; twigs slender to moderate; sap watery .... R. *copallina*
(Figure 74, Plate 90)
1. Leaf scars U-shaped, nearly surrounding the bud; twigs very stout; sap milky 2
  2. Twigs densely hairy, round .... R. *typhina*
(Figure 76, Plate 90)
  2. Twigs smooth with whitish bloom, slightly flattened ..... R. *glabra*
(Figure 75, Plate 90)

Salix

1. Lateral buds blunt .... S. *sericea*
1. Lateral buds sharp-pointed............................... 2
  2. Bark smooth with shallow longitudinal fissures on larger stems...
....S. *floridana*
  2. Bark rough, furrowed into scaly ridges 3
    3. Twigs brittle, glabrous; usually a tree.............. S. *nigra*
(Figure 78, Plate 90)
    3. Twigs not brittle, usually hairy; shrubby....... S. *caroliniana*

Stewartia

1. Winter buds about ¼″ long; persistent fruits 5-angled and beaked at the summit; mountains or Piedmont.................... S. *ovata*
(Figure 83, Plate 91)
1. Winter buds minute; persistent fruits, not angled or beaked at the summit; Coastal Plain or lower Piedmont........ S. *malacodendron*

Styrax

1. Twigs densely hairy or scaly...................... S. *grandifolius*
(Figure 84, Plate 91)
1. Twigs hairless or nearly so....................... S. *americanus*

Ulmus

1. Some twigs with corky ridges or wings...................... 2
    2. Buds greater than ⅛″ long .... *U. serotina*
        (Figure 91, Plate 92)
    2. Buds less than ⅛″ long........................... *U. alata*
        (Figure 88, Plate 91)
1. Twigs without corky ridges or wings........................ 3
    3. Buds purplish brown to black and covered with reddish woolly hairs or with rusty hairs at least at tip, ovoid, blunt; mature bark dark brown..................................... *U. rubra*
        (Figure 90, Plate 92)
    3. Buds chestnut-brown, glabrous or essentially so, ovoid, acute; mature bark light gray .... *U. americana*
        (Figure 89, Plate 92)

Viburnum

1. Leaves persistent, terminal buds ¼″ or less long; twigs with strong odor when crushed .... *V. obovatum*
1. Leaves deciduous, terminal buds greater than ½″ long; not strongly scented 2
    2. Mature bark smooth; flower buds narrow and long pointed...
        .... *V. nudum*
        (Figure 92, Plate 92)
    2. Bark fissured into a blocky pattern; flower buds swollen at the base 3
        3. Buds with rusty-woolly hairs; twigs with rusty hairs.......
            .... *V. rufidulum*
            (Figure 93, Plate 92)
        3. Buds smooth or scurfy, brown to reddish gray; twigs smooth with spinelike spurs .... *V. prunifolium*

Zanthoxylum

1. Buds reddish brown, hairy; leaves falling in fall; bark smooth ....
    .... *Z. americanum*
    (Figure 94, Plate 92)
1. Buds black or dark brown, not hairy; leaves often persisting through winter; bark with prominent conical, spiny knobs .... *Z. clava-herculis*
    (Figure 95, Plate 92)

List of Some Common Introduced and Naturalized Trees in Georgia

Ailanthus altissima (Miller) Swingle (SIMAROUBACEAE)
Tree-of-Heaven
Albizia julibrissin Durazzini (FABACEAE)
Mimosa
Aleurites fordii Hemsl. (EUPHORBIACEAE)
Tung-oil Tree
Broussonetia papyrifera (L.) Vent. (MORACEAE)
Paper Mulberry
Carya illinoensis (Wangengh.) K. Koch (JUGLANDACEAE)
Pecan
Catalpa speciosa (Warder ex Barney) Engelm. (BIGNONIACEAE)
Northern Catalpa
Cinnamomum camphora (L.) J. Presl. (LAURACEAE)
Camphor-tree
Citrus aurantium L. (RUTACEAE)
Sour Orange
Firmiana simplex (L.) W. F. Wright (STERCULIACEAE)
Chinese Parasoltree
Lagerstroemia indica L. (LYTHRACEAE)
Crapemyrtle
Ligustrum sinense Lour. (OLEACEAE)
Chinese Privet
Maclura pomifera (Raf.) Schneider (MORACEAE)
Osage-orange
Melia azedarach L. (MELIACEAE)
Chinaberry
Morus alba L. (MORACEAE)
White Mulberry
Paulownia tomentosa (Thunb.) Siebold & Zucc. ex Steud. (SCROPHULARIACEAE)
Princess-Tree
Pinus clausa Vasey ex Sarg. (PINACEAE)
Sand Pine
Poncirus trifoliata (L.) Raf. (RUTACEAE)
Trifoliate Orange

Populus alba L. (SALICACEAE)
　　White Poplar
Populus nigra L.
　　Black Poplar
Sapium sebiferum (L.) Roxb. (EUPHORBIACEAE)
　　Chinese Tallowtree
Tamarix gallica L. (TAMARICACEAE)
　　Tamarisk
Ulmus parvifolia Jacq. (ULMACEAE)
　　Chinese Elm

Glossary

Achene. A small dry, indehiscent, one seeded fruit.

Acuminate. Gradually tapering to a slender point.

Acute. Sharp pointed, sides of the tapered apex less than 90 degrees.

Aggregate fruit. Cluster of ripened ovaries traceable to separate pistils of a single flower inserted on a common receptacle; e.g., *Magnolia*.

Alternate. Arranged singly at different locations along an axis in a spiral manner.

Anther. Pollen bearing part of the stamen.

Apex. Tip or distal end.

Appressed. Closely pressed or lying flat against a surface.

Axil. The angle between a leaf and twig or between a twig and stem.

Axillary. Situated in an axil; e.g., an axillary bud is located in the axil of the leaf.

Axis. The central line of development of any plant or plant organ. The main stem.

Berry. A simple fleshy fruit with one or more seeds embedded in the pulpy ripened ovary; e.g., persimmon.

Bipinnate. Twice pinnate.

Bisexual. Having both sexes (pistils and stamens) in the same flower; perfect flower.

Blade. The flat expanded part of a leaf.

Bloom. A thin surface coating, usually a waxy substance, occurring on leaves, twigs or fruit.

Bole. Tree trunk.

Bract. A modified leaf subtending a flower or flower cluster; sometimes petal like.

Bud scales. Modified leaves that form the outer covering of dormant buds.

Bundle scar. A mark within the leaf scar indicating the former attachment of vascular bundles.

Buttress. Swollen base of a tree trunk.

Calyx. The outer whorl of a flower consisting of sepals; usually green.

Capsule. A dry fruit composed of 2 or more compartments; opening by sutures when mature.

Catkin. A spike-like inflorescence densely crowded with bracts.

Chambered pith. Center of twig with hollow compartments between cross walls.

Ciliate. Having a fringe of hair along the margin.

Compound leaf. A leaf divided into two or more leaflets.

Cordate. Heart-shaped.

Corymb. A flat topped inflorescence with the flower stalks arising at different levels on the main axis.

Crenate. Shallowly round-toothed or scalloped along leaf margin.

Crown. The upright mass of branches, twigs and leaves of a tree; the foliated portion.

Cultivar. A selected variety cultivated for some specific purpose.

Cuneate. Wedge shaped; narrowly acute at the base.

Cyme. A broadly rounded, almost flat topped flower cluster bearing pedicelled flowers.

Deciduous. Falling off or shedding seasonally.

Dehiscent. Opening along one or more lines of suture.

Dentate. Sharply toothed along margin with teeth pointing outward.

Diaphragmed pith. Solid pith with visible cross walls.

Dioecious. Having male and female flowers borne on different plants.

Drupe. A one seeded indehiscent fruit with seed enclosed in a stony wall; the outer ovary wall may be fleshy, dry, or leathery; e.g. Plum, Fringe Tree.

Elliptic. Shaped like an ellipse; widest at the middle with symmetrically curved sides.

Endemic. Native and restricted to a particular area or region.

Entire. Having a smooth margin, free of indentations.

Epicormic. A shoot arising from a dormant bud on the trunk or branches; water sprout.

Exfoliating bark. Bark that peels off or sloughs in flat plates or sheets.

Evergreen. Having foliage which remains green and functional through one or more winters.

Falcate. Sickle-shaped.

False terminal bud. A lateral bud that functions as a terminal bud following shoot tip abortion.

Fascicle. A bundle; e.g., pine needles.

Fascicle sheath. Basal scales which surround the base of fascicled needles in Pines.

Filament. Elongated stalk of the stamen which bears the anther.

Follicle. A dry, dehiscent fruit, opening along one line of suture; e.g. Hercules' Club, Magnolia.

Fruit. Mature ripened ovary; seed bearing organ of angiosperms.

Glabrous. Smooth; lacking hairs or projections.

Glaucous. Covered with a whitish waxy bloom.

Globose. Spherical.

Habit. General overall appearance of a plant; form.

Habitat. The environment in which a plant naturally grows.

Head. A compact mass of flowers.

Husk. Dry outer covering of a fruit or seed; hull.

Imbricate. Overlapping scales or parts.

Indehiscent. Not opening by lines of suture at maturity.

Indigenous. Occurring naturally in a given area.

Inflorescence. A flower cluster.

Internode. Portion of twig between two nodes.

Keeled. A central dorsal ridge, like the bottom of a boat.

Knee. Vertical outgrowths of lateral roots, as in cypress.

Lanceolate. Lance shaped; broadest at base and tapering toward the tip.

Lateral bud. Bud in axil of leaf or leaf scar.

Latex. A milky, often sticky, white exudate from various plant organs.

Leaflet. A single division of a compound leaf.

Leaf scar. A mark indicating former point of leaf attachment to the twig.

Legume. A dry, simple fruit of the pea family which usually dehisces along two suture lines at maturity.

Lenticel. A pore in the bark of a twig or stem which permits gas exchange; usually associated with a visible corky outgrowth.

Linear. Long and narrow; the two sides parallel or nearly so.

Mesic. Moderately moist habitat or environment.

Monoecious. Having male and female flowers borne on the same plant.

Monotypic. A genus having only one species.

Mucronate. Having a sharp terminal point or tip.

Multiple fruit. Fruit formed from several flowers whose ripened ovaries are inserted on a common receptacle; e.g. Sycamore.

Naked buds. Buds lacking true bud scales.

Node. Point of leaf attachment on twig.

Nut. An indehiscent, one seeded fruit with hard outer shell; e.g. Oaks, Hickories.

Nutlet. A small nut, often with accessary parts such as bracts or husks; e.g. Birch, Beech.

Oblanceolate. Reverse of lanceolate; widest at apex and tapering toward base.

Oblique. Having unequal sides, asymmetrical.

Obovate. Reverse of ovate; having a broad distal end and a narrower basal end.

Obtuse. Rounded at the tip.

Ovary. Ovule bearing portion of the pistil.

Oval. Broadly elliptical; egg shaped.

Ovoid. Egg shaped.

Ovulate cone. Young female or mature seed bearing cone of conifers.

Ovule. Egg containing structure in seed plants which develops into the seed after fertilization.

Palmate. Arranged in palmlike or handlike fashion; radiating from a common point.

Palmately compound leaf. A leaf with three or more leaflets radiating from a common point.

Palmately veined. Three or more veins originating at the same point near base of leaf.

Panicle. A branched flower cluster.

Pedicel. Supporting stalk of a single flower in a cluster; may be also spelled pedicle.

Peduncle. Stalk which bears a cluster of flowers or that of a solitary flower.

Perfect flower. Complete, with functional male and female parts; bisexual.

Perianth. Petals and sepals.

Persistent. Lasting for more than one season.

Petiole. Stalk of a leaf.

Pinnately compound leaf. A leaf with leaflets arranged oppositely or alternately along sides of the rachis.

Pistil. Female part of the flower, consisting of stigma, style, and ovary.

Pistillate. Having pistils but lacking functional stamens; unisexual.

Pith. Central spongy tissue of twigs and stems.

Polygamous. Bearing both perfect (bisexual) and unisexual flowers on the same plant.

Pome. A fleshy fruit resulting from a compound ovary with seeds encased in a papery inner wall; e.g. an apple.

Prickle. A sharp pointed outgrowth arising in an irregular manner from the epidermis or bark.

Pubescent. Covered with short hairs.

Raceme. An unbranched inflorescence with stalked flowers.

Rachis. The axis of a compound leaf bearing the leaflets.

Resinous. Producing resin which is often exuded.

Reticulate. Forming an interwoven netted appearance.

Revolute. Rolled under or downwards along margins.

Samara. A dry, indehiscent, winged fruit; e.g. Maples, Elms.

Scabrous. With short bristly hairs, rough to the touch.

Sepal. A modified leaf which comprises part of the calyx.

Serrate. With marginal, sharp teeth pointing toward the apex.

Sessile. Attached directly at the base, without a stalk.

Shell. Hard, outer covering of a fruit or seed.

Short shoot. A compact, non-elongated shoot with barely visible internodes; a spur or dwarf shoot with leaves and/or flowers.

Sinus. The recess or cleft between lobes of a leaf.

Spike. An elongated inflorescence with sessile flowers.

Spine. A sharp pointed, modified leaf or stipule occurring at the node.

Stamen. Pollen bearing organ of the flower, composed of the anther and filament.

Staminate. Having stamens and lacking pistils; male flower.

Stellate. Star shaped.

Stipules. Basal appendages of the leaf.

Stomate. A pore in the epidermal layer of the leaf permitting gas exchange.

Stone. A hard bony layer of a drupaceous fruit; e.g. the pit of a plum or peach.

Strobilus (pl. strobili). A cone-like structure composed of compact bracts or scales producing pollen or ovules in the conifers.

Style. The neck of the pistil with stigma at the distal end and ovary at the basal end.

Subglobose. Almost spherical, slightly flattened on opposite sides.

Subcordate. Nearly heart shaped.

Superposed bud. A bud located above the axillary bud.

Taxon (pl. taxa). A general term applied to any taxonomic unit, e.g., variety, species, genus, family, etc.

Terminal. Situated at the tip.

Thorn. A sharp, rigid or woody modified branch; arises from an axillary bud.

Tomentose. Densely woolly or pubescent, matted with soft hairs.

Trifoliate. A compound leaf composed of three leaflets.

Turbinate. Inversely conical; top-shaped.

Truncate. Appearing cut off or square at the apex or base.

Twig. The foliated portion of the current year shoot, or in the dormant condition, the last formed shoot of the previous season.

Umbel. A flat topped inflorescence with the flower stalks arising from a common point.

Unisexual. Individual male or female flowers.

Valvate. Meeting at the edges without overlapping, as in the scales of some buds.

Venation. Pattern of vein arrangement in leaves.

Wedge shaped. Narrowly acute at base; cuneate.

Whorled. Cyclic arrangement of parts around a point on the axis.

Wing. An extension of a membranous, foliar or corky outgrowth along a stem, fruit, seed of other part of a plant.

Woolly. Densely covered with long, matted hairs.

Bibliography

Argus, George W. 1986. The genus *Salix* (Salicaceae) in the southeastern United States. *Syst. Bot. Monogr.* 9: 1–170.

Bailey, Liberty H., compiler. 1976. *Hortus Third*, revised by the staff of Liberty Hyde Bailey Hortorium. Riverside, N.J.: MacMillan.

Billings, W. D., S. A. Caine and W. B. Drew. 1937. *Winter key to the trees of eastern Tennessee. Castanea* 2: 30–44.

Bishop, G. Norman. 1943. *Native trees of Georgia.* Athens, Ga.: Georgia Agricultural Extension Service.

Brizicky, George K. 1963. The genera of Sapindales in the southeastern United States. *J. Arnold Arbor.* 44: 462–501.

Clark, Ross C. 1971. The Woody Plants of Alabama. *Ann. Mo. Bot. Gard.* 58: 99–242.

Clewell, Andre F. 1985. *Guide to the vascular plants of the Florida Panhandle.* Tallahassee, Fl.: Florida State University Press.

Coker, W. C. and H. R. Totten. 1934. *Trees of the southeastern states.* Chapel Hill, N.C.: The University of North Carolina Press.

Dalle Torre, C. G. and H. Harms (1900–1907). *Genera siphonogamarum ad systema Englerianum conscripta.* Leipzig.: W. Engelmann.

Dirr, Michael A. 1977. *Manual of woody landscape plants: their identification, ornamental characteristics, culture, propagation and uses.* Champaign, Ill.: Stipes Publishing Company.

Duncan, Wilbur H. 1941. *Guide to Georgia trees.* Athens, Ga.: The University of Georgia Press.

Duncan, Wilbur H. and Marion B. Duncan. 1988. *Trees of the southeastern United States.* Athens, Ga.: University of Georgia Press.

Duncan, Wilbur H. and John T. Kartesz. 1981. *Vascular flora of Georgia: an annotated checklist.* Athens, Ga.: The University of Georgia Press.

Elias, Thomas S. 1971. The genera of Fagaceae in the southeastern United States. *J. Arnold Arbor.* 52: 159–195.

———. 1971. The genera of Myricaceae in the southeastern United States. *J. Arnold Arbor.* 52: 305–381.

———. 1972. The genera of Juglandaceae in the southeastern United States. *J. Arnold Arbor.* 53: 26–51.

———. 1980. *The complete trees of North America.* Field guide and natural history. New York: Van Nostrand Reinhold.

Eyde, Richard H. 1966. The Nyssaceae in the southeastern United States. *J. Arnold Arbor.* 47: 117–125.

Faircloth, Wayne R. 1979. An occurrence of *Elliottia* in central south Georgia. *Castanea* 35: 58–61.

Ferguson, I. K. 1966. The Cornaceae in the southeastern United States. *J. Arnold Arbor.* 47: 106–116.

Gleason, Henry A. and Arthur Cronquist. 1963. *Manual of vascular plants of northeastern United States and adjacent Canada.* New York: D. Van Nostrad.

Godfrey, Robert K. 1988. Trees, shrubs, and woody vines of northern Florida and adjacent Georgia and Alabama. Athens, Ga: University of Georgia Press.

Godfrey, Robert K. and Jean W. Wooten. 1981. *Aquatic and wetland plants of southeastern United States, Dicotyledons.* Athens, Ga.: University of Georgia Press.

Gonsoulin, Gene J. 1974. A revision of *Styrax* (Styracaceae) in North America, Central America, and the Caribbean. *Sida* 5: 191–258.

Haehnle, Garry G. and Steven M. Jones. Geographical distribution of *Quercus oglethorpensis*. *Castanea* 50: 26–31.

Halls, Lowell K. 1977. *Southern fruit-producing woody plants used by wildlife.* New Orleans, La.: USDA: Sou. For. Exp. Sta.

Hardin, James W. 1954. An analysis of variation within *Magnolia acuminata* L. *J. Elisha Mitchell Sci. Soc.* 70: 298–312.

————. 1957. A revision of the American Hippocastanaceae—II. *Brittonia* 9: 173–195.

————. 1971. Studies of the southeastern United States flora. I. Betulaceae. *J. Elisha Mitchel Sci. Soc.* 87: 39–41.

————. 1974. Studies on the southeastern United States flora. IV. Oleaceae. *Sida* 5: 274–285.

————. 1979. *Quercus prinus* L. Nomen ambiguum. *Taxon* 28: 355–357.

Harlow, William M. and Ellwood S. Harrar. 1969. *Textbook of dendrology.* 5th ed. New York and London.: McGraw-Hill.

Harper, Francis and Arthur N. Leeds. 1938. A supplementary chapter on *Franklinia alatamaha*. *Bartonia* 19: 1–13.

Harrar, Ellwood S. and J. George Harrar. 1962. *Guide to southern trees.* 2nd ed. New York: Dover Publications.

Heywood, V. H. (ed). 1978. *Flowering plants of the world.* New York: Mayflower Books, Inc.

Houghton, William M. 1988. *The systematics of section Cerophora of the genus Myrica (Myricaceae) in North America.* Master's thesis, Athens, Ga.: University of Georgia.

Hunt, David M. 1986. Distribution of *Quercus arkansana* in Georgia. *Castanea* 5: 183–187.

Jenkins, Charles F. 1943. Franklin's Tree. *Natl. Hort. Mag.* 22: 119–127.

Jones, Samuel B. and Nancy C. Coile. 1988. *The distribution of the vascular flora of Georgia*. Athens, Ga.: Department of Botany, University of Georgia.

Kopp, L. E. 1966. A taxonomic revision of the genus *Persea*. *Mem. New York Bot. Gard.* 14: 1–117.

Kopp, L. E. 1966. A taxonomic revision of the genus *Persea*. *Mem. New York Bot. Gard.* 14: 1–117.

Kral, Robert. 1960. A revision of *Asimina* and *Deeringothamnus* (Annonaceae). *Brittonia* 12: 233–278.

_____. 1983. *A report on some rare, threatened, or endangered forest-related vascular plants of the south*. 2 Vol. USDA, Forest Service, Tech. Publ. R8-TP 2. Atlanta, Ga.: USDA Forest Service.

Kurz, Herman and Robert K. Godfrey. 1962. *Trees of northern Florida*. Gainesville, Fl.: University of Florida Press.

Lawrence, George H. M. 1951. *Taxonomy of vascular plants*. New York: Macmillan.

Lawrence, G., et al. 1968. *B-P-H: Botanico-Periodicum-Huntianum*. Pittsburgh, Pa.: Hunt Institute for Botanical Documentation, Carnegia–Mellon University.

Little, Elbert L., Jr. 1971. *Atlas of United States trees, Vol. 1. Conifers and important hardwoods*. USDA, Forest Service, Misc. Publ. No. 1146. Washington, D.C., U.S. Gov't. Printing Office.

_____. 1977. *Atlas of United States trees*, Vol. 4, Minor eastern hardwoods. USDA, Forest Service, Misc. Publ. 1342. Washington, D.C.: U.S. Gov't. Printing Office.

_____. 1979. *Checklist of United States trees (native and naturalized)*. USDA, Forest Service. Handb. 541. Washington, D.C.: U.S. Gov't. Printing Office.

_____. 1980. *The Audubon Society field guide to North American trees (eastern region)*. New York: Alfred A. Knopf.

Mabberley, D. J. 1987. *The plant book*. Cambridge and New York: Cambridge University Press.

Murray, Edward. 1975. North American maples. *Kalmia* 7: 1–20.

Peattie, Donald C. 1950. A natural history of trees of eastern and central North America. Boston and New York: Houghton Mifflin.

Petrides, George A. 1972. *A field guide to trees and shrubs*. 2nd ed. Boston: Houghton Mifflin.

Porter, Duncan M. 1976. *Zanthoxylum* (Rutaceae) in North America north of Mexico. *Brittonia* 28: 443–447.

Preston, Richard J. 1976. *North American trees*. Ames, IA.: Iowa State University Press.

Preston, Richard J. and Valerie G. Wright. 1985. *Identification of southeastern trees in winter*. Raleigh, N.C.: The North Carolina Agricultural Extension Service.

Radford, Albert E., Harry E. Ahles and C. Ritchie Bell. 1968. *Manual of the vascular flora of the Carolinas*. Chapel Hill, N.C.: University of North Carolina Press.

Radford, Albert E., William C. Dickison, Jimmy R. Massey and C. Ritchie Bell. 1974. *Vascular plant systematics*. New York: Harper & Row.

Rehder, Alfred. 1940. *Manual of cultivated trees and shrubs*. 2nd. ed. New York: Macmillan.

Reveal, James L. and Margaret J. Seldin. 1976. On the identity of *Halesia carolina* L. (Styracaceae). *Taxon* 25: 123–140.

Sargent, Charles S. 1965. *Manual of trees of North America*. Vols. 1 and 2. New York: Dover Publications, Inc.

Small, John K. 1933. *Manual of the southeastern flora*. Chapel Hill, N.C.: University of North Carolina Press.

Spongberg, Stephen A. 1971. The Staphyleaceae in the southeastern United States. *J. Arnold Arbor.* 52: 196–203.

———. 1974. A review of deciduous-leaved species of *Stewartia* (Theaceae). *J. Arnold Arbor.* 55: 182–201.

Stafleu, F. A. (ed.), 1983. *International code of botanical nomenclature, Regnum Veg.*, Vol. III. The Hague. Bohn, Scheltema & Holkema, Utrecht/Antwerper Dr. W. Junk, Publishers.

The Herbarium, Royal Botanic Gardens, Kew. 1980. *Draft index of author abbreviations*. London: Her Majesty's Stationery Office.

Thomas, Joab L. 1960. A monographic Study of Cyrillaceae. *Harvard Univ., Contrib. Gray Herb.* 186: 1–114.

Wagner, W. H., Jr. 1974. Dwarf Hackberry (Ulmaceae: *Celtis tenuifolia*) in the Great Lakes Region. *Michigan Bot.* 13: 73–99.

Willis, J. C. 1973. *A dictionary of the flowering plants and ferns*, 8th ed., revised by H. G. A. Shaw. London: Cambridge University Press.

Wilson, James S. 1965. Variation of three taxonomic complexes of the genus *Cornus* in eastern United States. *Trans. Kansas Acad. Sci*, 67: 747–817.

Wiseman, James B., Jr. 1987. *Quercus oglethorpensis* in Mississippi. *Castanea* 52: 314.

Wood, Carroll E., Jr. 1959. The genera of Theaceae of the southeastern United States. *J. Arnold Arbor.* 40: 413–419.

Wunderlin, Richard P. and James E. Poppleton. 1977. The Florida species of *Ilex* (Aquifoliaceae). *Florida Sci.* 40: 7–21.

Index

Corrections

p. 31   *Vaccinium arboreum* differs from *Kalmia* in that midribs on both surfaces are usually pubescent and flowers are campanulate, about ¼" in
diameter

p. 91   Red Oaks *Quercus laurifolia* and *Q. myrtifolia* usually lack bristle tips

p. 92   *Quercus incana* differs from *Q. phellos* and *Q. laurifolia* in that leaves
have densely matted pubescence on lower surfaces and mature
leaves are bluish green

Fig. 47   mislabeled, is *Populus deltoides* × 1/8

Fig. 391   mislabeled, is *Fraxinus caroliniana* × 1/5

p. 260   *Carpinus caroliniana* may have catkins in late winter

p. 266   *Halesia carolina* bark of 2- to 3-year-old stems has white streaks

p. 283   Krakow, G. A. 1989. *A systematic study of Ilex ambigua, Ilex decidua and
related taxa.* Master's thesis, Athens, Ga.: University of Georgia.

Physical Provinces of Georgia: Cumberland Plateau (1), Ridge and Valley (2), Blue Ridge Mountains (3), Piedmont (4), and Coastal Plain (5).